Kinahan Assassins

ABOUT THE AUTHORS

Award-winning journalist Stephen Breen is crime editor of the *Irish Sun* and author and co-author of several bestselling books, including the No. 1 bestselling *The Cartel*, the definitive account of the rise of the Kinahan gang.

John Hand is news and crime correspondent at the *Irish Sun*. He was previously the *Irish Mirror*'s chief reporter. He has been short-listed across a number of categories in NewsBrands Ireland's annual awards, including crime journalist of the year and young journalist of the year. He regularly contributes to programmes on RTÉ radio and Newstalk. *Kinahan Assassins* is his first book.

Kinahan Assassins

*The Ruthless Hit Squads Who Brought
Terror to Dublin Streets and How
They Were Stopped*

STEPHEN BREEN AND
JOHN HAND

SANDYCOVE

an imprint of

PENGUIN BOOKS

SANDYCOVE

UK | USA | Canada | Ireland | Australia
India | New Zealand | South Africa

Sandycove is part of the Penguin Random House group of companies
whose addresses can be found at global.penguinrandomhouse.com

First published 2024
001

Copyright © Stephen Breen and John Hand, 2024

The moral right of the copyright holders has been asserted

Set in 13.5/16pt Garamond MT Std
Typeset by Jouve (UK), Milton Keynes
Printed and bound in Great Britain by Clays Ltd, Elcograf S.p.A.

The authorized representative in the EEA is Penguin Random House Ireland,
Morrison Chambers, 32 Nassau Street, Dublin D02 YH68

A CIP catalogue record for this book is available from the British Library

ISBN: 978–1–844–88680–7

For Ireland's frontline emergency workers
and the innocent victims of gangland violence.

Contents

Prologue: Open Fire   3

1. 'Who'd you kill, Jeff?'   10
    (29 February 2016: murder of Vincent Ryan)

2. Foot Soldiers   29
    (25 April 2016: murder of Michael Barr)

3. Family Business   45
    (24 May 2016: murder of Gareth Hutch)

4. Blood Brothers   63
    (13 June 2016: a murder revenge plot and a weapons seizure)

5. Young Guns   77
    (1 July 2016: murder of Daithi Douglas)

6. Serial Killer   95
    *(14 April 2016: murder of Martin O'Rourke and
    17 August 2016: murder of Trevor O'Neill)*

7. The Addict   109
    *(2 September 2016: attempted murder of John Hutch and
    26 March 2017: attempted murder of Eddie Staunton)*

8. The Innocent Target   125
    (22 December 2016: murder of Noel 'Duck Egg' Kirwan)

9. The Quartermaster   138
    (24 January 2017: Kinahan arms cache seizure)

I

CONTENTS

10. Business as Usual   157

    (12 January 2019: catching crime boss Thomas 'Bomber'
    Kavanagh and smashing a drug-trafficking network)

11. The Butcher   176

    (4 April 2017: plot to murder James Gately)

12. Border Patrols   191

    (2017: logistical support in the plot to kill James Gately)

13. 'Five World Cups and I'll be out'   207

    (10 May 2017: second assassination attempt on James Gately)

14. Disposable Assets   224

    (July and August 2017: hit teams target Michael Frazer
    and Caine Kirwan)

15. 'They're gonna get killed'   241

    (6 November 2017: conspiracy to murder Mr Z)

16. Following Orders   258

    (February 2018: planning to murder Patsy Hutch)

17. Planners and Professionals   274

    (28 February 2018 and 10 March 2018: conspiracies to
    murder Patsy Hutch)

Epilogue: Disrupt and Dismantle   290

Acknowledgements   305

Prologue: Open Fire

It was over.

Gary Hutch was one hell of a lucky man. He had made the serious mistake of deciding to take on the Kinahans in a direct hit. The plan was to take out Daniel, son and heir of Christy 'Dapper Don' Kinahan, and save his own life. Tensions had grown to a point where Hutch felt he had to strike first, before he was targeted. Not only had he made his own frustrations known after he had not seen a return on money he had invested in drugs with the cartel – cash he had earned from a tiger kidnapping in Dublin in 2009 – he had also been labelled as a 'rat'. But the attack he organized went wrong. Someone was shot, but it wasn't Daniel Kinahan. An innocent man, boxer Jamie Moore, was hit instead – another mistake – but he had lived to tell the tale. Gary Hutch had made a catastrophic error; he had squared up to the wrong family.

But it was all sorted now. Gary's brother Patrick had stood there and taken a bullet to the leg in a punishment shooting, and Gary had handed over a €200,000 compensation payment. He owed his life to his uncle, Gerry 'the Monk' Hutch, who had brokered the peace deal following a series of meetings with the Kinahans. It was a nasty episode that everyone could now put behind them. Gary could get back to Spain and resume his work in the drug-trafficking industry, though he knew he would have to start afresh, away from the Kinahans. But at least that was the end of it.

As Gary Hutch made his way back to his rented apartment on the Costa del Sol, he had forgotten two very important things: Daniel Kinahan hadn't got to where he was, his father's right-hand man in a multimillion-euro international drug cartel, by being the forgiving kind; and his credibility in gangland terms meant everything to him – he would not let this go.

25 September 2015

The man had been waiting in the basement car park for over two hours. The minutes continued to tick past, and he waited patiently.

Gary Hutch was heading out for a run. He left his place in the Angel de Miraflores apartment block, Estepona, on the Costa del Sol and made his way down to the basement to get his car. He was dressed in a bright orange top and shorts, all set for another warm, sunny day. He pressed the fob and the car beeped. He pulled open the door. And then it happened. The man was suddenly beside him, and Gary Hutch was looking down the barrel of a gun pointed at him. The tall man holding it was masked. He pulled the trigger.

The gun jammed.

Gary Hutch turned and fled for his life.

He pelted across the car park, leading his assassin only by yards. He sprinted towards the communal area and circled the pool twice, panic-stricken. The hitman kept coming, gun ready. He fired again and again at his moving target, letting off about fifteen shots in total. Residents looked up from their morning coffees, wondering what was causing the weird sounds they could hear. It was the bangs of the bullets and the clatters of the bullet casings hopping on the paving. Eye-witnesses who looked out from their apartments at the commotion thought it was a joke, but then they saw the tall man in black, wearing a balaclava, gloves, and holding a gun. They realized it was anything but a joke.

Gary Hutch kept running, trying to duck away from the bullets, attempting to put space between him and the man chasing him. His eyes darted about for an escape route. Then he saw it: the gateway. If he was first out through that, he'd make it.

He sprinted towards the gate and reached it before the hitman. He grabbed the handle. It was locked. He was trapped. No way out but past the man coming fast up behind him. He roared desperately, 'No, no, no!' He spun around, looking for any other way out.

The first bullet hit him in the back. Gary Hutch fell forward, collapsing on to the ground, and lay there, gasping, defenceless.

The hitman was out of breath too, but he paused metres away, steadied himself. He pointed his gun. Two head shots. Job done. It was over. We will never know if Gary Hutch recognized the killer as the man he had once shared wine, hookers and good times with not so long ago. But whoever he was, he had ensured there were no mistakes.

Now the assassin had to get away. He was so exhausted from the pursuit, he was sweating and breathless and could not run from the scene. Instead, he traipsed wearily up a hill, threw himself over a fence and climbed into a BMW X3 that was parked up and waiting. The stolen car was driven to a location in nearby Marbella and set alight.

This was when his luck ran out. A local spotted the blazing car and grabbed a fire extinguisher to tackle the flames.

The car was only partially burnt out. When the police searched it, they found a semi-automatic 9mm Glock pistol and a semi-automatic Colt 1911 pistol, and two baseball caps, one burnt and the other in good condition. It was all bagged up as evidence.

Back at the apartment complex, police were examining the scene of crime. Gary Hutch's body lay where he had fallen, and they found car keys beside him. They went down to the basement and there was his car, with the door standing open, and the events of the morning began to be pieced together.

Gary Hutch was dead. The peace deal hadn't held for long. For those who thought this daylight murder was finally an end to it, they were making the same old mistake. Three months later, the Kinahans came for the Monk. Gerry Hutch was celebrating New Year's Eve in Lanzarote when the assassins arrived. But he was quicker than his nephew and got away. It was an audacious move, though, an attempt to take out the criminal godfather in a bid to ensure he would not seek retribution for his nephew's murder. It couldn't go unanswered.

5 February 2016

The five gunmen stormed the Regency Hotel in north Dublin. They were well prepared, one dressed in drag, three in Garda SWAT-like uniforms and one undisguised. The Kinahan-associated MGM boxing outfit was holding a weigh-in ahead of the Clash of the Clans fight night later that week. Daniel Kinahan was in attendance. It was time for revenge.

In a hail of gunfire, Kinahan cartel lieutenant David Byrne

was shot six times – to the head, face, chest, stomach, hand and legs – and his body was left lying flat against the reception desk. Kinahan lieutenant Sean McGovern was shot in the leg. Daniel Kinahan managed to escape unscathed from the second Hutch gang attempt on his life.

The attack was daring and deadly. In the aftermath, a hit-list was compiled by leading Kinahan associates. Their strike-back came within three days. Eddie 'Neddie' Hutch, an older brother of the Monk, was assassinated outside his home on Poplar Row in Dublin's north inner city.

The Hutch family were left reeling and decided to make their feelings clear in a statement to the *Sunday Times*. It read:

> Gary had a falling out with the Kinahan organisation. This matter was resolved and €200,000 in cash was paid over to the Kinahans. We shook hands and agreed to walk away. Gary was then murdered for no reason. You cannot trust these people. The Kinahan organisation have attempted to kill Gerard on several occasions in recent months. We are being terrorised by the cartel. Kinahan's representatives said members of our family would be killed, or forced to leave their homes and Ireland if their demands for money were not met. We believe the Kinahan drugs cartel murdered Eddie at his home in Dublin having approached him days before with demands for money. Our extended family are under threat from these people. Our family are not involved in any drugs war. We are well known in the north inner city and have no involvement in drugs. Our family are involved in various charitable, religious and sports groups which help young people. We are not involved in drug dealing.

This move may have gained some sympathy among the public, but not with the cartel. A line had been crossed on both sides, and it would unleash a whole new type of violence never before seen in Irish society.

The Kinahan gang gathered dozens of killers and logistics men to target Hutch gang members, their families and their friends. They ranged from professional guns-for-hire, like the Estonian hitman known as 'The Butcher' and a former British army soldier to the strategic quartermaster 'Mr Nobody' and the desperate-for-cash foot soldiers on the streets. Money was their power, and the Kinahans were buying death.

11 June 2018

On the first day of his trial, James Quinn (b. 19 August 1982) stood accused of being the triggerman in the Gary Hutch murder. He was a close friend of Daniel and Christopher Kinahan Jnr from their childhood days in Dublin's south inner city. Quinn possessed a chilling persona, which even the most seasoned investigators feared. It was his DNA that had been found on one of the baseball caps recovered from the charred BMW getaway vehicle, which had led him to this moment: standing trial in a court in Málaga.

After a four-day trial, the jury opted to convict him of being a 'necessary participant' to murder but not the gunman, instead acting as lookout and getaway driver. He got twenty-two years.

During Quinn's trial, a senior Spanish investigator stated that Daniel Kinahan had ordered Gary Hutch's murder. Gardaí would later state, during a sentencing hearing in Dublin's Special Criminal Court, that the cartel was responsible for execution-type murders based on a perceived requirement to protect its core activities: drugs and firearms trafficking on an international scale. They described how the cartel operates on a hierarchical structure, which includes sub-cell structures. These units carry out specific tasks designed to enhance the capabilities of the organization and to advance its core activities. The sub-cells operate on the basis of directions issued by senior figures within the gang. Their aim is to segregate the activities of each group, limiting the overall knowledge of those further down the hierarchy. Each sub-cell also has an individual, internal hierarchy, and this structure has similar intent and purpose to that of the overall group.

The gardaí were describing a very organized, military-style approach to crime, a method that had ensured the Kinahan organized crime gang was feared and successful in equal measure. The revelations about the group's modus operandi and their level of wealth had been uncovered and established during extensive cross-border investigations of the gang.

But before that day in the Special Criminal Court would arrive, gardaí would spend years investigating a chain of murders and attempted killings that rocked Dublin city and destroyed lives and families. The feud had begun, and it was going to be a one-sided, bloody assault.

1. 'Who'd you kill, Jeff?'

(29 February 2016: murder of Vincent Ryan)

'I'm a prisoner in my own mind.'
— Kelly, partner of the victim

On the evening of 24 February 2016, a telephone call was made to Coolock Garda Station in north Dublin. Initially, the caller remained silent as the guard manning the phones asked them to explain their reason for contacting one of the busiest stations in the capital. Detective Superintendent Paul Scott, now retired, knows only too well how a shift went in that district. 'Coolock was an extremely busy station. No day was ever the same. The calls that came in were about drug-dealing, domestic violence, violent assaults, burglaries and other forms of serious crime. In 2016, Gardaí in Coolock also had major gangland figures such as Robbie Lawlor to contend with.'

This call was different. This time, career criminal Jeffrey Morrow was at the end of the line and he was pleading for help.

Dubliner Morrow (b. 21 March 1982) was regarded by one senior security source as a 'serious gangland criminal, with 115 previous convictions for some very serious offences, ranging from theft to armed robbery. He has a criminal career and network that spans throughout Dublin. He is violent and dangerous.' In another analysis of Morrow's involvement in organized crime, detectives described him as having 'a very violent disposition towards authority and he is known to have access to firearms. Jeffrey Morrow also associates with a number of violent criminals in the Finglas and greater Dublin area. It is not known if he is affiliated with any particular gang and would appear to have associates linked to many gangs.'

Among some of his more serious convictions was a 5-year sentence he received in March 2006 for possession of a shotgun, cocaine and a Garda baton. His links to serious organized crime gangs were exposed in November 2007 when he was arrested along with gang boss Eamon 'the Don' Dunne, who was murdered in April 2010 on the orders of the Kinahan cartel. On that occasion, both Morrow and Dunne were part of a gang that tried to steal €955,000 from a cash-in-transit van delivering to an ATM machine at the Tesco store in Celbridge, County Kildare, on 2 November 2007. As the raiders closed in on their target, gardaí moved in and made seven arrests.

Morrow, who was banned from driving for fifteen years in December 2006 for driving without insurance, was later charged with armed robbery. During his appearance at Dublin Circuit Court on 29 October 2009 he addressed the court and said: 'All I want to do here today is clear my name. I never said anything about anybody. It was not my fault other people were arrested that day.'

The prolific criminal, who claimed that he had been in Celbridge that day to steal a car, also addressed the issue of his guilty plea when he said: 'I pleaded not guilty all along. I only changed my plea to get it all over with.' He also claimed to have 'gone off his head on cocaine' after the death of a relative at the time of the incident. Following the conclusion of the court case, he received a 6-year sentence on top of the five years he had already received for possession of firearms.

During his time in the Irish prison system, which he spent entirely in Dublin's Mountjoy Prison, he was often placed in protective custody after being warned that his life was in danger from rival criminals. According to one senior prison source: 'Morrow just couldn't help himself. He was constantly issuing threats and mouthing off to other inmates. People were getting fed up with him and that's why he came under threat at different times during his incarceration.'

Released from custody in 2014, Morrow did not come to the attention of gardaí until his telephone call to Coolock Garda Station two years later. That didn't mean he was going straight. Detectives suspected that he had continued his association with senior figures in organized crime, including Eastern European criminals based in the Clondalkin area who were once aligned with gang boss Karl Breen before his death from a drugs overdose in February 2015. Morrow's gangland connections were kept below the radar, and he presented himself as a used-car dealer, often offering vehicles for sale on websites such as DoneDeal.ie. He also worked as a takeaway driver, delivering fast food across north Dublin.

In reality, gardaí suspected he was heavily involved in the stolen car trade across west Dublin. As one investigator pointed out: 'There was a lot of suspicion around Morrow's involvement in the stolen vehicles, especially across west Dublin, but nothing could ever be proven. He was also using aliases and even though he had spent a long time in prison, Gardaí knew that for Morrow, old habits die hard.'

Then he made that call to the gardaí in Coolock. During his bizarre telephone rant that day, the career criminal's conversation went as follows:

Morrow:	How ya, is that the guards?
Garda:	Coolock Garda Station, how can I help you?
Morrow, sounding agitated:	I was in a fight with one of the Ryan brothers. You know the ones from Donaghmede?

The garda who took the call asked him to elaborate, and Morrow went on to describe how he was convinced that his home at Burnell Court, on the Malahide Road in north Dublin, was 'under surveillance' by Real IRA leader Vincent Ryan and members of the dissident republican group.

A Garda patrol car was dispatched to Morrow's property and, following a search of the area, it was reported that 'nothing suspicious' was found. Once the search of outside his property had been completed, details of Morrow's bout of paranoia were logged to the Garda PULSE system. At the time of the call, and although suspicious of Morrow's ongoing involvement in organized crime, gardaí had no idea that he was plotting with others in the Kinahan cartel to commit yet another serious offence – murder.

At the time Morrow's erratic call was made, Vincent 'Vinnie' Ryan (b. 6 August 1990) was unemployed and had just become a father for the first time after his partner gave birth to the couple's daughter. Obsessed with health and fitness, Ryan consumed little alcohol and it was suspected he regularly used steroids. His other keen interest in 2016 was his love for scrambler bikes, which led him to make regular trips to the Wicklow Mountains with the Bikers for Life group. Influenced in his early years by his father Peter's support for the Provisional IRA during the Troubles and his strong opposition to the Northern Ireland peace process after the signing of the Good Friday Agreement in 1998, the youngest member of the Ryan family was the perfect recruit for the Real IRA.

Alongside his father's romantic tales of Ireland's struggle against the British, Ryan was also influenced by his older brother, Alan, who was fourteen years old when the IRA ceasefire was announced in 1994. Just four years later, Alan was caught with a loaded pistol at his family home, and in 1999 he was found at a suspected Real IRA training bunker in Stamullen, County Meath. Alan later received a 4-year sentence for possession of the firearm.

Released from custody in 2007, the same year in which their father, Peter, died, Alan Ryan continued his involvement with the dissident republican group. After turning eighteen in 2008, Alan's brother, Vincent, was also welcomed into the fold. It wasn't long before he was making a name for himself.

Over the next two years, the Real IRA's war in Dublin was waged against drugs gangs, including those with links to the Kinahan cartel. By 2010, the gardaí were well aware of Vincent Ryan and his associates in the republican group. As one source stated: 'It is believed that Vincent, his brother Alan and associates were engaged in many varied types of criminal and paramilitary activity on behalf of the Real IRA. They were actively involved in a process of widespread extortion from drug dealers and other members of the criminal fraternity in the Carlow and Dublin area for financial gain due to their Real IRA status and their capacity for violence. They previously made attempts, and in many cases succeeded, in extorting large sums of cash for their use. They were involved in the business of door security at a number of venues throughout the city.'

Even though the Real IRA's leaders maintained that cash from extortion rackets was donated to prisoner families and used for their 'war' in the North, investigators suspected that the 'tax' earned from criminal groups was used to fund a lavish lifestyle for members of the group, particularly the leader of its Dublin Brigade, Alan Ryan.

On 3 May 2010, Vincent Ryan's associates abducted a suspected drug dealer from west Dublin, who can't be named for legal reasons, and brought him to Fairview Park on the north side of the city. He refused to cough up the money they said he owed and they chopped two of his fingers off. At this time, those involved in drugs and other forms of organized crime were becoming more and more concerned by the dissident republican group's increasing use of violence against their associates. That concern led to the formation of a group calling itself the Criminal Action Force. This was a group established by Alan Wilson and his cousin John, who styled themselves as criminals who were taking on the republicans. Their response to the escalating Real IRA violence came on 26 July 2010.

A hitman got out of a car being driven by an accomplice and walked up to the entrance door of Player's Lounge pub in Fairview, north Dublin, armed with a special-calibre Smith & Wesson revolver and a Zastava semi-automatic pistol. He opened fire.

During the gun attack, three innocent people had miraculous escapes despite being shot. Doorman Wayne Barrett was shot twice in the head, three times in the left buttock and once in the thigh. One customer was shot in the chest, on the right side of his groin, in the foot and in the arm. A second customer was hit in the back and the forearm.

Within weeks of the attack, investigators had identified

their chief suspects: John Wilson and his cousin Alan Wilson, who was a Kinahan cartel gun-for-hire. Gardaí believe the pub, now closed and previously run by the father of former Ireland international footballer Anthony Stokes, was targeted because Alan Ryan was a regular customer there. Investigators suspected the attack was arranged by veteran criminal Sean Hunt, who blamed Alan and Vincent Ryan for the murder of his friend Collie Owens on 9 July 2010.

At the time, gardaí classified the shooting as 'one of the most reckless gun attacks ever carried out on a public street in this country'. Former Detective Superintendent Paul Scott also said: 'When I first looked at the CCTV footage of the shooting outside the Player's Lounge, I was astonished no one had lost their life. It was more akin to the narco-style drive-by shootings in Mexico or Mafia assassinations of the 1930s. While the crime attracted a lot of publicity at the time, due in part to the fact the shooting was connected with dissident republican leader Alan Ryan, the enormity of the possible fatal consequences of the attack was missed in the public eye. Not so, however, for its innocent victims who suffered life-changing injuries as a result.'

The attack was significant as well in that it was one of the first times in the history of the state in which those involved in organized crime had taken on republican paramilitaries. But it did not stop Alan Ryan and his associates from continuing their extortion rackets and targeting major gangland figures who refused to donate to their 'cause'. One such figure was 30-year-old Michael 'the Panda' Kelly, a close associate of Eamon 'the Don' Dunne and other major drug dealers operating across Dublin and the border counties. One meeting Kelly had with the Real IRA unit in Dublin, in

August 2011, ended abruptly when Kelly refused to hand over any cash.

Unbeknownst to him at the time, Kelly had signed his own death warrant. On 15 September, he was targeted by a Real IRA hit team in the Clongriffin area just after he had visited his girlfriend, Caoimhe Robinson (who would go on to marry cartel leader Daniel Kinahan at the luxurious Burj Al Arab Hotel in 2017). As he walked away from his girlfriend's home, a gunman opened fire with an AK47 assault rifle. Kelly slumped to the ground, and the gunman shot him once in the head. The killer and his accomplice made sure their target was dead by reversing their getaway car over him as he lay bleeding on the ground.

Kelly's killing boosted morale among the two Ryan siblings, but the Real IRA's position of strength over the coming months would not last long. In the shadows, the drug lord nicknamed 'Mr Big', who has no convictions but has been linked to thirteen murders since 2000, had put the wheels in motion to kill the republican group's leader, Alan Ryan.

Recruited for the murder was Kenneth Finn, from the Coolock area of north Dublin, who had previously been caught with firearms and ecstasy during a lengthy criminal career. Their plan was put into motion on 3 September 2012 when Finn – who would be murdered in March 2018 by hitman Robbie Lawlor – approached Ryan and shot him in the head at point-blank range in Grange Lodge Avenue, north Dublin. Following the shooting dead of Alan Ryan, the Real IRA in Dublin went into freefall, with the balance of power now resting with those involved in serious and organized crime.

Ahead of Ryan's paramilitary-style funeral, a crowd of around five hundred people gathered outside his family home in north Dublin. As they did so, six men emerged from the crowd in combat uniforms with their faces covered and fired shots over the dissident leader's coffin. Then the six men melted back into the crowd.

Just a few weeks after the funeral, on 22 September the surviving Ryan brother, Vincent, was charged with possession of an AK47 assault rifle and membership of an illegal organization on the same day that Kelly was murdered. When charged in connection with the Kelly murder, Vincent Ryan, who was unemployed at the time, was receiving his social welfare payments through the post. The decision had been made for him to receive the payments in this way because of Garda concerns for staff and other people visiting the local welfare offices based in Kilbarrack, north Dublin. No one wanted another reckless gun attack on the streets of Dublin.

Vincent Ryan received a welcome boost on 16 March 2013 when the Director of Public Prosecutions (DPP) ruled there would be no prosecution with regard to offences relating to membership of an illegal organization arising from the funeral. His good fortune before the courts continued on 24 October that year when, seventeen days after his trial for the firearms offences in connection with the Kelly murder started, the trial collapsed due to lack of evidence.

Following his victories before the courts, Vincent Ryan continued to associate with members of the Real IRA in Dublin, with gardaí assessing that he was 'part of a somewhat fragmented group of the IRA in the Dublin region'. Since the murder of his brother, Alan, the Dublin unit of the Real IRA had imploded, with many of its members going their separate ways. Some continued to align themselves with key dissident figures in the North, while Vincent Ryan concentrated on his career as a barber and his passion for motorbikes. His only interaction with dissident republicans appeared to be at commemorations. By the summer of 2015, he was preparing to become a father for the first time and perhaps hoping to put his past behind him.

On 29 October 2015, Vincent Ryan had just left a check-up with his partner at the Rotunda Hospital. As the couple walked along Parnell Square North, he was attacked by a man with a knife and sliced up the right side of the face, from his chin to the base of his right ear. He was taken to the Mater Hospital for treatment, and later discharged and left with permanent scarring as a reminder. The gangster known as 'Mr Big' and an associate of his were later arrested by detectives in connection with the attack but did not face any charges due to lack of evidence.

Following the incident, Ryan did not return to work and maintained a low profile as he prepared to welcome his daughter into the world. Just three years after the murder of his brother, the latest attack on another member of the Ryan family proved the Real IRA were no longer major players in the world of organized crime.

Although first targeted by 'Mr Big', it was the turn of Daniel Kinahan's transnational gang to have him in their sights after the murder of cartel lieutenant David Byrne at the Regency Hotel in Dublin on 5 February 2016. Following Byrne's killing, gardaí believe Kinahan's associates compiled a list of individuals they thought could declare support for the Hutch gang in their ongoing feud, as former Assistant Commissioner Michael O'Sullivan explained: 'The Kinahan Organized Crime Group were targeting people because they could. They had the resources to offer people huge amounts of cash to kill people. If they perceived someone to be a threat, even without any shred of evidence, that person would be a target for murder. It didn't matter who you were or if you weren't involved in anything, you could still be killed just because a Kinahan gang member had a certain thought – that's how cheap life was to them.'

Unfortunately for Vincent Ryan, and despite having no connection to Gerry 'the Monk' Hutch, he was one of a number of individuals identified as a cartel target simply because of his previous involvement in violent dissident republican activity. The plan to eliminate him as a potential recruit to the cartel's enemies was under way in the days after a cartel hit team from north Dublin murdered the Monk's brother Eddie on 8 February.

On 29 February 2016, Ryan and his partner, along with their new baby daughter, spent the morning and enjoyed lunch at the Ryan family home in Grange Abbey Drive. They had stayed there the previous night, talking about their plans to marry. At 2.45 p.m. that day, the couple and their child left Donaghmede in Ryan's distinctive white Volkswagen Golf. (Ironically, the white Golf was registered to LS Active Car Sales, a company run by senior Kinahan cartel figures Liam Byrne and Sean McGovern before its assets were seized by the Criminal Assets Bureau under Operation Lamp.)

The family arrived at his partner's family home in McKee Road, Finglas, north Dublin, at 3.07 p.m., and the mother and child walked into the house while Ryan remained in the car, waving at Ms Smyth's brother, Keith. As Ryan sat in his car, a silver Volkswagen Golf pulled up alongside.

At 3.10 p.m. the passenger in the silver car opened fire

from a 9mm Makarov RAK submachine gun, hitting Ryan in the right shoulder, right temple and right hand. In total, fourteen shots were fired, with one stray bullet later recovered from the Smyth family home. Three minutes after the gunman opened fire, the first of four 999 calls to gardaí reported hearing a 'noise of shots and screaming'. Brought to the Mater Hospital, Vincent Ryan was pronounced dead at five past nine that evening.

Following the shooting, an incident room was established at Finglas Garda Station under the command of Senior Investigating Officer Detective Inspector Colm Murphy, now a Detective Superintendent. Among the first pieces of information investigators received were reports of a silver Golf found burnt out at Red Lane, Newhall, Naas, County Kildare. A firefighter with Naas Fire Station extinguished the blaze and managed to identify the vehicle's chassis number. Gardaí also recovered a registration plate beside the vehicle. The following day, detectives established that the registration plates were false as the chassis number matched a vehicle stolen on 13 October 2015 from a house in Carbury, also County Kildare.

The investigation focused on the sourcing of CCTV from nearby premises and properties. Analysis of the footage showed the stolen car in the McKee Road area on 27 and 28 February and at thirty-two different locations that day. Gardaí were also able to use the Automatic Number Plate Recognition (ANPR) system as part of their efforts to track the movement of the getaway car. The system works by cameras placed at fixed locations across the capital recording, and logging, the registration of each vehicle that passes.

As the investigation continued in the days following the

murder, detectives received a boost when the hit team's stolen car was logged on the ANPR system travelling out of the Palmerstown Bypass and on to the N4 road. Crucially, the Volkswagen Golf was also caught on the ANPR driving in convoy with a Kia Sorento at 3.59 p.m. that day. The two vehicles were also captured at an ANPR site in Kill, County Kildare, at 4.12 p.m. Following the discovery of the burnt-out car at 4.30 p.m. on the day of the murder, the Kia Sorento, including details of its registration, was then captured by another ANPR camera in the Clondalkin area at 4.46 p.m., travelling towards Dublin city. As part of their extensive CCTV analysis gardaí also established that the stolen Golf had followed a car similar to the murder victim's on the M50. Unbeknownst to the hit team, that car belonged to an off-duty garda.

In a breakthrough for gardaí, officers further established that the Kia had been registered to Natalie Byrne from Colepark Drive in Ballyfermot. Although Ms Byrne was not involved in organized crime, the same could not be said of her partner – Paul O'Beirne.

At the same time, an analysis of the Garda PULSE system led the detectives to Morrow's bizarre phone call on the evening of 24 February, five days before the murder. From that moment on, Morrow became a 'person of interest' to the investigation team. The Garda team's suspicions were further raised when intelligence on Morrow identified O'Beirne as one of his key associates.

At the time of the killing of Vincent Ryan, O'Beirne (b. 17 September 1982) was not regarded as a major gangland player despite his association with major criminals, including Jeffrey Morrow, in the capital. Gardaí also suspected that he was a heavy drinker and frequent cocaine user, which led to him suffering from bouts of paranoia. Gardaí were made aware of his paranoia on two occasions in 2014 when he was brought to Tallaght Garda Station after claiming he was 'being tracked by men with guns' and that his 'house was bugged'. The father of six admitted to gardaí at the time that he had been 'consuming large quantities of cocaine'.

His sixteen previous convictions included a 240-hour community service order for assault causing harm in 2003, while the rest were fines for road traffic matters. Due to O'Beirne's links to Morrow and to the car that drove in convoy with the getaway vehicle, and Morrow's complaint about Ryan, gardaí were satisfied they had enough to arrest their prime suspects.

At 9 a.m. on 15 March 2016, investigators from Finglas Garda Station made their move, swooping on O'Beirne's home in Colepark Drive in Ballyfermot and Morrow's apartment in Burnell Court in Coolock. Five days before the raids, gardaí also recovered the Kia Sorento from a major gangland figure, who can't be named for legal reasons, in the Ballymun area of north Dublin. On the day of the Garda operation, O'Beirne was arrested by Detective Sergeant Gavin Ross, now a Detective Inspector, for withholding information in relation to a serious offence, while Morrow was arrested by Detective Sergeant Alan Brady, now a Superintendent, on suspicion of Ryan's murder.

During the search of O'Beirne's home, the Garda team established that the hard drive from the extensive CCTV system the suspect had installed at the property due to his 'paranoia' had been removed. They also discovered a partially burnt mobile phone in a barbecue. It was a setback in their hunt for clues. But the following day they had a stroke of luck when they established that a man known as 'Pat' had installed the CCTV at O'Beirne's home and had been socializing with O'Beirne at the Silver Granite pub the night before gardaí arrived to conduct the search of his home.

Gardaí obtained a warrant to recover the CCTV from the pub. When they examined it, they identified Morrow, O'Beirne and 'Pat' enjoying drinks. Although there was no sound on the footage, judging by their actions, gardaí believed Morrow and O'Beirne were demonstrating Ryan's murder to their friend.

As the murder suspects remained in Garda custody, detectives identified the mystery man 'Pat', who cannot be named for legal reasons, and searched his home in Kinnegad, County Westmeath, on 17 March. During a search of that property, gardaí also gained access to a van. They found the CCTV hard drive from O'Beirne's home in the passenger footwell of the van. Once analysed, the CCTV displayed the movements of people at the Ballyfermot property on the day of Vincent Ryan's murder.

At 2.10 p.m. the CCTV captured Morrow arriving at the house in the stolen Volkswagen Golf. Then it showed O'Beirne removing a green seat cover from the vehicle's boot and placing it in a wheelie bin, located in the front garden. In their analysis of the CCTV gardaí were supported by Acume Forensics Ltd in Leeds, UK. The company was able to identify, and also show, that mobile phone numbers associated with the suspects were pinging off masts in the same area where the cars were travelling. The company, which assists law enforcement agencies around the world, was also able to confirm that Morrow was the individual who collected O'Beirne from Colepark Drive.

During the raid on the suspect's home, the green cover

was seized, along with mobile phones and electronic devices. The raid on Morrow's home also turned up mobile phones. In an examination of one of the phones seized at Morrow's property, gardaí recovered two messages sent on 7 March which both read: 'Who did you murder Jeff'.

On 12 March, gardaí were given an insight into the relationships of both men during an examination of O'Beirne's partner's phone when she sent a text to Morrow's partner, Amy Brown:

'Jeff's and him together after fckn off out. If he's not back in twenty minutes there be fckn murder.'

Amy Brown texted back: 'He goes out at like 3 o'clock in the morning telling me Paul n his mates ar up drinking. Full lies. Karma a bitch. Leave them be.'

Following the arrests, Paul O'Beirne was held for two days before being released without charge. However, he was re-arrested at his home on 19 March, this time on suspicion of murder after gardaí had viewed the CCTV from the hard drive. During his time in custody he was interviewed twenty-two times, replying, 'No comment,' to all of the questions and evidence presented to him, before being released for a second time as the investigating team prepared their file for the DPP. Jeff Morrow, who also made no reply to the questions put to him during his nineteen interviews, including a question about the phone call he made to Coolock Garda Station, was also released on 21 March.

As the investigation continued, gardaí had another breakthrough when the owner of the stolen Volkswagen Golf told them that the green cover was his and was used for his dogs to lie on. The green cover was analysed by Weatherby's Animal DNA Service, based in Kildare, and dog hairs recovered from it were matched to the car owner's two dogs. This tied the stolen car directly to O'Beirne.

As the weeks passed, the major gangster who had possession of the Kia Sorento met with gardaí on 15 June 2016 and denied all knowledge of the murder, but he did admit that he knew one of the suspects, that he had contacted a friend and asked him to try to help Vincent Ryan immediately after he was shot and also that he had bought the Kia from a man known as 'Padji'.

His interactions with gardaí were not complete when he was arrested on 21 July 2016 for possession of information in relation to the murder of Vincent Ryan. At the time of his arrest, gardaí had concluded that this man 'had serious criminal links and is known to gardaí throughout Dublin. He has recently been arrested in relation to a murder which involves the feud between the Kinahan and Hutch gangs. It is suggested that he is a hired gun for the Kinahan crew.'

During his arrest period, he was interviewed five times and admitted that the Real IRA had demanded €20,000 from him due to his involvement in drugs and that he knew Alan Ryan from the Player's Lounge and that Vincent Ryan had been in a local GAA club before his murder, 'hassling lads' who were taking drugs. Later released without charge, the major gangland figure was classified as a 'person of interest' as the investigation continued.

Once the extensive Garda file had been completed in 2017, it was sent to the DPP to consider. In the meantime, Morrow had moved to the Manchester area while O'Beirne continued to live in Dublin. In 2018, two years after the murder, the DPP contacted gardaí to inform them that there was enough evidence to charge both men. Morrow was arrested in Manchester on a European Arrest Warrant on 12 March 2018. On the same day, O'Beirne appeared before a special sitting of Dublin District Court and was charged with murder.

Ten days later, Morrow was brought back to Ireland, where he was also charged with the killing. Remanded in custody, on 24 June 2019 both men went on trial at the Central Criminal Court for the murder. Evidence was presented to the court for seven days before the case was dominated by legal argument for a two-week period. On 23 July 2019, both men pleaded guilty to helping a criminal organization murder Vincent Ryan.

Remanded in custody again, the pair returned to the court on 31 July 2019 to learn their fate. Morrow received an 11-year sentence, and O'Beirne received a 9-year sentence. In his address to the court, Mr Justice Michael White said: 'I find it difficult to understand why a man with no history of criminal activity got involved in such a serious crime. Every human life is valuable and these criminal organizations, by the way they behave, have no respect for human life.'

In a message to those convicted over the shooting, Ryan's partner said: 'You have gained nothing because you never knew Vincent and he never knew you.'

Addressing the media after the guilty pleas, Detective Superintendent Murphy said: 'The sentencing shows An Garda Síochána's determination in combating organized crime gangs. Vincent Ryan's murder was brutal, callous and shocking, carried out in broad daylight as young children made their way home from school. I would like to thank the many people who gave evidence during the trial and I would also like to acknowledge the words of Justice Michael White in commending the members of An Garda Síochána who investigated this murder to the highest professionalism.'

In her victim impact statement Ryan's partner spoke of the heartbreak of those left behind: 'He lived for his family, but he only had five weeks with his daughter. He was such a proud dad and loved showing her off. I watched Vincent fighting for his life, struggling for every breath. It's an image that will stay with me forever. I'm a prisoner in my own mind. How do I explain to a 3-year-old girl that her daddy is never coming home?'

In those very early days of the Kinahan and Hutch feud, Vincent Ryan became the first dissident republican to be targeted by the Kinahan assassins – he would not be the last.

2. Foot Soldiers

(25 April 2016: murder of Michael Barr)

'How can a life be measured in drugs or money?'
— Noeleen Barr, sister of the victim

Shortly after 11 p.m. on 31 December 2015, an Irish pub in Lanzarote was packed with revellers preparing to welcome in the New Year. The pub, located in the resort of Puerto del Carmen, was a popular venue for Irish holidaymakers from all walks of life who were enjoying a bit of winter sun. One of the sunseekers in the pub that night was Gerry 'the Monk' Hutch, who spent many months of the year at his apartment on the island. Throughout the course of 2014 and 2015, Hutch was a well-known figure in the Irish pub, and in other pubs around the resort, as he contemplated 'retirement' from a life at the heart of organized crime in Ireland.

On that particular New Year's Eve, however, Hutch's demeanour was different. This time, the confidence and carefree manner he usually displayed on the holiday island had evaporated following the murder of his nephew, Gary. On top of this the Kinahan cartel, now being run by eldest son, Daniel, had made the veteran criminal their number-one target, placing a €1 million bounty on his head. For the Kinahan cartel leadership, which included people like Ross Browning, later named in court as the gang's 'principal representative' in Ireland and Hutch's old neighbour, the Monk would always present a threat due to his standing in the criminal underworld, the international connections he had made over the years and his links to heavily armed dissident republican paramilitary groups.

Following his nephew's murder, Hutch had made the decision to keep on the move, often travelling between different locations in Spain and elsewhere on the Continent. But over the Christmas period in 2015 he had made the decision to stay in Lanzarote, a place that he was familiar with. Despite the threat hanging over him, he still decided to go out that night – a decision that almost cost him his life.

As he drank with friends in the bar, with a clear view of the front door and constantly monitoring those arriving at the premises, he noticed two men walk into the pub. The men, wearing baseball caps, stopped and surveyed the place, before having a look in the toilets of the premises. In an instant, Hutch recognized one of the men as Eamon Cumberton (b. 12 January 1987) from Dublin's north inner city. Hutch knew Cumberton as a close associate of Browning. Cumberton had a brief stint as a professional mixed martial arts fighter, and had continued to train with Browning, a fitness fanatic, after stepping away from the paid ranks.

The other man that night was not known to Hutch. He was Christopher Slator (b. 4 October 1984), a violent criminal from the Cabra area of the capital. Acting on an instinct gained over years of involvement in the underworld, Hutch hid behind his pals in the pub as he watched the men leave before he fled.

Later, when assessing the attempted hit, Spanish police concluded that: 'It is commonly understood that both Eamon Cumberton and Christopher Slator flew to Lanzarote in December 2015 with a view to shooting Gerry "the

Monk" Hutch.' Despite their failure in Lanzarote, the two assassins offered their services to the cartel for a second time just four months later, ready to have another go.

On the evening of 25 April 2016 there were around twenty people inside the Sunset House pub, located in the heart of Dublin's north inner city. Those present were there for a raffle in aid of the Irish Republican Welfare Association, a group established to support the families of dissident republican prisoners. Others in the pub that night included locals there to watch an English Premiership game between Tottenham Hotspur and West Brom. Also there was 35-year-old bar manager Michael Barr, who had been in the premises from 5.20 p.m. that day.

Originally from Strabane in County Tyrone, Barr, who had previously worked as a joiner during the nine years he had lived in Dublin, had been working in the Sunset House for around a year, as his sister Noeleen explained: 'Michael was in his element working in that bar. He loved GAA and to be working so close to Croke Park was a dream for him – he loved it. He got the job because he was doing a job for the owner and when he said he didn't want to be paid, the owner offered him the bar job. He was a bit disillusioned with the building trade, so he jumped at the opportunity to do something different.' Off-duty that night, Barr had left the pub but then returned for the raffle.

At the time, he was suspected by gardaí of being a member of the Real IRA. On 18 July 2014, the father of five was charged with membership of an unlawful organization, the Irish Republican Army, and of handling stolen property at Finnstown House, Lucan, County Dublin. One of the reasons he was hit with the membership charge was the gardaí's belief that he had helped restructure the Dublin Brigade of the Real IRA following the murder of Alan Ryan.

He later pleaded guilty to the theft charge, but the DPP ruled that there was not enough evidence to charge him with membership of a proscribed organization. Noeleen explained: 'Michael had been a republican all his life – these are the views he held. He was never charged with the membership in the end and he was vehemently anti-drugs. He may have been a republican who was opposed to the Good Friday Agreement, but in 2016 the only thing that he cared about were his children, family, GAA and the pub. He wasn't involved in anything else.'

In the pub, people were chatting and Barr was talking to a customer about their holiday plans when two men walked in at 9.30 p.m. Turning to Barr, the woman he was talking to said: 'There's two kissograms for you.' The customers had no idea that both men were armed with Makarov handguns fitted with silencers. One of the men stood guard at the entrance, while the other singled out Barr, shooting him five times in the head, once in the shoulder and once in the left thigh. An eighth bullet was later found lodged in a mirror. The woman who had moments before been chatting and laughing with Michael Barr would later tell gardaí: 'We didn't know what was going on. There was blood everywhere. I realized there was a shooting. The glass was all over me. We were all shouting, in shock. I crawled over and blessed him. He was on the ground, all the blood coming from his head.'

The first 999 call was made at 9.33 p.m., with gardaí arriving at the scene at 9.36 p.m. Due to the nature of the gun attack, gardaí were left in no doubt that they were dealing with another murder in the ongoing Kinahan and Hutch feud. In the days that followed the shooting, rumours were rife that Barr had been targeted because he had helped source the weapons used in the Regency Hotel attack. This theory was discounted by Senior Investigating Officer and Detective Inspector John Bates (now retired), who told the authors: 'There was no information available to suggest that Michael Barr was involved in the planning or logistics around the Regency Hotel incident. Michael Barr was not a suspect in the Regency investigation at any time.'

Barr's sister Noeleen also offered her views on the cartel's decision to kill her brother: 'At the time we were worried about the situation in Dublin and when we mentioned it to Michael he said he was fine in Dublin because the feud had absolutely nothing to do with him. He did not feel under threat and if he did, he would have come home. It looks as if my brother was murdered simply because he came from the same town as one of the gunmen involved in the Regency.'

When analysing the killing, Mr Bates also said: 'The murder was cold and calculated. It was meticulously planned, perfectly timed and implemented with the utmost precision. That is, until it came to the disposal of the getaway vehicle, clothing, firearms and disguises used in the murder. Michael Barr had no chance of surviving this shooting. The murder was over in seconds. The hit team banked on the getaway vehicle being completely destroyed.'

Also responding to the shooting that night was Dublin Fire Brigade. At 9.39 p.m. they frantically tried to save Barr's life. Their efforts were in vain. Due to the extent of his injuries, he never stood a chance. He was pronounced dead at 10.12 p.m.

As the attempts were being made to save Barr, another 999 call was made, with the caller stating that 'possibly a light blue Audi' was on fire on Walsh Road. As gardaí on the north side of the city responded to the latest shooting, Detective Garda (now Sergeant) Michael Harkin and Garda Sheila O'Brien, from Ballymun Garda Station, were on patrol. In response to the 999 call they arrived at Walsh Road at 9.42 p.m., suspecting this might have been the car used by the hit team to escape.

They found an Audi A6 with smoke billowing from the front passenger-side window. Acting swiftly, Detective Garda Harkin used a fire extinguisher to put out the blaze before it could take hold. As he did so, he noticed a Nokia 106 mobile phone at the rear of the car, lying on the ground. The phone began to ring, then stopped, then began to ring again. Detective Garda Harkin took note of the incoming number before placing the phone in an evidence bag. Inside the bag, it began to ring for a third time from a different number.

The car was brought to a compound at Santry Garda Station for a full examination by the Garda National Technical Bureau. It wasn't long before more items were recovered. These included two boiler suits, a pair of Air Tech trainers, a Dublin GAA football scarf, two baseball caps, three rubber face masks, a black ski mask, two petrol cans, three cigarette butts and a protein drink. Even more significantly, officers also recovered two 9mm Makarov handguns fitted with silencers and two 9mm Glock pistols.

The day after the murder, the decision was made by senior gardaí for the investigation to be run by detectives from the Bridewell Garda Station due to the pressure officers from Mountjoy and Store Street Garda Stations were under investigating the murders of Eddie Hutch and Martin O'Rourke (which feature in Chapter 6). Thanks to CCTV footage from cameras placed along the North Circular Road, the investigating team identified the Audi A6 arriving at the pub and also travelling at speed along the Ballybough Road. Gardaí were in no doubt this was the gang's getaway car.

Satisfied that the items recovered from the car were used by the hit team, gardaí became aware of rumours sweeping the north inner city naming Cumberton and Slator as Barr's killers. As gardaí investigated the pair's possible involvement in the killing, they also established that the pair were booked on flight EK164 from Dublin to Dubai, and then on to Bangkok, just twenty-four hours after the murder. Slator had left Ireland on 26 April, but Cumberton had been forced to return to his home because his passport had expired. He was issued with an emergency travel document and left Ireland on 27 April. Investigators would also establish how their €900 flights had been booked only on 26 April by a female friend of Cumberton and that both men had arrived at the airport without any luggage.

As the prime suspects remained in hiding, gardaí received further information that Jonathan Keogh was also in the bar that night. Keogh was a close friend of Cumberton and had previously boasted of being a member of the INLA before he was removed from the paramilitary group's wing in Portlaoise Prison between 2010 and 2011 due to his connections to organized criminals. Unfortunately for gardaí, they were unable to confirm their suspicions that Keogh had been a 'spotter' in the bar as the pub's CCTV system wasn't in place at the time of the shooting. Their suspicions of Cumberton and Keogh's links were also confirmed by investigators in Spain.

According to the Spanish, it was their belief that Keogh and Cumberton were paid €50,000 each by the Kinahan cartel to identify a list of targets for execution and that they had been making inquiries about four people living in the north inner city. The investigators also established that the pair were 'surveillance conscious and had travelled to Spain for meetings'. They discovered the €1 million bounty the cartel had placed on Gerry Hutch's head and also that there was a €250,000 bounty on the head of James 'Mago' Gately, a lifelong friend of Gary Hutch and the wider Hutch family from the north inner city. Once Keogh's name had been linked to the Barr murder, he was approached by gardaí, but he refused to make a statement or agree to any meetings.

As the investigation focused on different strands, another breakthrough came when gardaí established that the mobile phone found at the getaway car had been registered at the FoneZone shop in the Ilac Shopping Centre in Dublin city centre. At the request of gardaí, the phone's IMEI (serial) number was checked and it was confirmed that it matched a device sold on 23 April 2016. Gardaí further established that two other phones were also sold that day to the same male customer. CCTV images from the shop showed the man who purchased the items. Once obtained, that image was quickly shared on a Garda bulletin, and it wasn't long before low-level criminal Martin Aylmer (b. 15 November 1986), from the Marino area of Dublin, was identified as the man who bought the phones. The identification of Aylmer meant that three people were now linked to the murder of Michael Barr.

A key focus of the investigation was using CCTV footage to track the movements of the Audi in the hours before the hitmen arrived at the pub. In one section of the footage, gardaí identified the car parked in Dorset Lane, off North Circular Road. This was of significant interest to the investigation team due to the location of the car near a lock-up garage. As the examination of the CCTV footage continued, gardaí identified the getaway car outside the same lock-up and a man directing the vehicle. By now, gardaí had well-founded suspicions that the lock-up had been used by the hit team to prepare for the murder. They were getting closer.

At 12.17 p.m. on 20 May 2016, a Garda search team swooped on the property. Inside the lock-up they recovered three .38 Smith & Wesson revolvers, mobile phone chargers and clothing. Examination of these satisfied the team that the garage had been used as a base for the gang before they embarked on their mission to kill Barr.

The evidence was starting to mount, but then detectives struck gold: a DNA sample taken from one of the masks and one of the baseball caps matched Cumberton's profile, which was stored on a database due to a previous conviction for assault, and Slator's DNA profile was matched to a sample taken from one of two rubber masks and from runners recovered from the getaway vehicle. In addition, though, gardaí recovered DNA from a Freddie Krueger-style rubber mask that did not match any on their database. As in similar cases, the unmatched DNA was sent on to Interpol and to the police in the UK. It wasn't long before gardaí received a call informing them that the DNA samples matched the same profile as Liverpool-born drug addict, car thief and burglar David Hunter (b. 5 September 1978). Thanks to the DNA evidence, gardaí now had the three hit-team members firmly in their sights: Cumberton, Slator and Hunter.

Unaware of the intense investigation taking place in the background, Cumberton had remained in Thailand since April, but now decided it was time to come home. He returned to Ireland on 25 May. By that stage, gardaí had intelligence of his involvement and had also identified the DNA from two of the items in the car. Within hours of arriving back in Ireland, the investigation team had received information of his return. Their prime suspect was also the subject of a bench warrant over his failure to appear in court on an assault charge. Fearful of him slipping the net again, Cumberton was arrested on 27 May at a property in the north inner city.

He was informed that he was being held on suspicion of breach of his bench warrant. That no doubt put him at his ease, and the former Hutch family neighbour dropped his guard and asked for a cigarette. The investigators were determined to present a watertight case and here was another chance: they took a DNA sample from the cigarette.

While Cumberton remained in custody, a positive match was made between the cigarette and one of the masks in the getaway car. Consultations were held with the DPP and then on 29 May the MMA cage-fighter was brought to court and formally charged with the murder of Michael Barr. One member of the hit team had been taken out of commission.

Just nineteen days later it was the turn of Aylmer to be arrested. He was hauled in for questioning on suspicion of providing logistical support for the gang and was held for three days before being released without charge as gardaí prepared another file for the DPP. Once the case had been examined by the DPP, they accepted the investigation team's contention that: 'The Kinahan criminal organization has shown ruthlessness in its efforts to wipe out its adversaries and their associates.'

Over the next eighteen months the investigation team

would complete their case before Cumberton's trial got under way at the Special Criminal Court on 20 November 2017. In his opening remarks for the prosecution, Dominic McGinn SC told the court that Cumberton was 'inextricably linked to the items found in the Audi, themselves inextricably linked' to the shooting. Over the course of the next month, evidence linking Cumberton to the crime scene was presented to the court. The three-judge panel ruled on 21 December that they would return to the court on 29 January 2018 with their verdict.

In his address to the court in January, Mr Justice Tony Hunt read from a sixty-four-page judgement which found Cumberton guilty of a 'deliberate and planned execution' and that there was 'no basis to conclude his DNA was present in the car for some innocent reason'. Mr Justice Hunt also referred to Cumberton's 'highly unusual' flight to Thailand. However, Mr Justice Hunt said the court 'could not determine' which role Cumberton had played in the shooting, which subjected those in the pub that night to a 'very traumatic spectacle'. The senior judge also noted that the hit team's masks were 'eye-catching, lurid and distinctive'. Before the case concluded, Noeleen Barr told the court how the murder of her brother had 'torn our family apart. It's left a huge hole behind and we will never get him back.' In his final address to the court, Mr Justice Hunt expressed his condolences to the Barr family, describing the murder as a 'truly shocking crime'.

When Cumberton was receiving his life sentence for murder, both Hunter and Slator were still in hiding. That meant Martin Aylmer would be the next member of the gang to face justice. He appeared before the non-jury court on 7 March 2018, charged with participating in or contributing to activity intending to facilitate the commission by a criminal organization or any of its members of a serious offence, namely the murder of Michael Barr. Remanded on continuing bail, Aylmer was back before the court on 25 July, when he pleaded guilty. Following his admission, he was remanded in custody and on 15 October was handed down a 3-year-and-9-month sentence for providing logistical support to the gang. The DPP later appealed this sentence, arguing that it was 'unduly lenient'. When the appeal was heard, Aylmer's sentence was increased to six years, with the last fifteen months suspended. This would not be the last time Aylmer would appear before the Special Criminal Court on Kinahan cartel business (see Chapters 8 and 12), but for now he too was taken out of action and put behind bars.

Following Cumberton's and Aylmer's convictions, the investigation to apprehend Slator and Hunter continued. The next member of the murder squad to be arrested was Hunter, when he was detained by UK police in the Liverpool area on 16 October 2019. He was brought back to Ireland the same day and appeared before the Special Criminal Court, where he was charged with the murder.

His trial started on 10 June 2020 and his defence team insisted that he was 'no James Bond or Ethan Hunt' – the fictional characters from the Bond and *Mission Impossible* movies. In fact, Hunter had previously worked as a carer, but the death of his brother Paul in 2007 had led him to the world of drugs and addiction, culminating in his involvement in serious and organized crime. Gardaí were satisfied, however, that he was part of the cartel's UK branch, based in the north-west of England. Investigators also established that he had flown on a 'last minute' Ryanair flight to Dublin three days after the murder of David Byrne, also the day Eddie Hutch was murdered. His other travels included flying to Spain three days after the Barr murder.

During his trial, the Special Criminal Court heard how he had returned to Ireland on 23 April 2016 – the same day that Aylmer bought the phones in the Ilac Shopping Centre. The court also heard how Hunter had bought a new phone in Holyhead before he boarded the ferry with his then girl-friend, Jordanna Kiely. Upon arrival, they booked into the Travelodge Hotel in Swords, north Dublin, and spent much of the time drinking and taking drugs. The trial then focused on the day of the murder, outlining how Hunter had dropped a phone in Walsh Road. When the caller failed to get through to the discarded phone, they had then called Hunter on his personal UK mobile, which was the same number noted by Detective Garda Harkin.

Towards the end of his trial, the court heard details about Hunter's DNA being found on three of the items recovered from the getaway car. In reference to one of the items, the ski mask, Hunter claimed that he was an 'avid skier' and had the mask because he planned 'to steal a car to order in a nice housing estate'.

The case concluded on 30 July 2020 as the judges con-sidered their verdict. Back in court on 11 September, Mr Justice Alexander Owens told the court that Hunter's claims regarding his reasons for being in Ireland were 'unbeliev-able', 'untrue', 'implausible', 'peculiar' and 'not credible' and that his involvement in the murder had been 'fully proved'. He handed down the mandatory life sentence.

Following Hunter's conviction for murder, Michael Barr's father, Colin, thanked gardaí for their efforts in bringing his son's killers to justice and said: 'He [Hunter] left England to come here to murder an Irishman. He should definitely be made to serve his sentence here. We know who's behind this. Everyone knows who is paying these men and people are prepared to take money to take a human life; at the end of the day, that's what it's all about, killing for money, it's ridiculous. I have no fear of them, they can do what they want.'

Noeleen Barr added to her father's statement, asking: 'How can a life be measured in drugs or money?'

Hunter had become yet another 'disposable foot soldier', the term coined by Mr Justice Tony Hunt during his address to the court when he referred to the 'cynicism of the Kinahan Organized Crime Group'. He explained: 'The risks are subcontracted to vulnerable, desperate and foolish individuals . . . and for very little gain.'

For the investigating team it was three down, one to go.

Gardaí did not have to wait long for their next arrest. On the morning of 21 December 2020 an anonymous 999 call informed gardaí that Christopher Slator was back in Dublin and visiting a relative in Cabra. Within minutes, Garda units from Cabra Garda Station were dispatched to a house in the area, where they found Slator enjoying a cup of tea. This was the first sighting of him by gardaí since Barr's murder.

Like Cumberton, he was arrested on suspicion of breach of a bench warrant over an old drugs charge for which he had failed to appear in court. Before being brought to court for the bench warrant hearing, detectives seized his trainers, trousers, mobile phone, reading glasses and a €50 note.

However, when he was again arrested at 2.52 p.m., this time on suspicion of murder, he replied: 'Sure everyone knew this was going to happen, probably going to stitch me up like the other lads.'

Slator was brought back to court the following day and remanded in custody until the start of his trial on 25 April. It concluded on 2 July, and the three-judge panel convened on 15 July to deliver its verdict: guilty.

Ms Justice Tara Burns said: 'The joint effect of DNA being on both the mask and the runners and the runners being found on top of the guns used in the murder satisfied the court that the accused wore both and was involved in the murder of Mr Barr. There is no other rational explanation.'

The work of the investigation team had been thorough and undeniable. The Garda Representatives Association's National Executive member at the time for the DMR North Division, Declan O'Carolan, praised the actions of his colleagues that night: 'It's fortuitous there wasn't an explosion when Detective Garda Michael Harkin put his life on the line when he was extinguishing the fire in the car. His professionalism and his commitment to extinguishing the fire was crucial in the preservation of evidence. Without the intervention of Det Garda Harkin and Det Garda O'Brien that night, valuable evidence may have been lost and future prosecution jeopardized. Their actions that night also reflected the realities of frontline policing in what was a very difficult period.'

The initial investigation at the time of the murder was undertaken by detectives from the Bridewell Garda Station. The case was then transferred as officers from the North Central Division were already investigating the feud-related murders of Eddie Hutch and Martin O'Rourke and trying to prevent further bloodshed. The probe was run by Detective Inspector John Bates, Superintendent Dan Flavin, Detective Superintendent Eunan Dolan, Chief Superintendent Sean Ward and Assistant Commissioner Pat Leahy, who are all now retired.

The latter stages of the investigations into Hunter and Slator were undertaken by Detective Inspector Mark Jordan, Superintendent Martin Mooney, Superintendent Jonathan O'Brien, Detective Superintendent Colm Murphy and their teams, with support from Garda national units.

Superintendent Mooney, now retired, noted: 'The murder of Michael Barr was cold, calculated and callous. It was well planned but thwarted through the quick-thinking actions of Det Garda Harkin and Det Garda O'Brien who prevented vital evidence from being destroyed. I would like to commend everyone involved in this investigation for their perseverance and determination and I would also like to thank the community for all of their assistance.'

In a damning statement against Daniel Kinahan's narco-terrorist gang, Noeleen Barr said: 'The drugs cartel that murdered my brother do not understand the importance of a loving family. All that matters to them is drugs and wealth. A family's love is more valuable than anything and I am proud to call the loveable rogue Michael Barr my brother.'

What the Kinahan cartel seemed to understand best was that there were enough guns-for-hire in Dublin to do their bidding and eliminate anyone they cared to name – and they were far from done.

3. Family Business

(24 May 2016: murder of Gareth Hutch)

'It's the fucking feud.'
— Ross Hutch, cousin of victim

His cousin Gary Hutch and his uncle Eddie Hutch were dead, and in May 2016 Gareth Hutch had serious concerns for his own life. The Kinahan cartel didn't seem inclined to forgive and forget and Dublin was awash with rumour and counter-rumour, everyone looking over their shoulders and wondering who would be next.

Gareth Hutch was a nephew of the Monk and he had come to Garda attention before when he was arrested over a botched cash-in-transit robbery in Lucan in 2009 during which one man, Gareth Molloy, was shot dead by gardaí. Gareth Hutch had fled the country but was extradited from the Netherlands, and he was later acquitted of the charges. His cousin Derek 'Del Boy' Hutch was handed down a 16-year prison term for orchestrating the heist.

Gareth kept his head down over the following years, but that wouldn't save him if his surname was enough to land him on a hitlist. He knew the Kinahan cartel wanted him dead, but his main concern was for his 7-year-old son's safety. Gareth Hutch had been warned by gardaí that his life was under threat and was seeking to be moved from his flat, 13A at Avondale House. Gareth's home was less than a two-minute walk from the home of another uncle, Patsy, who lived on Champions Avenue, around 450 metres from O'Connell Street. Despite living in the heartland of the Hutch territory, events in the past months meant that neither he nor any Hutch relative or associate could trust anyone. There didn't seem to be any safe place for the family any more.

Tormented by thoughts of what might come to pass, Gareth turned to the former Lord Mayor and Dublin city councillor Nial Ring for help. Cllr Ring told the authors: 'Gareth was a lovely guy and he came up to my office in May. And he just sat down, and he was quite calm about it. He had a foreboding feeling. He said, "I think they're going to get me, but I don't want them to do it in front of me kid." He had a little fellow at the time who was living with him in Avondale House. And he said, "The security in the place is absolutely terrible. There's CCTV for other parts, I'm totally exposed . . . people can get in the window, people can get in the front." But it was just all about his kid. And that was the sad part about it. I mean, here was a guy knowing he was under threat, but at the same time his only concern wasn't his own life, it was his kid, making sure his kid didn't see him being shot in front of them.'

Gareth Hutch spent ninety minutes at Cllr Ring's office as the politician helped him write a letter to Dublin City Council. The letter read: 'This situation is a cause of worry, concern and anxiety for me and, more importantly, is possibly putting my child at risk. This is the most important issue for me and for this reason I am asking for a welfare priority and transfer from the flat. You should be aware of the background issues surrounding my family and I have been advised by the Gardaí about my personal safety. Indeed, the house number is with the Emergency Response Unit in case of any incident.'

The next morning, 24 May 2016, was a warm summer's day and Gareth Hutch emerged from his flat at 9.53 a.m., which was over an hour later than he ordinarily would. He walked to his Volkswagen Passat car and opened the rear passenger door to place his jacket on the back seat.

Two hooded men appeared suddenly and ran towards the car. Gareth Hutch never even got to turn around and look them in the eye. From behind, he was shot four times: two bullets to the back of his neck, one to his lower back and another to his chest. Smoke rose from one of the guns as spent cartridges hit the ground. The victim lay unmoving on the ground.

The assassins ran over to a black 02-D BMW in the car park, which appeared to have had its rear windows spray-painted. They leapt in, but the vehicle choked and after a minute of trying to start it, the pair abandoned it and began to run on foot.

At that moment, Ross Hutch drove into the car park, parked, got out and then saw his cousin's body on the ground. He spotted the two attackers and chased after them as they fled through a pedestrian exit and raced off. Ross Hutch turned and came back to his cousin. Stunned residents making their way down to the gruesome scene heard him roar, 'Oh, no, no, no!' as he clutched his head. Gareth Hutch was dead.

All the while, the hitmen ran away, heading to Seán McDermott Street and then on to Champions Avenue, where an 05-D Skoda Octavia was parked. The car reversed out at 9.56 a.m., three minutes after the execution, and drove off to nearby Rutland Street, where one of the men got out of the car and ran to Summerhill. The driver then went to the Bal-lymun area. The vehicle was found burnt out at Dubber Cross in Finglas later that day.

The shock of Gareth Hutch's murder soon turned to fury among residents at Avondale, as the first two gardaí on the scene, who arrived just after 10 a.m., discovered. Asked who the victim was, Ross Hutch told one of the officers, 'You fucking know who it is. Do your job.' When questioned as to what had happened, he snapped, 'It's the fucking feud.' The hitmen had both flung down their weapons – two semi-automatic Makarov 9mm guns of Russian origin and fitted with silencers – at the scene and they were recovered by investigators. Bullets had been fired from just one of them; the second firearm still had its safety catch on and six full rounds of ammunition.

Cllr Ring heard about the shooting minutes after it had happened and he knew that Gareth had been heading to deliver the letter they had drafted the day before. He said: 'He was actually going to that meeting. That was the real scary part. But the fact that I had set him up with a meeting which ended up with him being shot as he was coming out of the flat complex, that was very upsetting.' A neighbour of Gareth's wrapped his body in a sheet while his father, John, and brother Jonathan were later seen crying and shaking at the scene.

As this fresh murder investigation got under way, gardaí were also concerned that Gareth's cousin Ross would seek revenge. Ross Hutch was a volatile character who had strug-gled with drug addiction, and he was all too aware that he too was a marked man. Less than a year earlier he had looked healthy and content when he appeared on RTÉ's *Winning*

Streak game show on behalf of his older brother Eddie (who died of natural causes in May 2024) and won €33,000 in prize money. But fortunes for him and his family had taken a dramatic turn just six days later when his cousin Gary Hutch was gunned down in Spain, while his father was Eddie Snr, who had been assassinated earlier that year.

Ross did not, as gardaí had feared, commit any crimes the day of Gareth Hutch's murder, but in his fit of anger at the scene he mentioned the name of Jonathan Keogh (who featured in Chapter 2) as being one of the men in the hit team he recognized.

Keogh (b. 29 July 1985) lived in the area and was a serious criminal with convictions dating back to 2002. A father of two, he had strong links to the INLA since 2006, striking up a friendship with another dangerous figure, Gerard Mackin, and had become an enforcer for the terror group. Keogh had an active role in it, taking part in paramilitary parades and colour parties, resulting in him being given an 8-year jail term at the Special Criminal Court in 2009 after being caught making bombs. He was later released, and gardaí soon became aware that, although not a member, he was working for the Kinahan cartel for money. Keogh had been paid from cartel coffers to go up north and kill Kevin 'Flatcap' Murray, the dissident republican who had been one of the Regency Hotel gunmen on behalf of the Hutch organized crime gang. However, Keogh had never carried out that hit because he was afraid that Tyrone native Murray – who died from motor neurone disease in August 2017 – was under surveillance from the Police Service of Northern Ireland (PSNI). At the time of the latest feud murder, he was also taking money from the state, on job-seeker's allowance.

With Keogh's name in the mix, it was pertinent to the

investigation that his older sister Regina had lived in Avondale House for many years. The eldest of seven, Regina (b.
26 May 1977) was not involved in crime and she knew Gareth
Hutch personally. Gardaí searched the Keoghs' father's home
on Upper Seán McDermott Street on the day of the murder
at around 3.30 p.m. While they were there, Regina turned up
and said to a detective sergeant present, 'You will probably
be searching my house next.' They did, but nothing of evidential value was found there.

Thomas 'Tossy' Fox also came on to the Garda radar as a
suspect. Aged twenty-nine at the time and a low-level criminal, he had been friends with Jonathan Keogh and had
become closer to him in recent months. He often associated
with criminal figures in the north inner city and had over a
hundred convictions, including for drugs and criminal
damage, and also, more significantly, for the possession of a
firearm in suspicious circumstances. He had served a 1-year
sentence for that. In the aftermath of Gary Hutch's murder,
Fox's family home at Rutland Court, in Dublin's north inner
city, and another address he was linked to were raided too.
Some hours later he handed himself into Mountjoy Garda
Station, claiming he was there to clear his name. Detectives
arrested and detained him on suspicion of murder with a
firearm at 7.01 p.m. on the evening of the killing.

Before Regina Keogh had gone to her father's home that
day, she had called to the flat of her brother Jonathan's ex-
partner, Denise King. The relationship between Denise and
Jonathan had ended in November 2015 and she'd had no
contact with him until March 2016, a week before their baby
daughter was born. At that point, Keogh began staying at her
flat regularly, telling his ex he had a threat on his life and he
felt safe there. He stayed there the night before Hutch's

murder, when she overheard him on the phone telling someone he had had a 'fight with the Hutch fella'. He had also
told Denise King that he had planned leaving the country on
Tuesday, 24 May.

That day, when Regina called round, she handed Denise
King around €2,000 in cash and told her to bring it up to
Jonathan, who was in Belfast. After a sunbed session, a trip
to the shops and dropping in to a pal to collect some DVDs,
Denise King decided to make the trip up north, getting a bus
at 7 p.m. As she made her way there, Keogh was in a pub
gulping pints: he was captured on camera footage at Fibber
Magee's pub in Great Victoria Street at 9.54 p.m. Denise
King later handed him the money in a hotel room, booked
through a female associate of his. When Denise King asked
Keogh if he had murdered Hutch, he denied it. The following morning, Keogh got a haircut before he caught a ferry at
the Stena Line Port Terminal in Belfast and travelled to
Cairnryan, Scotland.

Chilling CCTV of Hutch's murder had made its way on to
social media, adding further pressure on the gardaí as people
commented on the depravity of the killing. Officers trawled
through extensive footage of the periods before and after
the murder and established that the BMW had been parked
in the Avondale complex the day before the killing, strategically placed there at 10.28 a.m. Keogh, they established, was
one of the two men in the car. On the day of the hit, a
Honda Civic arrived on Champions Avenue at 6.35 a.m. and
a second car, a Skoda Octavia, was also seen on camera travelling from Ballymun at 6.24 a.m. and landing at the same
location around twenty minutes later. The two drivers got
out and walked from there. At 6.46 a.m. they walked past the

front gate of Avondale House and a minute later they went up a stairwell, one of them holding a plastic bag, and went in the direction of a first-floor flat, number 18A. They only emerged again from that flat when they went to kill Gareth Hutch.

The flat was that of Mary McDonnell, aged forty-three at the time, who had lived a life that centred around the flats and her family. She was best friends with Regina Keogh, who lived in 6A, and they had known each other since Mary McDonnell had moved into the complex over fifteen years earlier. McDonnell had ongoing medical issues relating to epilepsy and also suffered with depression, but Regina had been there for her when she had suicidal thoughts. When she had stints in hospital, Regina looked after her children. On the day of the murder, McDonnell's home was declared a crime scene, so that night she stayed with Regina.

The day after the murder, 25 May 2016, gardaí obtained a warrant to search Mary McDonnell's home. When they arrived, they saw her putting a black bag into the bins. This was later retrieved and found to contain cigarette butts, baby wipes and surgical gloves; more baby wipes were seized from her home. A pink dressing-gown from her main bedroom with pairs of latex gloves in the pockets was also later recovered.

As the search was ongoing, McDonnell engaged in general conversation with gardaí, during which she revealed information about a row on the evening prior to the murder. The gardaí asked her to make a statement about it, and she agreed to do so. In making her statement, she left officers stunned as she disclosed further specific details about the planning and execution of the murder of Gareth Hutch. The gardaí cautioned her, but she kept on talking. The investigators were so shocked at what she had come out with that they were struggling to believe it at first. Mary McDonnell had just willingly implicated herself in a murder.

McDonnell later explained that she was in her flat on the day before the shooting when she heard an argument in the car park of the Avondale complex. When she looked out the window, she saw Jonathan Keogh arguing with Gareth Hutch. Keogh, who had arrived in his Honda Civic with 'Tossy' Fox, confronted a man in the car park who was apparently waiting to meet Gareth Hutch and his cousin Ross over the sale of a motor. Keogh had become paranoid when he saw the man talking on a phone and pointing in the direction of the flats. He chased the man out of the complex before Gareth Hutch stood in as a mediator. There then followed a heated exchange between him and Hutch. McDonnell said Keogh pointed towards his sister Regina's flat and she recalled him saying, 'If anything happens to her or any of my family, I'm coming after you.' As she watched, Hutch and Keogh seemed to reach an understanding and shook hands.

Regina had then arrived up to McDonnell's flat for a 'relaxer' – a Valium. She had also witnessed the row and seemed upset by it. McDonnell recalled telling her, 'It's over, like, they're shaking hands,' to which Regina had responded, 'No, that's only the beginning.'

Gareth had called Regina Keogh over to his apartment and handed her a note with a phone number to pass on to her brother. McDonnell said the note told him to call Gareth's uncle, described as 'Mega'. Jonathan Keogh, along with 'Tossy' Fox, came up to McDonnell's flat and he rang the number. McDonnell overheard Gareth's uncle on the phone saying, 'I've nothing to do with them two gobshites.' Keogh was on the phone again later in the day and she listened to him saying, 'I'm going to get him before he gets me.' She believed this was a reference to Gareth Hutch.

The weekend before all this, McDonnell said she was asked by Regina to do something for her brother Jonathan. Then on 23 May she found out what the 'something' was: McDonnell said that Jonathan told his sister to 'give Mary €1,000 out of that money that you have belonging to me and I'll give her the €4,000 when I come back'. McDonnell was effectively being asked to give up her flat to Keogh for cash, for reasons she now knew about, but did not know at the time. She thought this was a joke at first, but when she realized it was a serious request, she told Regina that she would not allow the men to use her flat because her husband and twin daughters wouldn't like it. Regina had tried persuading her by saying, 'That's the only way it is going to happen. If not, Jonathan is going to be shot.' By then, Keogh and Fox had already left and Regina then left to return to her own flat to feed her children.

That evening, 23 May, McDonnell went over to Regina's flat for a time, during which Keogh and Fox arrived. When Mary got up to leave, Regina said, 'They'll be up to you.' Almost immediately after she got home, Keogh and 'Tossy' Fox arrived at her flat and spent five minutes inside. They asked for baby wipes, and she thought it was for them to wipe their hands, but she recalled: 'Next of all I looked in their hands and saw two guns, they were using the baby wipes to clean them. I was shaking at the door. I was just praying they would get out of my house with them.' She said one of the men told the other to 'make sure not to leave the silencer on'. She gave them an Aldi-branded bag to put the guns in and they then left with the firearms.

Terrified after what had just happened, McDonnell rang
Regina and told her that she had already said that she did not
want 'anything up in my house'. Soon after, Regina arrived at
her flat, using the excuse that she needed teabags. She gave
McDonnell a handful of surgical gloves and said, 'Give them
to Johnny for tomorrow.' McDonnell refused and told
Regina, 'It's not happening here, it's not, because [her hus-
band] won't let it happen here or nothing like it, and neither
will the twins.' However, McDonnell did take the gloves from
Regina and left them on the counter.

The next morning, the morning of the murder, a knock
came, and McDonnell recalled that when she opened it, 'the
door nearly came in on top' of her. The second man with
Keogh was not 'Tossy' Fox this time, like the night before, it
was another young man who she did not recognize: he will
be referred to as 'AB' from here on. Keogh asked for the
gloves 'Gina gave you' and he and AB put them on. Over the
next three hours Keogh was in and out of her sitting room
and into her bedroom, which overlooked the car park at the
complex, making sure the BMW would not be blocked in.
She heard Keogh warning his associate AB 'not to leave any
evidence' around after he threw a cigarette butt into the bin
while he watched Gareth Hutch's apartment from her kitchen window.

During this time Keogh received a number of calls from
Fox, who she said was nearby in a van, saying he wanted to
leave. 'Tossy was telling him to hurry up, Johnny was saying
they would be up in five minutes and not to leave,' according
to McDonnell. She said that Keogh was annoyed at Fox and
she heard him say to AB: 'That fucking eejit Tossy, he wants
to go now, 'cause everyone is coming out looking at the van.'
At 9.53 a.m. the men saw Gareth Hutch emerge from his

apartment. McDonnell recalled AB saying to Keogh, 'Right Johnny, we are on.'

Mary McDonnell had herself been accomplice to a murder, but she was also in a very dangerous place and accessible by either side of the feud. Concerned for her safety, gardaí brought her to Mountjoy Garda Station and in the meantime they began viewing CCTV to corroborate the details of what she had told them in her initial statement. That evening, she was arrested on suspicion of murder with a firearm and brought to the Bridewell Garda Station. McDonnell's information was vital to building the picture of what exactly had happened. The use of her flat had been a key part of that plan, because of its clear view of Gareth Hutch's home, and while Jonathan Keogh was now the prime suspect, Regina Keogh had known about the intent of her brother and had, in fact, been involved in the planning of the killing.

'Tossy' Fox had remained in the Mountjoy Garda Station since handing himself in on the evening of the murder, after being persuaded to do so by his mother, and he was ready to spin his own tale to gardaí.

Gardaí had quickly established that an 04-D Ford Transit van had been strategically parked on Wellington Street, Dublin 7, the day before the murder. This vehicle, gardaí believed, was going to be the 'switch': the two men would flee the scene in the BMW to a location where the BMW could be burned out and Fox would be waiting there to drive them away as the car, and its evidence, went up in flames. The morning of the murder, Fox drove a relative's 03-D Toyota Avensis before taking up his role as the driver of the van. The van was seen throughout the morning moving to different locations, including on to St Mary's Place North and later on to Mountjoy Street. However, the BMW not starting caused a significant breakdown in the hit team's plan, forcing Keogh and AB to use the Skoda Octavia, which meant Fox and his van were no longer needed. When that became apparent, he parked the van back at Wellington Street and drove off in the Toyota Avensis.

'Tossy' Fox was expecting a child with his girlfriend at that time. When he sat down with gardaí to give his version of events, he claimed to have been in his aunt's home on the morning of the murder and that he went down to the area after hearing about it just because he was being 'nosey'. His father, Michael Taylor, had been shot dead in front of his mother in 2011 and he claimed this meant it was not in him to shoot anyone: 'It's not in me to retaliate.' Fox said he didn't have 'the stomach or the balls' to pull the trigger of a gun and he asked, 'What kind of thick would hand himself in?'

Fox admitted that he knew Keogh, but claimed he never got involved in his business. He said Keogh had told him about the threat on his life but seemed relaxed about it, telling him, 'Fuck it, if they are going to get me, they are going to get me.' Fox denied any involvement in the murder, insisting that he'd never raise his baby on 'blood money'.

Crucially, though, Fox identified himself and Keogh on CCTV walking to McDonnell's flat on the night before the murder. He said that once they were inside, he realized Keogh had two guns in his trousers. Fox claimed that Keogh said, 'You'll get it yourself' if he did not do what he was told. He said to gardaí: 'If I wasn't under pressure I wouldn't have done it. The gun was pushed into my hand.'

He further confirmed that he and Keogh had left McDonnell's flat that night at ten forty-five. He protested his innocence, saying he did not foresee what was going to happen and that he had not sourced guns for the hit.

The abandoned BMW had been seized by gardaí and they had found a red petrol can inside it that was two thirds full and had Fox's DNA on it. When this was put to him, Fox claimed Keogh must have got it from his garden and worn gloves while doing so, because he had definitely not given it to him with the knowledge that it was going to be used for murder. A tin of spray paint had also been seized, which was relevant due to the rear windows being blacked out with such a substance, and this also had Fox's DNA on it. He did admit giving the spray paint to Keogh but said he had never asked what it was for and he rejected the suggestion that he was the one who had done the job.

The evidence against Fox would soon be added to when CCTV later recovered showed Fox in the company of Keogh on 22 May 2016 in a Tesco shop, buying a bottle of Milton sterilizing fluid. The bottle was recovered from the Ford Transit van.

During his time in custody, Fox was found unresponsive in his cell with a ligature around his neck, but he was brought to hospital and discharged back to the garda station on the same day. He would still have to face further questions and provide answers.

On foot of Mary McDonnell's explosive statement, Regina Keogh was arrested on 26 May on suspicion of murder and taken to Store Street Garda Station. The mum-of-five told gardaí she had a good relationship with Gareth Hutch but that the Hutch family were feared by everyone in the Avondale flats complex.

When questioned about the run of events leading up to

the murder of Gareth Hutch, Regina claimed she didn't recognize the two men who came out of Mary McDonnell's flat
on the morning of the murder and she denied that her
brother Jonathan had said the previous day that he was going
to shoot Hutch. Regina said she did not know who carried
out the hit, but she was sure of one thing: 'I had no part in it.
I'm not losing my kids for anybody.'

Gardaí put it to her that her brother was one of the
gunmen and she said, 'I don't believe it, I don't.' When they
suggested that she knew the murder was going to happen
and allowed it to go ahead, she fumed, 'I'm not guilty of any
of this.' She also rejected the allegation that she gave money
to her brother's ex-partner, Denise King, to bring to him in
Belfast. When she was told the details of McDonnell's statement she branded her old pal a liar. In fact, she claimed,
Jonathan had told her that Ross Hutch was out to kill him.

Regina was later released without charge, but it was by no
means the end of the matter for her.

On 31 May 2016, Mary McDonnell appeared in court and
was charged with withholding information. She was brought
into the Dóchas Centre after being remanded in custody.
The next day, 'Tossy' Fox was in the dock to answer a charge
of unlawful possession of a handgun. McDonnell gave further detailed statements to gardaí on 10, 11 and 13 June and
was subsequently granted bail. Given the security concerns
that existed, she and her family had to be relocated in October that year. Her charge was later withdrawn as McDonnell
was given immunity and became a witness for the state.

As 2016 came to a close, Jonathan Keogh remained a free
man, outside the jurisdiction. The gardaí were granted a
European Arrest Warrant for him and began liaising with
their counterparts abroad to track him down.

In January 2017, Fox was arrested from prison and hit with a fresh charge: this time, for the murder of Gareth Hutch.

Seven days after the first anniversary of Gareth's murder, on 31 May 2017 the Hutch gang claimed revenge for his death by targeting Michael Keogh, a brother of Regina and Jonathan. He was blasted in his head, chest, neck and trunk. The dad of two was found dead in his Volkswagen Golf in an underground car park at the Sheridan Court flat complex, off Dorset Street in the north inner city. Jason 'Buda' Molyneux was one of the prime suspects in the 36-year-old's murder and his home was searched as part of that investigation. (Molyneux would be murdered in January 2018.) Three other arrests were made in relation to the Michael Keogh case, but gardaí were never able to bring charges.

Ten days later, on 10 June 2017, gardaí swooped on Regina Keogh and arrested her at 9.29 a.m., and she later appeared in court charged with the murder of Gareth Hutch. Gardaí had become increasingly concerned that Jonathan Keogh might return to Ireland to commit further crimes for the cartel, before skipping the jurisdiction again. But as it turned out, he wouldn't get the chance. In the early hours of the morning after Regina was charged, Jonathan Keogh was arrested at 1.00 a.m. in the Romford area of Essex, London, by officers from the UK's National Crime Agency on foot of the European Arrest Warrant. In August, Keogh was extradited to Ireland on a military plane and immediately hit with a murder rap.

The information about his location in Romford had been gathered after he made an online passport application. Gardaí seized the ear plugs Keogh had worn on the flight back to Ireland for the purpose of getting his DNA. It was later found to match samples on the latex gloves taken from McDonnell's dressing-gown and a number of items in the BMW car: a balaclava, a biker's neck warmer and a baseball cap. Gardaí finally had the evidence that unequivocally put Jonathan Keogh at the murder scene of Gareth Hutch.

In 2018, Jonathan Keogh, his sister Regina and 'Tossy' Fox faced a murder trial before the Special Criminal Court.

In June, the murder trial heard testimony from witness Mary McDonnell. Over a number of days she gave her account of the events that had taken place in the Avondale complex. She made a number of identifications on CCTV, including Keogh having the argument with Hutch on the day before the shooting, Keogh with Fox at her flat that night, and Keogh and AB as the shooters on the day. Other witnesses, two of whom knew Jonathan Keogh, gave evidence of seeing him running shortly after the murder, after he had got out of the Skoda Octavia on Rutland Street and went on to Summerhill. Fresh phone evidence also linked the three accused together, along with AB.

It was a lengthy trial and the culmination of it saw all three convicted. Mr Justice Tony Hunt said that Jonathan Keogh was the triggerman on the day and 'had a hand in almost every aspect' of the planning in the run-up to the murder. The court found that Regina Keogh had 'colluded' with her brother, that she had taken advantage of her 'good friendship' with McDonnell, and that she had brought the latex gloves to her best pal's flat on the night before the killing knowing what was afoot. Fox had put forward a defence that his involvement in the planning of the hit was through coercion by Keogh but that was 'counteracted' by him pulling out late on the day. However, the court found that an intention to withdraw from a criminal enterprise must be unequivocal, that to withdraw because of panic does not suffice as a defence.

A victim impact statement was read out on behalf of Vera Hutch, the mother of Gareth, in which she said: 'We struggle every day as a family and can't comprehend why this happened. There are many times I have even wished that I had died that morning with Gareth.' As a garda read out Vera's statement, Jonathan Keogh shouted, 'What about everyone else's families? What about all the other families? Sorry, Judge. Fucking bastards, rats.'

It was Keogh's final insult to the family of the man he had murdered before he was led away, with his accomplices, to begin his life sentence in Mountjoy. His part in the Kinahan feud against the Hutch family was over, although there were others who had stepped up to take his place.

4. Blood Brothers

(13 June 2016: a murder revenge plot and a weapons seizure)

'Lads, I just want you to know, this wasn't for financial gain. David Byrne was my best friend. I miss him. I really miss him.'
   – Mr X, friend of victim

On 13 June 2016 the Ireland football team got off to a decent start in their opening game at the European Championship finals with a one–one draw against Sweden. Following the result, fans across the country were feeling optimistic about the chances of the boys in green making the last sixteen as they looked ahead to the game against European heavyweights Belgium. With kick-off against the Belgians scheduled at 5 p.m. that Saturday, pubs and clubs would be packed with fans cheering on their heroes. The whole country would come to a standstill as then manager Martin O'Neill's men took to the field.

On Saturday, as fans eagerly awaited kick-off, one man had no interest in the big match. Mr X (who can't be named for legal reasons) had only one thing on his mind that day: revenge for the murder of his friend David Byrne. Since the high-profile killing at the Regency Hotel that had shocked the whole country, Mr X had been left devastated by Byrne's murder. He had stood alongside cartel heavyweights at his friend's funeral that previous February, and he was left reeling by the assassination. As one former detective told us: 'Mr X was a nobody in the overall structure of the cartel, but he was well respected because him and Byrne were inseparable. Mr X knew full well how ingrained Byrne was in organized crime but they still maintained a very close relationship. When Byrne wasn't in Spain, he would always be with Mr X. Anytime Byrne was stopped at a checkpoint, most of the time Mr X was with him. When Byrne was murdered the locals in the street were saying that [Mr X] had gone into a deep depression and just couldn't cope.'

Just under four months on from the Regency gun attack, and with the cartel in the midst of an all-out war on anyone even remotely connected to Gerry 'the Monk' Hutch, a grief-stricken Mr X offered his services to Daniel Kinahan's gang. An eye for an eye.

On the morning of the big game, the Garda National Drugs and Organised Crime Bureau (GNDOCB) received confidential information that Mr X, along with another man, who also cannot be named for legal reasons, had access to a Volkswagen Golf and a Nissan Qashqai for the purpose of moving firearms to be used in an attack against an unnamed member of the Hutch family. After analysing the intelligence, the GNDOCB instigated an immediate 'threat to life' operation. An operation of this type is when gardaí are mobilized to prevent someone being shot. It would be one of twenty operations undertaken that year.

The operation started at 1.10 p.m., with gardaí placing Mr X's associate under surveillance as he arrived at Mr X's house in a green Ford Focus. The associate left the property alone before returning at 1.47 p.m. Both men then left the property together and drove a short distance before doing a U-turn when they noticed a Garda checkpoint. Unaware that they were under constant surveillance, the pair drove to the Lansdowne Valley Crescent area, where Mr X was spotted at 1.50 p.m. taking a red petrol can from a wheelie bin and placing it in the passenger-side footwell of the Focus. The pair then drove off towards the M7 and headed in the direction of Sallins in County Kildare, arriving at the Oldbridge Estate at 2.16 p.m.

Once there, Mr X left the car and got into a black Volkswagen Golf and drove off in the direction of Dublin, following the other car. The Ford Focus pulled into the Esso garage before Junction 7 and Mr X, wearing a black baseball cap, black hooded jacket and black gloves, continued on his journey towards the capital and made his way along Walkinstown Avenue.

As the black Golf drove along Walkinstown Avenue at 2.40 p.m., the order to intercept the vehicle was given by Detective Inspector Gerard McGrath. Five minutes later the Emergency Response Unit, part of the Garda's Special Tactics and Operations Command (STOC), made their move. Mr X quickly found himself lying on the ground, hands cuffed behind his back.

Once the target had been apprehended, investigators searched the car. In the glove box they found a 9mm Glock handgun along with thirteen rounds of ammunition. A single live round was also recovered from the back seat, an encrypted BlackBerry phone from the front passenger seat, which gardaí were unable to unlock, and a red petrol can from the boot. When searched, Mr X also had a key to a Nissan Qashqai, confirming the gardaí's earlier suspicions.

Once the vehicle had been secured, Mr X was formally arrested by Detective Sergeant Greg Sheehan – who was involved in investigations into the Kinahan cartel for twenty

years but is now retired – on suspicion of possession of firearms in suspicious circumstances. In an interview with the
authors, the retired officer recalled his encounter with Mr X:
'He seemed to be visibly upset and it looked as if he was totally out of his depth. He had one previous charge for
possession of stolen property, but yet here he was, being
caught up in this feud.'

Mr X was brought to a waiting patrol car and driven the
short journey to Crumlin Garda Station for questioning.
Even though he had made no reply when formally charged,
he spoke for the first time that day when he asked Detective
Garda Ian Pemberton and Detective Garda Conor O'Sullivan
to remove his cap, saying: 'Take this stupid thing off my head.'
As he continued to sit in the car with his head bowed, he
spoke again to the investigators: 'Lads, I just want you to
know, this wasn't for financial gain. David Byrne was my best
friend. I miss him. I really miss him.'

In his first interview at the station with Detectives Pemberton and O'Sullivan, which lasted from 6.49 p.m. to 7.50
p.m., Mr X again expressed his sadness over Byrne's murder:
'I miss him now and I'll miss him for the rest of my life. You
caught me. I'm not a rat. I can't sleep. I won't be able to see
him again, go shopping, or a bite to eat. He was a close friend.
If David was still here, would I be here today?' The man was
then shown the firearm and he replied: 'Yeah, that's it.'

The second interview took place between 10.40 p.m. and
11.46 p.m. During it, Mr X again referred to Byrne's murder
when he said, 'I was in work. It was the worst day of my life.
I don't talk about it,' before referring to his own situation
when he said, 'I'm financially sound, I don't live outside my
means.' When asked if there was 'anger in him', he replied:
'Yeah, that's all I feel. It's all I show. I wished when I put my

hands up you lot would crack me in the head, that's why I did it when I stopped today.'

When questioned about the gun for a second time, he adopted a self-defence mode: 'I didn't have a gun in my hand today.' He then moved on to the ongoing feud, outlining his views when he said: 'It's never going to stop. Enda Kenny [then Taoiseach and head of government] says it's two feuding families. It's never going to stop. Would you let something happen to your loved ones and not do anything about it? I was loyal to David. You see others at the funeral, once it was finished, they were gone. If you don't have loyalty, you die with your loyalty.'

Once the interviews were completed, Mr X rested for the evening before being brought back into his third interview at 8.57 a.m. the following day. Within seconds of taking his seat, Mr X was shown the surveillance footage of him from the previous day. He again asked to speak and this time he made a request to 'clarify' his position. Granting his request, the two officers listened intently as he said: 'I wanted to clarify straight away – this wasn't gangland or anything like that, before you make me out to be some sort of killer. How would you feel if one of your loved ones and that happened to them? It would send you off in a different direction. Before anything is said about it in court or whatever, I just wanted to clarify that.'

His state of mind was evident when he admitted frankly to the interviewing detectives: 'I wished I had been killed yesterday in "suicide by cop". You should have killed me yesterday with all this bollix. David Byrne's death was the worst day of my life.'

During Mr X's continued detention, other members of the Garda investigation team established that the Volkswagen

Golf had been stolen from the Terenure area of Dublin and fitted with a false tax document, counterfeit insurance document and false registration plates. Aware the car had been stolen, they questioned Mr X about his intentions: 'You travelled from Dublin to Naas, collected a stolen car with a firearm in the vehicle and returned to Dublin with serious intent to cause injury or death to another father, best friend or multiples. You put planning into it.' When asked what 'emotion' he was feeling, he replied: 'Nothing – doesn't faze me at all. It's never going to go back to the way it was before all this happened.'

The questioning then switched to Mr X's capacity to kill someone when he was asked: 'Do you think you would have been able to kill someone yesterday? Would the grief have pushed you that far? The anger that's inside you?' In response to the question, Mr X replied: 'I don't know, my mind is never going to be the same again. I wish they never did that. I wish I never met you and I was back in my normal life, but it's not going to be like that.'

Following the conclusion of his third interview, Mr X remained silent during his three remaining interviews. He was charged at 11.05 p.m. on 19 June with possession of firearms in suspicious circumstances. Appearing in court the following day, he was remanded in custody until his appearance at Dublin Circuit Court in February 2017, where he pleaded guilty to the charge. Before the guilty plea, the Garda investigation team had concluded that 'The planning that went into this operation was precise. The intent relates to an ongoing feud within Dublin city between two organized criminal groupings.'

At Mr X's sentence hearing on 30 March 2017, in which he received a 6-year jail term, the court heard how he had gone into an 'emotional tailspin' after Byrne's murder, with Judge Martin Nolan insisting that he could 'infer from the evidence in the case that if the right occasion had occurred, the defendant had intended to use a lethal weapon'.

Mr X's defence barrister, Michael Bowman SC, indicated that his client had experienced an 'emotional crisis' and made a 'catastrophic error', explaining how Mr X had identified the death of his friend as the 'sole trigger' for possession of the gun, before concluding that his client now 'hangs his head in shame' over the incident. The court was also told that Mr X's DNA wasn't discovered on the firearm.

Following his sentencing, the *Irish Independent* reported that Ross Hutch – who is currently serving a 10-year sentence for two violent attacks on a man and woman over a two-day period in 2021 – was the intended target, to be hit after he had gone to a city-centre pub to watch the match that day.

Whoever was the intended target, Mr X did his time and was released from custody in 2020, but he continued to mourn his friend. He was photographed outside the Regency Hotel on 5 February 2021, when Bryne's friends gathered to remember him. At the time of writing in 2024, Mr X had appeared at Dublin Circuit Court on 22 January 2024, where he was sent forward for trial in 2026 on drugs charges. The would-be assassin never got to pull the trigger.

Mr X was not the last of David Byrne's close friends to come to the attention of gardaí in 2016. On the afternoon of 5 November, Detective Superintendent Dave Gallagher from the GNDOCB received confidential information that members of the Kinahan cartel based in the Cabra and north inner-city areas of Dublin had access to a Ford Focus van for the purpose of moving drugs, and possibly firearms. Once the intelligence had been shared with his colleagues, Detective Superintendent Gallagher initiated a covert operation that involved investigators patrolling those areas in unmarked cars as they searched for the suspect van.

A few hours into the operation, a Garda patrol in Cabra identified two males in a silver Ford Focus van driving in the St Attracta Road area. After driving along the road for a few minutes, the van stopped suddenly as it passed a man walking along the footpath. The man on the path leaned into the passenger window to talk to the van driver and his passenger. The Garda team saw their opportunity and pounced. They arrested all three men and brought them to Mountjoy Garda Station to be searched.

Once inside the station, the man who had been out walking was identified as Graham Gardner (b. 21 October 1984), who had previously been identified as a Kinahan cartel associate and a close friend of David Byrne. The duo in the van were identified as Vincent Maher (b. 28 April 1972), then partner of Regina Keogh, and another cartel associate, who can't be named for legal reasons. Maher and his passenger were released without charge.

A search of Gardner found that he was wearing a bullet-proof vest in which was stashed a Mass card in memory of David Byrne. Also tucked into Gardner's vest was the key to a Subaru vehicle. At the same time, gardaí were searching the Ford Focus and discovered a hidden compartment. It was activated by a pull-cord system concealed between the passenger and driver seats. When pulled, the cord released a catch that caused a section of the rear-floor panel to rise upwards. However, the hidden compartment was empty.

Gardner maintained that he had found the Subaru key while 'out walking his dog' and replied 'No comment' to all other questions. So it fell to Garda Redmond O'Leary and Garda Darren Coller to try to locate the Subaru that would fit the key.

Garda O'Leary recalled seeing a Subaru in the underground car park of the Homestead Court Apartments off the Quarry Road. They headed over there and identified a Subaru Outback parked in the corner of the car park. Garda O'Leary had the key taken from Gardner and when he pressed it the vehicle's lights flashed, confirming they had found the right vehicle.

Pulling on their latex gloves, they began to examine the interior of the Subaru. Garda Coller noticed how the seats had been sliced open, which is a tactic used by criminals to allow petrol to soak into the vehicle before it is set on fire. When Garda O'Leary opened the boot of the vehicle, he discovered a black hold-all, with a magazine and a number of rounds of ammunition sitting on top of the bag. Cautiously opening the bag, Garda O'Leary discovered two MP9 machine guns, two silencers, three Smith & Wesson revolvers, 107 rounds of ammunition and three loaded magazines. The find was relayed back to the station. When the interviewing gardaí asked Gardner about these weapons, he again replied, 'No comment' and continued to insist that he had found the key while out walking.

Gardner was released two days later as gardaí awaited the results of a forensic examination of the weapons. After examining more than 400 hours of CCTV footage, the investigation team established that the vehicle had been parked at the complex on 28 October, but they were unable to identify the driver, who had made sure to conceal their identity.

*

Gardner stayed at different locations throughout the capital, fearful that he would be targeted by the Hutch gang following his arrest. Meanwhile, his friend Maher soon found himself at the centre of another Garda investigation.

Shortly after seven o'clock on the morning of 6 December, gardaí called to the hostel accommodation in North Frederick Street where Maher was staying, but he was not there. Determined to locate him, officers drove around the north inner city, looking out for him. They noticed a Volkswagen Polo pull into the laneway off Mountjoy Street, beside the Berkeley pub. At 9.10 a.m. a team from the Special Crime Task Force arrested Maher as he left the area. He was being targeted by gardaí as they wanted to re-interview him about the weapons seizure the previous month.

However, as Maher was being questioned at the station, a member of the public rang 999 to say they had discovered a firearm in the laneway beside the Berkeley pub on Mountjoy Street. At the time, a member of the Special Detective Unit happened to be driving nearby and was the first to arrive at the scene, where he found a fully loaded Smith & Wesson revolver buried in a pile of sand at the end of the laneway. Once recovered, the weapon was sent immediately for forensic examination; gardaí had already obtained Maher's DNA from the previous arrest. The examination was fast-tracked and it was quickly established that Maher's DNA was a positive match to the sample recovered from the weapon.

In the interview room the conversation changed direction to the question of the recovered Smith & Wesson. It was pointed out to Maher that: 'Your DNA sample has been matched with a DNA sample from the handle of the firearm. You're in serious bother now. I think you should come clean when you have one last chance and tell us the right account of what occurred in relation to the firearm.' In response, Maher made an admission about the firearm when he said: 'I have GIM letters, as you know, and people are out to get me. My girlfriend had to go to England with the baby, so I had it for my own protection. I got it last Thursday. I had been looking for one and I got it in Phibsboro, in the bushes.'

When asked who had supplied the weapon, he said: 'Got the lend of it from a friend. I told him Gina [Keogh] had to go to England and I couldn't go yet. So I asked him could he get me a lend of a gun. I was after being threatened on the Wednesday. It was on the phone and he said he'd kill me, Gina, the baby and the whole family. You said yourself you'd protect your family, all my family are good people. I'm the only one that was ever in trouble.' When questioned about his role in the feud, he replied: 'It wasn't the feud but it was threats coming from people who are involved in the feud. My family won't let me stay with them because I'm a criminal and on drugs.' Asked where he slept at night, he replied: 'In my car.'

Referring back to the seizure in November, Maher was asked if he was scared of the 'capabilities' of the MP9's fire-power and he replied: 'Course it would, it would scare anyone.' The suspect was then asked why he had a balaclava and gloves when he was arrested in November and he said: 'It was Hallowe'en a few nights before and I had it for frightening the kids.' Asked what he would bring 'to shoot someone', he replied: 'A gun and myself.'

As his interviews came to an end that night, Maher was asked if it 'would be a fair assumption, given the people that you're associating with who would be heavily involved in the ongoing Kinahan and Hutch feud, have you been caught up in the feud?' He replied: 'No comment.' His interviews finished with him being asked if he accepted 'full responsibility' for the firearm, to which he replied: 'Yeah.'

At 7 p.m. on 7 December, Maher was formally charged with unlawful possession of a loaded firearm.

With Maher in custody, now it was the turn of the investigation team to try and locate Gardner. By that stage, DNA samples recovered from the revolvers and one of the submachine guns had proven a positive match to the suspect. Gardaí had also established that the Subaru had been falsely registered. On the morning of 13 December, Gardner was arrested at a shop in Cabra and hauled in for questioning once again.

Starting the interview process, he was asked if he was 'under threat', to which he replied: 'Not that I know of.'

Moving on to the Subaru and his DNA, Gardner was asked: 'You find yourself in a position of being in possession of the key to a car which has five guns and your DNA is on three of them. What have you to say about that?' Gardner said: 'I don't know how the DNA got there. I can't explain it because I never touched them.' Gardaí ended that part of the conversation by insisting: 'So you think you've been framed by someone? You expect us to believe that?'

Gardner was asked again if he was under threat and he gave the same answer: 'The [bulletproof] vest is nothing to do with anything. I wear it every day. When David was killed, we just got them then.' The interview concluded with Gardner being asked if he intended to use the firearms in 'reprisal' for the killing of his friend, to which he replied: 'Nope.'

During his next phase of interviews, Gardner was again asked about the Subaru and his clothing when he was first arrested: 'I found the key, that was why it was in my pocket. The gloves and the hat, I wear them when cycling when it's cold.' Returning to Byrne's murder, Gardner was then asked: 'Have you ever been asked to commit a criminal act as a result of David's murder?' He replied: 'No. I know David about ten years. Just knew him from being out and in the pub. His ma gave the Mass cards to family and friends he knew. Stick it in the vest, keeps me safe probably. After David was shot loads of his friends and stuff were getting shot, so it was just better to wear it and be safe than sorry. If you were going for a long walk, you wouldn't wear the plates [vest], but if you were sitting in a car you'd wear them.'

When asked if he was part of the Kinahan and Hutch feud, he gave the same response: 'No comment.'

Satisfied with the evidence they had obtained, gardaí received the green light from the DPP to charge Gardner with possession of firearms. He appeared at Dublin District Court the following day. He remained in custody until the following month before receiving bail at the High Court, under strict conditions. He attended court hearings throughout 2017, and was due to attend court in August 2017 to learn the date of his trial. He failed to appear and a European Arrest Warrant was issued.

At the same time, a female friend of Gardner's reported him as a missing person. Unbeknownst to gardaí, as the warrant was being issued Gardner was on his way to the UK, where he would stay in cartel safe houses in the north-west of England for the next two years or so.

Two months after Gardner failed to attend court, Maher was back before Dublin Circuit Court to learn his fate after pleading guilty to possession of a firearm. On 10 October 2017, Maher, who had also served a 4-year sentence in the UK after he was convicted at Leeds Crown Court for robbery and false imprisonment, received a 7-year sentence for the offence. During the hearing, Maher also pleaded guilty to possessing €4,658 worth of heroin for personal use on 22 November 2015 and possessing heroin for sale and supply on 15 March 2016. The court heard how Maher, who had become addicted to heroin at the age of eleven, had been 'systematically destroyed' by the drug.

Maher's story was on hold for seven years, but Gardner was still on the run. In September 2019 he called time on his period in hiding and handed himself in to Merseyside Police, in Liverpool. He was flown to Ireland in a military plane, brought to Dublin Circuit Court and remanded once again.

This time, there would be no bail. Gardner remained in custody until he appeared in court at the beginning of April 2020, where he pleaded guilty to possession of the firearms and ammunition. He returned to the court on 18 May 2020, when he received a 9-year sentence. During the hearing, Detective Garda Ronan Doolan told the court that Gardner had claimed he'd fled to England because his life was under threat. The investigator also accepted that the firearms 'belonged to a large organization' which Gardner was 'taking direction from'. In conclusion, Judge Martin Nolan said: 'He must have known the purpose of these guns was to cause serious harm or death to others.'

The discovery of Gardner's weapons cache provided gardaí with an insight into some of the firearms at the assassins' disposal. It also affirmed the importance of the work the gardaí were doing in warning those who were being targeted and foiling these attempted murders. They were the third angle of the feud, working hard to contain the violence of both the Kinahan and the Hutch organized crime gangs and prevent them from acting with impunity.

5. Young Guns

(1 July 2016: murder of Daithi Douglas)

'You're not top dog any more – the Kinahans are . . .
Now you're surrounded by a bunch of apes.'
– Specialist Garda interviewer

The two men who walked into Little Caesar's restaurant, off Grafton Street in Dublin city centre, at 7.38 p.m. on 1 July 2016 were in great spirits. As they strolled through the busy restaurant, the building's CCTV system captured their smiles as senior Kinahan cartel figure 'Fat' Freddie Thompson and his 'driver' Lee Canavan made their way towards two other diners. At the table they joined their friends, one of whom was the teenage killer of Lorcan O'Reilly, who was killed at a Hallowe'en bonfire in 2015; the other a senior cartel associate who is currently, in 2024, before the courts on drugs charges. The jovial atmosphere was evident in their high-fives and warm embraces. A short time later, they were joined by another man, Nathan Foley. The other diners enjoying their evening were completely unaware that the group of men who sat close to them were there to celebrate a murder – the killing of former Provisional IRA man Daithi Douglas.

Douglas was still recovering from being shot three times in the chest as he was walking his dog close to his home in Cabra, north Dublin, in November 2015. He had only just returned to work at his wife Yumei's toy and shoe shop, called Shoestown, in Bridgefoot Street, south inner-city Dublin. Shoestown was located close to the Kinahans' old powerbase in the Oliver Bond flats complex and beside a children's crèche. Douglas had no idea that 'Fat' Freddie Thompson, who was classified by gardaí as being 'no stranger to murder', suspected him of being one of two gunmen who had tried to kill Thompson's first cousin and cartel associate Liam 'Bop' Roe at the Red Cow Hotel back in November 2015. That attempted hit had been carried out because the Hutch gang were seeking revenge for the murder of Gary Hutch by targeting members of the Kinahan cartel. They fired shots from a car as Roe and others were standing outside the hotel. They missed because the shots were indiscriminate. Douglas's old friend 33-year-old Darren Kearns was executed by a Kinahan cartel hit team in Blackhorse Avenue in Dublin on 30 December 2015 because they blamed him for Roe's attempted murder. Thompson blamed the two friends, Douglas and Kearns, for the botched hit without a single shred of evidence. In fact, gardaí would later obtain CCTV footage of the two men socializing in different pubs in Dublin at the time the gunman singled Roe out and tried to end him. Douglas and Kearns couldn't have done it.

Despite Kearns' murder and the fact that the Kinahan cartel's murder machine was in full flow in the summer of 2016, Douglas did not alter his routine or accept the Garda Information Message that he was under threat, which was delivered to him after he was injured in the 2015 shooting incident.

Ironically, Douglas had been caught with €2 million worth of the Kinahan group's cocaine on 13 April 2008 and had done time for it. He was released from custody in 2014 and seemed to have changed his ways. By all accounts, he was leading a normal life in 2016, as his wife later described to gardaí: 'Since he is out of prison, he didn't do anything wrong. I know he has some background history, but that's in the past. Everybody wants to change.'

What his wife didn't know was that the 55-year-old had fallen far from favour and had now been placed on the cartel's kill list. Thompson would see to it. For the job he recruited a few low-level south inner-city criminals: Lee Canavan, Canavan's half-brother Gareth Brophy, and Nathan Foley, who was caught in June 2016 with €8,000 worth of cocaine. Each member of this inexperienced hit team was given a specific role before and after the murder.

On the morning of 1 July 2016, Douglas started his day with a walk in north Dublin before joining his teenage daughter Seoidi at the shop for the day's afternoon trade. He chatted with customers throughout the day and was in good form. At 4 p.m., Douglas decided to have an early dinner and went out for a takeaway curry. As he enjoyed his meal at the front counter of the shop, a gunman, dressed from head to toe in black and with his face partially covered, walked towards the shop. At 4.11 p.m. the gunman calmly took a step inside, pulled out his 9mm Star pistol and opened fire. He hit his target in the right side of his face, the left side of his chin, the neck, twice in the torso and once in the right elbow. He had completed his mission in seconds, then he placed his weapon beside the victim's head and escaped in a Mercedes CLA, which drove a short distance away to Spitalfields. Once there, the getaway driver's trousers caught fire as he attempted to burn the Mercedes. He patted out the flames with his hands. Then the pair got into a Suzuki Swift and drove off.

Back at the shop, Douglas's teenage daughter was comforting her father as he lay in a pool of blood. She told gardaí: 'There was blood all around. I went to my dad. He didn't say anything to me. I knew he had been shot. When I went over to Dad, I saw a gun on the ground. I don't know guns. There was bullets all around him.'

In her interview with gardaí, his wife, Yuemi, said: 'As far as I know he didn't owe money or had fallen out with anybody – I don't know why he was shot.'

Eyewitness Shane Egan would also tell gardaí: 'I noticed a man, a bit all over the place. I just thought he didn't look right. Then I saw him shoot and he put the gun down beside the man's head. He smirked as he walked away. About five seconds later, I heard a young lady scream.'

Douglas was rushed from the shop to the nearby St James's Hospital for emergency treatment but was pronounced dead at 4.55 p.m. The Kinahan–Hutch feud had claimed its tenth victim.

The responsibility to catch the hit team lay with investigators from the South Central Division. They had already enjoyed success disrupting drug-dealing and money-laundering networks in the south inner city under Operation Thistle and had arrested Dutch crime boss Naoufal 'the Belly' Fassih in Daniel Kinahan's apartment in Baggot Street when he was on the run from the Dutch authorities. Fassih is now serving a life sentence after he was convicted of ordering the murder of a suspected Iranian spy, Ali Motamed, in the Netherlands.

The investigation team, under the command of Senior Investigating Officer Detective Inspector Paul Cleary (now Assistant Commissioner), Superintendent Patrick McMenamin (now Chief Superintendent) and Detective Superintendent

Peter O'Boyle (now retired), met to discuss the feud and their plan of action. Just three days after the murder of Daithi Douglas they would unwittingly have their first inter-action with two members of Thompson's hit team.

Nathan Foley, one of Thompson's associates, who had enjoyed their get-together in Little Caesar's, had parked his Mitsubishi Mirage at Stephen's Green Shopping Centre over the weekend. Shortly after 11.30 p.m. on 4 July, Lee Canavan and Foley drove the Mitsubishi to the beach-front car park in Sandymount, south Dublin.

Once there, Foley reversed his car into a Suzuki Swift, then got out carrying a can of petrol and saying: 'Should I pour it?' Canavan replied: 'Yeah, yeah, faster.' As he carried the can, he was approached by another motorist, who tried to intervene but was told to 'go away'. Foley then set fire to the car as the witness dialled 999 and provided details of the Mitsubishi's registration plate. Fleeing from the scene, and unaware that their attempts to destroy the vehicle had failed and it had not caught fire properly, the pair were later stopped by members of the South Divisional Crime Task Force as they drove along the canal towards Rathmines. Arrested on suspicion of criminal damage, the pair were brought in for questioning before being released without charge. Both ve-hicles were also seized for a technical examination.

In the days after the killing, a key priority for Garda Ciaran Byrne and the investigation team was to trawl through images from 160 different CCTV systems, comprising more than 1,500 hours of footage. As part of their efforts to track the movements of the Mercedes CLA the gunman had used to flee the scene, they focused on the hours leading up to the murder. They worked around the clock on the CCTV footage and established that the Mercedes had travelled in convoy with a Suzuki Swift on the day of the murder. They also identified a Ford Fiesta travelling with a Mitsubishi Mirage and the Mercedes at different intervals throughout the day.

However, the investigation team's biggest breakthrough came when CCTV showed Freddie Thompson driving the Fiesta, which was registered to a man in west Dublin. Gardaí also identified Canavan driving the same vehicle. The Fiesta was seized on 15 July; Thompson was in the UK on that date. In yet another CCTV discovery, low-level criminal Nathan Foley was identified driving the Mitsubishi Mirage and also buying two Nokia Lumia Rm1132 mobile phones at 1.38 p.m. from the Cell Hub phone shop in Meath Street. On top of that, the CCTV also allowed officers to identify Gareth Brophy, Canavan's half-brother, as the passenger in the Suzuki after the shooting.

There was one image that provided key evidence: it came from the Little Flower Old Folks Centre, a charity that provides meals for the homeless community and is located a short distance from Shoestown, and it showed Freddie Thompson breaking up a mobile phone. The footage was shown to Detective Sergeant Adrian Whitelaw (now retired). In an instant, the experienced gangland investigator identified the man in the image as Freddie Thompson.

The decision was made to show the images to the Garda team who'd had the most recent encounter with the gangster. The task fell to Garda Seamus O'Donovan, who along with Detective Superintendent Paul Murphy had brought Thompson back to Ireland from the Netherlands in 2015 to stand trial for violent disorder at a funeral in Dublin. The two officers scrutinized the images and both confirmed it was Thompson in the stills.

Alongside the CCTV evidence, a technical examination of the vehicles was also undertaken by the Garda National Technical Bureau. Once completed, the crime scene investigators had recovered Thompson's DNA from an air-freshener cap and hand sanitizer in the Ford Fiesta and his left thumbprint on the rear-view mirror. His DNA was also recovered from an inhaler in Foley's Mitsubishi Mirage. In further examinations, they recovered Canavan's DNA from a Sellotape lift in the Suzuki Swift and also two marks of his left thumb on the rear-view mirror of the Fiesta. Canavan's DNA was also recovered from a cigarette butt found in the Fiesta, while Brophy's left palm print was found on the inside of the passenger door of the Suzuki Swift.

Unlike in previous years, when Thompson had escaped justice, gardaí were convinced they had enough evidence to build a case against one of Ireland's most senior gangland figures and his three associates. On the morning of 26 July, gardaí made their move, but there was no sign of Thompson at his home or at a safe house he had been using. Canavan and Brophy were also in the wind, although they knew exactly where Foley was: held on remand at Cloverhill Prison on separate drugs charges.

As three of the suspects remained in hiding over the coming months, Thompson made the mistake of returning to Ireland on Tuesday, 1 November 2016, flying into Belfast.

Thompson didn't know that SIO Paul Cleary and Detective Sergeant Whitelaw had received information that the returning Thompson was due to have a meeting at the City North Hotel outside Dublin. Rushing to the hotel, along with colleagues Sergeant Stephen Daly and Sergeant Linda Williams, they arrived at 2.40 p.m. By the time the investigation team arrived, Thompson had been under surveillance by the Garda National Surveillance Unit as soon as he crossed the border. As the investigation team entered the hotel, Thompson spotted them and tried to hide. He was tracked into the gents' toilets by Paul Cleary and apprehended there. The murder suspect's bid to avoid arrest had ended in failure. He had just become the most senior member of the Kinahan organization to be arrested since the outbreak of the violent feud.

Thompson was brought to Kevin Street Garda Station for questioning about Douglas's murder, where he was interrogated by specialist interviewers from the Garda National Bureau of Criminal Investigation. The interview began by addressing the issue of the Douglas killing, and detectives asked Thompson if he had been the 'manufacturer' of the killing when they said: 'Whether you're on the outside or inside – murder is murder.' Focusing on the movements of the hit team's vehicles that day, the detectives said: 'The vehicles are all recovered by gardaí. Where was the planning and expertise? You were all sitting down for dinner, drinking and chatting about the murder, but you hadn't got rid of any of the evidence. You didn't plan that very well. From what we are seeing on CCTV, it's obvious you are organizing the murder of Daithi Douglas. You are an experienced guy. You know how this works. Did you not check the CCTV? You are seen coming and going from the car that was used to murder Daithi Douglas. Why would you be so obvious? Why would you do that?'

Thompson said nothing.

Referring to the hit team during the second day of his detention, Thompson was asked why he had 'surrounded himself with young lads' and said that if 'they wanted to be the next Freddie Thompson', they would have to 'bulk up'.

Thompson said nothing.

Moving on to the actual murder of Daithi Douglas and the Kinahan cartel, the interview team said: 'There's no excuse for that – you ruined his daughter. How would your son feel seeing you shot dead eating a bowl of curry? You're not top dog any more – the Kinahans are. Were you told to murder Daithi? Maybe they wanted him murdered. Did they come to you? Did they ask Freddie Thompson to plan, organize and direct this murder? You conspired to have Daithi killed. You are the man who pulled the strings. You were cocky and careless – two things that will get you caught.'

Thompson said nothing.

Referring once again to the Kinahan gang on the fourth day of his detention and questioning, the detectives said: 'There was a time when you were cock of the walk, but the Kinahan boys have come on leaps and bounds. You were the main man ten years ago but now you're surrounded by a bunch of apes. You're using the likes of Nathan Foley to carry out a murder in a town where everyone knows him and your fall from grace is bad. You planned this, and look where we are now. You have no one to blame but yourself. You picked some prize beauties. Instead of burning the car – your man burned himself.'

Thompson said nothing.

As the interviews were taking place, gardaí also kept in constant contact with the DPP's office, informing them of their belief that: 'There can be little doubt that, with his standing in the criminal world, he [Thompson] is the one who orchestrated the murder of Daithi Douglas. He has the motive and the criminal muscle to put everything into place – cars and guns etc. While it is all set up by Thompson, he then used his less experienced associates to carry out the murder.

Three of the other suspects, Lee Canavan, Nathan Foley and Gareth Brophy, are low-level street criminals who would be used by Freddie Thompson as his so called "gillies". They would be involved in the sale and supply of drugs on Freddie Thompson's behalf – he uses them to do his dirty work for him. Lee Canavan is generally used to drive Freddie Thompson around and Canavan and Foley would associate with Thompson on a regular basis but Brophy not as much. It's suggested Brophy owed Freddie Thompson a drug debt for which his life was under threat and that this is the reason he is involved in this murder, in order to pay off his debt.' In their final submission to the DPP, gardaí concluded: 'Frederick Thompson has been one of the most notorious gangland figures in this country for the past fifteen years. He is a senior member of the Kinahan organized crime gang. Freddie Thompson would be used as an enforcer for the Kinahan gang.'

While Thompson was being interrogated, Nathan Foley was also brought from Cloverhill Prison for questioning. Like his mentor before him, he too made no reply to any of the questions put to him. But by that stage, gardaí had secured the CCTV footage of Foley buying the mobile phones, footage of Thompson breaking up his phones along with Canavan, and footage of Brophy driving in convoy in the vehicles used in the killing.

As the end of Thompson's detention period edged ever closer, the DPP made the decision to charge him with the murder of Daithi Douglas. On 7 November 2016, the major criminal appeared at Dublin District Court charged with the murder – the first time he had ever been charged with taking a life. One month later, Thompson's protégé Nathan Foley was also charged with the former IRA man's murder. Both men were remanded in custody until their respective trial dates in 2018 and 2019.

In 2017, Thompson failed in repeated attempts to receive bail, with one hearing at the High Court being told that the experienced criminal 'was operating at the very top level of serious organized crime. He is engaged in a wide variety of serious criminal activity, namely the importation, sale, supply and distribution of drugs and firearms, international money laundering, murder and witness intimidation. Frederick Thompson and this criminal grouping are involved in a murderous feud with another criminal grouping – the Hutch organized crime gang.'

Unlike his previous court appearances in a criminal career spanning twenty years, Thompson faced a life sentence when his trial started at the Special Criminal Court on 2 May 2018. The eagerly awaited trial opened with prosecuting barrister Sean Gillane SC telling the court: 'The prosecution does not say he carried out the physical act of the killing. One hand might have been on the gun, but many fingers were on the trigger. It is our case that one of these fingers belonged to Mr Thompson. The accused and others were working closely in a carefully planned execution of another human being. Four vehicles and their occupants were operating in concert that day.' Over the course of the next fifteen days, ten of those days would deal with the case, while the others were set aside for legal argument.

After an adjournment on 17 May, the court returned on 1 June. At that hearing the prosecution concluded that Thompson should be found guilty of the murder, while his defence team insisted he should be found not guilty because there was 'no forensic connection' between their client and two of the cars involved in the crime – the Suzuki Swift and the Mercedes. The case was adjourned once again to allow the three-judge panel to consider their verdict.

The trial resumed on 30 August 2018. Addressing the packed courtroom, Mr Justice Tony Hunt informed the court that the judgement was sixty-five pages and would take 'some time to read'. The senior judge said: 'This was, in effect, an execution and, as in all such cases, it is the prosecution's case that this murder involved intricate planning and co-ordination.' As the judge continued, he referred to Nathan Foley as the man who delivered the gunman and the getaway driver to the Mercedes and referenced the CCTV footage of Thompson in Meath Street appearing to be 'smiling and happy'. Completing his comments on the Fiesta, Mr Justice Hunt told the court that it was 'inherently improbable' that someone other than Freddie Thompson was driving the car that day.

In further extracts from the judgement, Mr Justice Hunt also referred to the gathering at Little Caesar's: 'There is no doubt that, viewed in retrospect, this was a disturbing and unpleasant occasion. We have no doubt whatsoever that the presence of Mr Thompson, together with Mr Foley and Mr C [Canavan] in the Mirage and subsequently in the restaurant, was not explicable by unlikely coincidence but because the three of them were inextricably linked together on that day by their joint participation in the murder of Mr Douglas.'

Thompson's hopes of a positive outcome were erased when Mr Justice Hunt concluded: 'We are satisfied that the totality of the evidence establishes the necessary proof beyond reasonable doubt of the guilt of the accused. There is no reasonably possible scenario which could explain Mr Thompson's actions and associations except that for which the prosecution contend.' As Mr Justice Hunt finalized the proceedings, Thompson had heard enough and he left the court, before returning a short time later.

In his final address to the court, Mr Justice Hunt said: 'What we do know is that this man was killed, if not in front of his daughter, who was very young, when she was around, and she came upon her dead parent in the immediate aftermath of his execution, because that's what it was. That's a terrible thing to happen to anyone and Mr Gillane, if you would, convey on to her the Court's sympathies. I hope that she will be able to recover from it – I can't think of a worse thing.' Referring to the Garda team, the senior judge said: 'The standard of the investigation was second to none and we want to pay particular tribute to Garda Byrne and the entirety of the CCTV team. It doesn't take a big leap of imagination to think that the two hours that we saw was produced on the back of an awful lot of slog and boring footwork.'

By the end of the proceedings, Thompson's position in the Kinahan cartel was over. He was given a life sentence, taking him out of circulation for a long time. His luck with the judicial process seemed to have finally run out.

He later appealed his conviction, with his lawyers arguing in April 2023 that his sentence should be overturned due to the lack of records stating and verifying that he was identified from CCTV footage. His case returned to the Court of Appeal on 30 January 2024, where Ms Justice Ní Raifeartaigh outlined how the original trial's approach to recognition evidence was 'legally correct and carefully considered. The appeal was dismissed. Thompson remains behind bars, serving out his time.

*

Attention now turned to the three remaining members of the hit team. With Canavan and Brophy still at large, gardaí didn't have long to wait before their next move. By that stage, the DPP had already given instructions for the pair to be charged. After receiving intelligence that Brophy was back in Dublin, the investigation team swooped on the Barn House pub in Dolphin's Barn at 11.58 p.m. on 18 November and arrested the 24-year-old.

When charged by detectives with the murder, Brophy replied: 'Sorry for his loss, if that means anything.'

As he was remanded in custody the following day, gardaí prepared for Foley's appearance at the Special Criminal Court on 22 November. Just fifteen minutes after Foley being brought to the court, State Solicitor Michael O'Donovan told the hearing that the DPP would now accept a new charge for Foley, that of helping a criminal organization commit the murder of David (Daithi) Douglas. The new charge of participating in or contributing to activity intending to facilitate the commission by a criminal organization of a serious offence was put to the defendant and Foley, who was just twenty years old at the time, replied, 'Guilty'.

Remanded in custody, Foley was back before the non-jury court in January where he was described as a 'foot soldier' and 'runner' for a criminal organization, as well as being 'friendly' with one of the main organizers of the Douglas murder. In his defence, Foley's barrister, Paul Greene SC, told the court that his client was not in the 'front rank of planning and strategizing'. In a reply, Detective Superintendent Paul Murphy said: 'He certainly would have been a runner for the main organizer in the particular organization.' Foley's defence barrister also told the court how his client had addictions to crystal meth and cocaine and that both of his parents were also battling with addiction. In a further statement, the defence barrister outlined how one psychiatrist had suggested that Foley had a 'mental disability', resulting in his capacity to only undertake 'limited tasks'. Concluding his mitigation plea, the barrister also suggested that his client was 'Not a man who is at the front of the queue in his ability'. Judge Hunt replied: 'Perhaps he was more of a foot soldier out at the front line. He was performing an important task and there was no getting away from that.'

Remanded in custody once again, Foley eventually learned his fate on 25 January 2019. Mr Justice Hunt outlined how Foley had played a 'significant role' in 'an intrinsically planned and pre-meditated murder, with the most heinous aspect being the fact that Mr Douglas was discovered by his daughter within seconds of being shot. The exposure of a child to the murder of their parent was a risk the organizer in this escapade was prepared to run.' Turning to Foley, the senior judge referred to his 'limited cognitive' abilities, his guilty plea, young age and remorse before handing down a 6-year sentence for his role in the Douglas murder.

The young man found himself before the court again on 3 April 2019 when he received an extra year's sentence after being caught with a mobile phone in Mountjoy Prison for the eighth time in two years. At the time of writing, in early 2024, Foley is back living in the south inner city after being released from prison before Christmas 2022.

Speaking after Foley's sentencing, SIO Paul Cleary said: 'I have spoken to the family of Daithi Douglas – they are satisfied with the result. I would like to thank the community of Dublin 8 who assisted us, which was invaluable. People involved in these murders and the organized criminal gangs need people to arrange logistics. There are other people we are pursuing and we will continue to pursue and we are optimistic there would be further arrests down the line.'

The gardaí were indeed still in pursuit of the remaining members of the hit team. It wasn't over just yet.

Brophy, the getaway driver, was brought to the Special Criminal Court on 13 December 2019 for the start of the proceedings against him. He adopted the same stance as his friend Foley and pleaded guilty to facilitating Douglas's murder.

Before Brophy learned his fate, there was a dramatic twist in the story of Canavan's successful disappearance. Based on intelligence provided to their colleagues in the UK's National Crime Agency, Canavan was arrested by the European Network Fugitive Active Search team on 18 January 2020. He was brought before Westminster Magistrates' Court in London and ordered forward for extradition. Canavan had spent time on the run in Scotland and Liverpool before being caught after the issue of a European Arrest Warrant.

In the meantime, Brophy returned to the court on 17 February 2020, where he was handed a 10-year sentence for his role as the gunman's getaway driver. During the proceedings, Mr Justice Paul Coffey told the court how the accused had played a 'critical role' at a 'critical phase' of the Douglas murder, accusing him of being at the 'higher end of the top end of the gravity'. Before his role in the Douglas murder, the court heard how he had amassed twenty previous convictions, including robbery, assault causing harm, public order offences and violent behaviour at a Garda station. In mitigation, Michael Bowman SC said his client had come from a disadvantaged background and had 'difficulties' with drugs. Brophy was taken to Mountjoy Prison to serve his time.

That left Canavan.

He was held at Belmarsh Prison following his arrest and agreed to the Garda's extradition request on 12 May 2020. That process was completed on 19 May and the 30-year-old appeared at Dublin District Court charged with murder. His trial started on 1 March 2021 and he pleaded not guilty. On the opening day of the trial, prosecution barrister Mr Sean Gillane SC described the feud killing as a 'meticulously and carefully planned assassination' before arguing that the man dressed in black who had entered the shop was Canavan and that the CCTV footage was 'crystal clear regarding the vehicles and individuals involved'. Over the course of the next twenty-nine days, the DNA and CCTV evidence against Canavan was outlined to the court. The prosecution concluded their case on 30 March 2021 and insisted that Canavan was 'crucially and significantly' involved in the planning of the murder and 'up to his neck in the enterprise' due to the 'overwhelming evidence' as 'the person who literally pulled the trigger'.

The three-judge panel retired to consider their verdict. On 20 May they revealed their verdict: guilty of murder and criminal damage. However, the court indicated that they could not agree with the prosecution that Canavan was the gunman, owing to lack of forensic or identification evidence. As a result, Canavan was found guilty of murder due to his 'active participation' in the 'shared intention' of the murder of Daithi Douglas.

The court reconvened for sentencing on 3 June 2021. Canavan became the latest cartel foot soldier to receive a life sentence.

That is nothing compared to the life sentence visited on Douglas's wife and daughter, but the cartel didn't care about such things. There was a list of names that had to be ticked off and that was what mattered to them. The feud may have lost some soldiers, but that didn't mean the war had ended.

6. Serial Killer

(14 April 2016: murder of Martin O'Rourke and
17 August 2016: murder of Trevor O'Neill)

*'I don't have to explain to my children what happened because
they were there – they saw it. Any of us could have been killed
that night – the gunman put the gun over my daughter's
shoulder before opening fire.'*
– Suzanne Power, partner of Trevor O'Neill

The feud had taken hold and there was a sense around Dublin
that a murder could take place at any time – people were on a
knife edge and the gardaí were operating a huge number of
lines of inquiry at once, while also delivering GIMs (Garda
Information Messages, which gardaí are obliged to give an individual if they receive intelligence that the person is under
threat) to those suspected of being next. After Daithi Douglas's murder, only weeks would pass before the next hit. But the
roots of that hit went back a few years, to the summer of 2013.

That summer, 21-year-old Dean Johnson from Clondalkin,
west Dublin, was considering a new life in Australia. At the
time, Johnson was unemployed and a number of his friends
had already made the move Down Under. However, it was
not a plan that his mother, Elizabeth, endorsed: 'All his friends
went to Australia, but I wouldn't let him go because I thought
it was too dangerous. He was my youngest and he was my
baby, I always worried for him. Dean was loved by everyone

and he was a lovely chap. He was the type of fella that if someone was cold, he would have given them his jacket.'

Similar sentiments were shared by his brother, Andrew. In an interview with one of the authors, he said: 'Dean was a very popular lad and the only thing he was into was music, football, his friends and his family. There's no doubt he had a bright future ahead of him.' Despite his mother's concerns, the popular young man still harboured hopes of a new life in a new country.

Those hopes, and his mother's worries, would never materialize. Dean Johnson was shot dead shortly after midnight on 24 August 2013.

He had spent the day socializing with his friends and close to midnight he left Finches pub to make the short journey home on foot. As he did so, he phoned his mother to say: 'Ma, don't worry. I'll be home soon.' Shortly after ending the call, he was approached by two gunmen, who both opened fire with handguns, letting off ten shots. Johnson was hit six times, in the head and chest, and pronounced dead a short time later at the hospital.

In the days that followed the shooting, gardaí struggled to find a motive for the brazen killing because the country's latest gun-attack victim had no involvement in or connections to organized crime.

However, it wasn't long before they established that the intended target of the murder was James 'Nellie' Walsh, who at the time was involved in a feud with senior Kinahan cartel figure Peadar Keating over the sale of drugs in west Dublin. Thirteen days after the murder, the *Irish Independent* ran an article in which Dean Johnson's mother claimed the intended target had contacted her family and said: 'So sorry what happened – that was meant for me.' In a further statement about her son, Elizabeth also said: 'Dean worried a lot about me when I had cancer. He was very close to me. I worried about him and I'd ring him every day.'

Although investigators followed 530 lines of inquiry, took 400 witness statements and made 10 arrests over the years, no one was ever charged with the murder. Two extensive files were also sent to the DPP in 2016 and 2022, but on both occasions the DPP ruled there was insufficient evidence to bring any charges in the case. At the inquest into Dean Johnson's death at Dublin Coroner's Court, his older brother Andrew revealed how the murder victim had been 'full of energy' a few days before his death: 'He appeared to be happy in the days before his death. He was a promising footballer who had won many trophies, was mentioned in the newspapers and was a great uncle to my children. He was the best brother you could ever have.'

His sentiments were shared by his sister Audrey: 'I still think it is all a bad dream. That Dean is just going to walk in that door. He's my baby brother. I was seventeen when he was born so I was more like a second mother to him. He looked out for my own children – he always protected them.'

In both files to the DPP, Glen Clarke, a petty criminal who had twenty-seven previous convictions, mainly for criminal damage, public order and traffic offences, was identified by gardaí as one of the two gunmen who murdered Dean. This was based on intelligence received after the murder. Hauled in for questioning after the murder, Clarke was later released due to lack of evidence.

At the time, the 23-year-old Clarke was a close associate of senior cartel figure Peadar Keating and was anxious to make a name for himself in the world of organized crime. Clarke had acted as an enforcer for a west Dublin drugs gang and had only minor convictions, as one investigator told the authors: 'Glen Clarke was up-and-coming then, but because he was known to Keating he was trusted. There just wasn't enough evidence to bring charges against him for the Johnson murder and he was still determined to take human life. He was a bit of a loner and it looked as if he was maintaining his association with Keating and his associates because he wanted to be a big man in the underworld. Clarke didn't have the intelligence to realize that someone like him would simply be used by the likes of Keating and more senior cartel figures.'

The 'mistaken identity' Johnson murder and the public revulsion that came with it did not deter Clarke from continuing his involvement with the cartel. Following the Byrne murder at the Regency Hotel, and like many other criminals, Clarke spotted the opportunity to take a step up the ladder and was keen to prove his worth to the cartel leaders. He offered his services.

His chance came in April 2016. This time the gang's target was Hutch gang member and convicted armed robber Keith Murtagh. He had been identified by the cartel as 'potential spotter' on the day of the Regency attack, even though they didn't have any evidence to back up that assertion. Gardaí would later confirm that there was no evidence to support the cartel's theory, with his family also pleading with the investigating team to produce the CCTV evidence that would show he was in a different part of the city on the day Byrne was murdered and had definitely not been involved.

By April 2016, Murtagh, who was severely wounded by gardaí in 2009 during an attempted raid of a cash-in-transit van, was back living in the north inner city after spending some time in the UK following his release from prison at the start of 2016. He had been officially warned by the Garda Síochána that his life was under threat, with the cartel placing a €30,000 bounty on his head. Like many of those under threat, Murtagh felt safer at his home in north inner-city Dublin, but the cartel had other ideas.

On the morning of 14 April 2016, Murtagh left the safe house he had been staying in for a number of meetings with associates. As he made his way home around 12.30 p.m. that day, he was standing outside Noctor's pub on Sheriff Street when a man dressed in black cycled towards him. The cyclist had a scarf wrapped around his face and a gun in his hand. Standing close to Murtagh at the time was Martin O'Rourke, a 24-year-old man who gardaí believe was in the area to buy drugs. Spotting the imminent danger, Murtagh ran as the gunman opened fire, wildly firing thirteen shots.

One of the rounds hit Martin O'Rourke above the left eye, killing him instantly. Murtagh managed to dive between two cars and he survived unscathed. The blundering assassin hopped on to his bicycle and fled, dumping it down the street and throwing his gun into a wheelie bin. Within minutes of the shooting, gardaí had responded, and narrowly missed the gunman as he was brought to safety by his associates. The feud had claimed its first innocent victim not connected to organized crime or dissident republican activity.

That same night, cartel heavyweight Freddie Thompson was stopped at a checkpoint and said: 'It's terrible. The young fella got six bullets in the back and two in the face from a nine millimetre.' Asked how he could have such information, he replied: 'I just heard it.' O'Rourke's funeral, which was attended by then Taoiseach Enda Kenny, heard how the young father had been due to attend a drug rehabilitation course and then an FÁS programme in the hope of getting a job.

As the Garda investigation continued over the coming weeks, no DNA was recovered from the gunman's bike. But the investigation team made a breakthrough when a DNA sample was taken from the firearm found in the wheelie bin. Once analysed, gardaí had found their match: Glen Clarke's DNA was on the gun that killed Martin O'Rourke.

Over the course of the investigation, gardaí followed 657 lines of inquiry, collected 281 statements and made three arrests, but no one was ever charged with the murder. During the investigation, detectives obtained CCTV footage which showed that the suspected killer jumped in the back of a waiting van in the Sheriff Street area following the shooting. As a result of this, gardaí manning the Operation Hybrid patrols, which were established to counter the threat posed by the criminal organization in terms of moving weapons and targeting people, were asked to be on the lookout for suspected cartel killers travelling in vans, especially with a bike in the back.

Investigators also established that another cartel associate might have been assisting Clarke that day. That suspect's car was seized, but there was not enough evidence to bring any charges against him.

In an interview with one of the authors, Martin O'Rourke's father-in-law, Larry Power, explained how he had forgiven the killer: 'I forgive Martin's killer now because I know he didn't set out to kill him that day. If there were twenty men charged, it wouldn't bring Martin back. I don't even blame the Kinahans or Gerry Hutch's gang because I know they didn't arrange for Martin to be killed. I'd heard this man Clarke was meant to be the gunman but there's nothing I can do about it and our main focus is Martin's children. Martin's death was 100 per cent mistaken identity . . . I want to thank gardaí for everything they have put into this. To be honest, I'd prefer Martin to be where he is now.'

Former Assistant Commissioner Pat Leahy also told the authors: 'My sympathies will always be with the family of this innocent young man. The family and community deserved justice. The team in Store Street who worked on the investigation put a huge effort into solving this crime. Myself and the team would have liked to have someone before the courts to hold them publicly accountable for that killing.'

In the weeks after the murder, Clarke received sanctuary in Spain's Costa del Sol, thanks to the support of cartel kingpin Thomas 'Bomber' Kavanagh. This was his second failed murder – yet again he had hit the wrong person – and he was keen to make amends. He didn't have long to wait for another chance to prove his worth as an assassin to his paymasters. His opportunity came in August 2016, when one of the cartel's representatives in southern Spain, Eamon Cumberton's brother Michael, established that Jonathan Hutch, brother to Gareth, who had been shot dead in May of that year, was staying in the Costa de la Calma resort in Mallorca. Once Hutch's location had been positively identified, Clarke was sent to the island on 16 August to complete his third mission for the cartel.

On the evening of 17 August, Clarke made the decision to strike. Shortly after 8 p.m., Jonathan Hutch and his family left their apartment block to walk to a nearby restaurant. Dublin City Council worker Trevor O'Neill, along with his partner Suzanne and the couple's three children, were just a few yards in front of them. Trevor's family had only recently decided to travel to Spain, after abandoning their initial plans of a holiday to Turkey. The two families had encountered each other earlier and exchanged pleasantries, and they now happened to be walking in the same direction. Trevor O'Neill and his family had no idea that the man they had just met, who was walking along the path behind them, was being targeted by the Kinahan cartel.

As the two families walked along in the balmy evening air, Suzanne noticed a man dressed in dark clothing and wearing a hoodie. He came towards them. Within seconds, he opened fire, hitting Trevor O'Neill once in the back. As the gunman fled on foot, still holding his firearm, the families erupted into screams and pure panic. The police arrived within minutes.

The father of three was rushed to a hospital, while the Hutch family and the O'Neill family were brought to a safe house by the Spanish authorities. It was a confusing and frightening time, as Suzanne explained to co-author Stephen Breen: 'We were treated in an appalling fashion after the shooting and someone has to be held accountable for this. The last time I saw Trevor was when he lay in my arms on the ground before the ambulance took him away. They told me I could see him, but I never got the chance. I don't even know where he was brought to. How do I know where he was brought to? No one from Spain even told me he had passed away – I had to learn it from family. Someone in Spain has to be held accountable for the way we were treated. Trevor came back to Ireland thirteen days later with a death certificate in Spanish, but this isn't good enough.'

Hours after the shooting, a relative of the innocent man contacted the *Irish Sun* and said: 'Please, please let people know that Trevor had nothing to do with the Hutches or the Kinahans or gangland or any of that. He was never in his life in trouble with the Gardaí. We can't bear to think that people would associate him with them. This was mistaken identity. He was only over on holiday with his three children. This is the result of this feud. This is what happens – innocent people get killed.'

Once under the protection of the Spanish authorities, Hutch told officers he was the 'intended target' before apologizing and offering his condolences to O'Neill's family. As Suzanne described it: 'The Spanish police took us to a "safe place" and my family, along with Jonathan Hutch and his family, were all kept in the same room. When we were there he said he was sorry twice, but I was too upset to speak to him. He also tried to apologize again at the airport, but I just couldn't talk to him. He knew the bullet was for him. I wasn't happy with the way we were treated in Spain and I can't believe they brought the intended target of a gang back to the same location as the victim's family. We were just sitting there in that room and we didn't even know if Trevor was alive or dead. I have a great family support network around me and can't thank everyone enough for all the kindness they have shown us.'

Reflecting on the callous nature of the cartel attack, Suzanne also said: 'I don't have to explain to my children what happened because they were there – they saw it. Any of us could have been killed that night – the gunman put the gun over my daughter's shoulder before opening fire. Trevor was just so outgoing, friendly and decent and this is what cost him his life. His biggest problem was that he talked to everyone – that's why he's in a grave today. We always knew he was popular, but we never knew how popular he was until the day of his funeral. Even people from Belfast we met on holiday turned up at his funeral. Each and every one of his friends are broken-hearted. My neighbours still can't believe he's not coming in because he looked after everyone in this area.'

Former Dublin Lord Mayor Brendan Carr also voiced strong views on the murder: 'The murder of Trevor was the darkest time of my tenure as Lord Mayor. We also remember another innocent father, Martin O'Rourke, who was murdered by these bastards. This disgusting murder hurt everyone at the Council – it was also an attack on the people of Dublin.'

A few weeks after the killing, investigators from the Guardia Civil compiled an early file on the case, stating they had a 'keen interest' in it and were 'very anxious to solve it with no resource being spared in an attempt to apprehend the killers and several lines of inquiry ongoing. A full investigation is ongoing.' Details of Jonathan Hutch's exchanges with Spanish police were also included, with Hutch stating that a 'well-built male in a hooded top passed the women and children and something was not right. I grabbed my son as the male pointed the gun in my direction and I stepped to the side. I also felt I was being watched in the pub the night before the shooting. I recognized a man from the north inner city of Dublin and he spent the evening on his mobile phone.'

Through cooperation with Gardaí and following examination of CCTV images, investigators in Spain were satisfied that the man who had been on his phone in the pub was Eamon Cumberton's younger brother, Michael. (Eamon Cumberton was one of the hitmen in Chapter 2.) Michael Cumberton was staying in Spain after receiving a warning that his life was in danger. (He later lost his life, in December 2018, when he fell off a balcony at an apartment in Marbella.) His behaviour suggested he was the spotter for the hit. Spanish police believed at the time that James Quinn was the man supplying the weapons to the assassins who had travelled to

Spain to kill Gerry and Jonathan Hutch. One investigator previously involved in the case told the authors they were satisfied Clarke was the gunman due to his 'movements' before and after the killing and because of his previous history.

The file, which included CCTV images of the suspect, described him 'covered from head to toe in black attire' and that he could be seen 'running down the road' after the shooting. 'CCTV has been requested and has been taken from all relevant businesses and private properties on any possible routes taken by the killers.' The file also referred to witnesses, with detectives establishing how one witness 'who was watching from a balcony in Trevor O'Neill's hotel saw everything from start to finish'. Another witness also provided a photofit of the suspect who 'had run past her'. As part of the investigation, detectives obtained the details of residents of every hotel on the island, along with the details of passengers of all incoming and outgoing flights in the days before and after the murder. They also examined 1.5 million hits from the Spanish Automatic Number Plate Recognition system in a bid to establish the killer's movements.

Their hard work paid off when they got their first breakthrough: known cartel associate Glen Clarke had taken a flight from the island the day after the killing to Belfast in Northern Ireland. From that moment on, Clarke became, and remains, the prime suspect in this unsolved murder of an innocent man.

This is cold comfort to Trevor's widow, who wants and needs 'proof' that Glen Clarke pulled the trigger on the gun that killed her husband: 'I need someone to stand in front of me and tell me who killed Trevor. Clarke's DNA was found in another murder investigation, but we don't have that level of proof. We might never get to know who pulled the trigger.'

In another interview with one of the authors, Sinn Féin TD Aengus Ó Snodaigh confirmed that he had written to Minister for Justice Helen McEntee, asking: 'I hope Minister McEntee will inquire as to the state of play with the investigations both here in Ireland and with the Spanish authorities. While it has been reported that the suspected shooter has passed away, there were more than him involved and Trevor's partner Suzanne has sought answers to many questions over the years. I would ask the Minister to consider meeting Suzanne to reassure her An Garda Síochána still have an ongoing investigation and that they will try to impress on their Spanish counterparts the need to follow up leads from their early investigation into this callous murder.'

Despite the Spanish authorities' stated determination to prosecute all of those involved in the killing of Trevor O'Neill, at the time of writing in 2024, no one has ever been brought before a court. Trevor's heartbroken father, Vincent, passed away in February 2021 without seeing justice for his son.

In the autumn of 2016, Glen Clarke was back in Dublin. Gardaí believe he was still being used by the Kinahan cartel sub-cell being directed by Peadar Keating in west Dublin. Although he now had three failed hits under his belt, it appeared the cartel did not consider him a liability. As one investigator explained: 'The fact that Clarke had been implicated in the murder of three innocent men didn't seem to bother the cartel leaders. They used anyone at that time because they had all the money in the world. It didn't matter if you were a drug addict or a petty criminal – they would have recruited anyone to kill. The only thing Clarke had in common with many of the other assassins was that he was expendable.'

As the end of 2016 approached, gardaí believe Clarke was recruited once again for yet another murder. He never got his chance to 'prove' himself. Glen Clarke's body was found in a stolen Vauxhall Zafira in the Riverdale Estate in Leixlip, County Kildare, around 1.30 a.m. on 2 December 2016.

He was wearing a boiler suit, which led detectives to surmise that he had accidentally killed himself when examining his firearm, which was recovered from the footwell of the Vauxhall Zafira. The car, which had been fitted with false plates, had been stolen in the Blanchardstown area the previous October.

Following the discovery of Clarke's body, his mother, Carol Darcy, told *Sunday World* journalist Patrick O'Connell that she was convinced her son had been murdered: 'He didn't shoot himself. I believe my son was murdered. Glen didn't work for the Kinahans. He was on social welfare. Glen told me everything and there was no one after him – he'd no enemies. I think the clues to who killed my Glen are still in that car. Somebody killed him.'

At the inquest into his death on 11 March 2020, Senior Investigating Officer Frank Keenaghan (now retired) outlined to Dublin Coroner's Court how, despite 'extensive searches', the bullet which killed the 26-year-old was never recovered: 'In the aftermath, we tore every seat, panel and mat apart, the car was destroyed in the search for this piece of lead. My best guess is that it was taken away in the man's clothes as he was transferred to the hospital. It had all the hallmarks of someone looking down the barrel into the breach, a potential accidental discharge due to wearing gloves.'

As the senior detective addressed the court, which also heard how the suspected killer's DNA had been found on the firearm, members of Clarke's family called out from the public gallery, insisting that he would not have taken his own life. The detective superintendent also described the phone recovered alongside Clarke's body: 'The phone was an unusual type of phone – a burner phone that you throw away with no money in it.' At the time, gardaí believed that Clarke may have been recruited to target Noel 'Duck Egg' Kirwan, from the north inner city, after he was photographed along-side Gerry Hutch at his brother Eddie's funeral. The court also heard that the post-mortem had concluded the cause of death was 'massive intracranial damage' due to a bullet wound, along with evidence of recent cocaine use. Pathologist Professor Eamon Leen confirmed the bullet had entered just under Clarke's right eye and exited the back of his head and was consistent with a self-inflicted injury.

At the end of the proceedings, Coroner Dr Myra Cullinane returned an open verdict, reflecting the lack of evidence available for a suicide or misadventure verdict: 'There is insufficient evidence to fully explain what happened. The open verdict means there are unanswered questions.'

Glen Clarke left a lot of unanswered questions behind him from his short life – questions that the loved ones of those he targeted now have to live with for the rest of their lives. His death, however it happened, left Peadar Keating a man short, but there was more killing work afoot, and Keating would soon turn to others to get the job done.

7. The Addict

(2 September 2016: attempted murder of John Hutch and 26 March 2017: attempted murder of Eddie Staunton)

'We'll never forget what he's done. It's sad, things will never be the same. All over that scumbag in there.'
— Vera Hutch, wife of victim

By August 2016, over the course of just seven months, John Hutch's brother Eddie, son Gareth and nephew Gary had been murdered by Kinahan assassins. The targeting was relentless and included anyone with the Hutch surname or even remotely associated with the family, as former Dublin Lord Mayor Nial Ring recalled: 'It was such a terrifying time for the Hutch family. You had people like John Hutch and his wife, Vera, who weren't involved in anything, and yet here they were being hunted by ruthless killers just because of their name. There was [*sic*] also childhood friends of Gerry ['the Monk'] Hutch who were living in fear simply because they might have lived beside the Hutch family at one time in the past. John had lost his son, his brother and nephew and I honestly don't know how he was coping with the pressure his family were under. It was an awful way for anyone to live and it was clear the Kinahan crime group were throwing money at people from all over the place. They were simply killing and targeting people because they had the resources to do so.'

Even though three members of his family had been killed and his younger brother Gerry was in exile in the Canary Islands, John (b. 23 August 1953) did not have the financial resources to move his family, so they continued to live at the family home on Drumalee Avenue, on Dublin's north side. Following the murder of his brother in February that year, he stopped working as a taxi driver and claimed social welfare, insisting to the Department of Social Protection that this was a legitimate claim because, as court documents showed, his 'life was in danger'.

The only time he left the house was for essential errands or if his children needed help. Each time he left, he made sure the coast was clear before getting into his Nissan Note. In another measure to protect his family, the father of nine enlarged the rear wall of his back garden and installed a reinforced steel gate along with extensive CCTV cameras. He and his family were living under immense pressure and he was not taking any chances. The improved security at his home and the increased Garda patrols across the capital under Operation Hybrid might have offered some crumb of comfort, but as long as the feud was still running John Hutch would remain a 'legitimate' target for the Kinahan hit teams.

On 2 September 2016, Gerry Hutch's older brother had spent most of the day at his home. John and his wife left the house around 4 p.m. for an optician appointment. Afterwards, the couple travelled along the North Circular Road before turning into Drumalee Park, at the rear of the Hutch property, where John and other residents regularly parked their vehicles. It was 5.24 p.m. The couple got out of the car and began heading towards the safety of the reinforced gate and the sanctuary of home.

Within seconds, a red Opel Astra screeched to a halt behind them. Sensing danger, John Hutch ran towards his back garden. A gunman, armed with a German-made Walther PP semi-automatic pistol and a Japanese-made Miroku Brig-and six-shot revolver, chased after him. Hutch's wife ran in a different direction. In his panicked pursuit of his target, the gunman dropped one of his weapons.

John Hutch made it to his back garden and shut the gate, with his attacker on the other side. The frustrated gunman fired six indiscriminate shots into the back garden as his target, along with one of his daughters, who was at home that day, dived for cover. Miraculously, both father and daughter escaped injury. As bullets whizzed by, John Hutch's two other daughters watched the terrifying incident on the internal CCTV system, before rushing to the garden and helping their father and sister inside. The cartel target's 7-year-old grandson was also in the house at the time of the attack.

The first 999 call came from a neighbour as soon as the shots were fired at 5.24 p.m., followed a minute later by a call from Hutch's daughter, who told gardaí her father 'has been shot'. Three other calls were made that day, including one which described the red Opel, with a partial registration O5Y, leaving the scene.

Realizing his mission had failed, the gunman ran back to his getaway car, calmly picking up the discarded weapon on his way.

As the gunman fled, Vera Hutch, who had run in the other direction and bolted into a neighbour's house and was unaware of her husband's close escape, told a neighbour: 'They are after trying to get Johnny.' The neighbour ran to the Hutch property and jumped over the wall to check on John. When he saw that John Hutch was unharmed, the neighbour slumped to the ground, relieved, unaware that he had broken both of his ankles in his leap over the wall.

Gardaí arrived at the scene at 5.30 p.m. and John Hutch told them: 'They tried to get me. All members of my family are targets in this feud. They have killed my son and my brother.' In other interactions with gardaí, John Hutch described his attacker as 'stocky, with a scarf covering his face'.

In her conversation with investigators, Vera Hutch described how the gunman had 'looked at me before returning to his car. I believed my husband had been shot dead and I asked neighbours to check.' One of their daughters recalled 'feeling the bullets fly overhead'. By this time, the hitman's getaway car was making its way along Blackhorse Avenue. As it passed McKee barracks, it encountered heavy traffic due to roadworks, forcing it to make a U-turn. The getaway driver then drove into Regal Park, a laneway off Blackhorse Avenue. Once there, the vehicle was set on fire and the gunman and his accomplice, who has never been identified, fled on foot.

At the time of the shooting, gardaí from the Special Crime Task Force were monitoring the movements of senior cartel figure Dean Howe (b. 24 October 1984) as he drove a white Citroën Nemo van in the Watling Street area on the south side of the city. As news of the latest attempt on the life of a Hutch family member was distributed on the Garda communications network, the two officers received the order to stop Howe's van.

They were joined by two other colleagues, and they positioned their vehicles to prevent Howe from escaping. As Garda David Howard ordered Howe from the vehicle, the gangster opened a Nokia mobile phone and swallowed the SIM card. Howe, who was classified by gardaí at the time as being 'closely associated with a number of members of the

Kinahan crime gang and is suggested to have been involved in serious incidents including assault, drugs and attempted murder', was immediately arrested on suspicion of possession of a firearm in suspicious circumstances. Inside his van, the officers recovered a yellow bag containing petrol, even though the van was diesel operated. During his detention, Howe was interviewed nine times, replying 'No comment' to all of the questions put to him. He was released without charge at 4.35 p.m. on 4 September.

By the time he was released, gardaí had recovered two badly burnt firearms and a mobile phone from the Opel Astra, which had been stolen in Naas, County Kildare, just three days before the shooting. Gardaí also established that another vehicle had been stolen but was abandoned by the thieves because it broke down. An examination of the firearms showed that the serial numbers on both weapons had been removed.

Following the discovery of the car, two officers from the Special Crime Task Force searched pedestrian areas at Phoenix Park. As they entered the Laundry Gate Lodge, located just 300 metres from the burnt-out car, they found a small black mobile phone sitting on a bench. A witness told them that the phone had started ringing, so he answered it and a girl on the other end told him the phone was lost. He gave her the location and was waiting for her to arrive to collect it. When gardaí later established the identity of the girl who had contacted the phone, they knew her to be the relative of a man with known links to the Kinahan cartel in the south inner city. That man was Michael Carroll.

Carroll (b. 25 July 1979) came from a decent family in the Bride Street area of the capital but became addicted to heroin in his twenties. His only form of legitimate employment was a five-week period in 2000 when he worked on building sites. As his addiction grew, he turned to robberies to feed his habit. In 2000, he was the chief suspect for firing shots at a property in Mercer House. He received his most serious conviction in 2009, when he was jailed for eight years for robbing €1,405 during a spate of armed robberies in Usher's Quay. Carroll – described by gardaí as a 'volatile and dangerous criminal' – was only caught after a special operation was put in place. When he attempted to rob a garage in Usher's Quay, Detective Garda Richie Pender and Detective Sergeant John Brady were waiting for him. At the time, gardaí believed he was committing the robberies because he owed a €6,000 drug debt to 'Fat' Freddie Thompson. He received a further 2-year sentence in May 2009, for slashing the face of another inmate in Mountjoy Prison.

As well as his involvement in violent crime to feed his own habit, he was also involved in the drugs trade and was a suspect in eight drugs possession incidents with values ranging from €400 to €10,000. His forty-six other convictions were for possession of knives, assault, criminal damage, possession of drugs and theft. Released from custody on 19 March 2013, Carroll kept a low profile before he emerged as a chief suspect in the Hutch shooting three years later. Once he had been identified as a contract killer for the cartel, gardaí concluded that Carroll had been 'entangled in serious and organized crime for over sixteen years'. They believed that due to his involvement in the importation and distribution of controlled drugs Carroll 'became indebted to the Kinahan Crime Group in 2016 and was consequently used to do their bidding in lieu of monies owed. Carroll is linked to the targeting of persons on behalf of the Kinahan group and is a suspect in witness intimidation and the organizing of numerous serious assaults.' One of the cases involved Carroll trying to target a taxi driver who had links to the Hutch family.

As the investigation into the attempted murder of John Hutch continued, detectives made a huge discovery when Garda David Howard found a tracking device on the undercarriage of John Hutch's car. The device contained a printed circuit board and data SIM card. It confirmed the gardaí's fears that Hutch's movements were being tracked by the cartel hit team. The device underwent examination at the Electronic and Media Examination Unit at Garda HQ. Over the coming weeks and months, the investigation team would concentrate on the tracker and on CCTV footage.

Focusing on the tracker, the device's IMEI number allowed gardaí to establish that it had been bought on the website Gotek in November 2015 by a man who later sold it on. The man was tracked down and told officers that he had sold it to a man who used the name 'John Shughnessy'. This man was never identified but was suspected of being a cartel member. As the weeks progressed, investigators from Garda HQ accessed the device's data from its SIM card. The device had been active between 15 January and 4 September 2016, but for only short periods of time. On 25 August 2016 the device's GPS system placed it in the Bride Street area of the south inner city – a Kinahan stronghold. On 30 August, it had left the School Street flats area of the south inner city before arriving at Drumalee Park at 6.32 a.m. The CCTV from Hutch's property on that date showed a man lying underneath the Nissan Note.

The device remained on the car until 2 September, when CCTV from the Hutch household showed a man arriving at

2.32 a.m. and climbing under the car. The signal was then picked up at School Street flats at 2.59 a.m., before leaving the south side at 6.01 a.m. and returning to Drumalee Park at 6.18 a.m., with CCTV once again showing the man getting under the car. Investigators had no doubt that the device had been retrieved by the hit team so that it could be recharged and replaced on Hutch's car to continue monitoring his movements. As the tracker was being returned to Drumalee, a mobile phone number linked to Carroll was pinging off a mast just 450 metres away in the Aughrim Street area. The information from the tracker being taken to the School Street flats also pointed gardaí in the direction of Carroll, particularly since his partner was living there at the time.

The mobile phone and tracker weren't the only evidence gathered against Carroll. There was CCTV footage that would also play a role in the gardaí's case against him. In the first piece of CCTV evidence, images showed a man leaving School Street flats on 2 September at 2.01 a.m. and returning by taxi at 2.34 a.m. He was wearing the same clothing as the man who had been underneath John Hutch's car. At 11.15 a.m. on the day of the shooting, CCTV captured Carroll leaving School Street flats with a yellow bag before talking with a close associate of 'Fat' Freddie Thompson. The footage showed him wearing grey cotton tracksuit bottoms and white trainers – the same clothing worn by the hitman during the attempted murder.

By the end of 2016, detectives had amassed a huge amount of CCTV evidence, including footage of Howe's van driving in convoy before the attack. Other images from the day included a man running in Phoenix Park at 5.39 p.m. in black bottoms and black top. However, two minutes later, an image of the same man was captured but wearing green shorts.

Gardaí believed the suspect, who was heading in the direction of Islandbridge in the south inner city, had changed into the green shorts in an area not covered by any cameras. The suspect, whose face was not clear in any of the images, was then captured in Islandbridge at 5.50 p.m. However, as he walked past the Patriot's Inn on the Old Kilmainham Road, the images were clear – and gardaí were in no doubt that it was Carroll. To confirm it fully, the image was shown to detectives in Kevin Street Garda Station, who had dealt with Carroll during his criminal career. Every one of the detectives confirmed that it was Carroll in the footage.

At 6.05 p.m., the suspect, wearing the same clothes as Carroll, was captured crawling along the ground at School Street flats, before knocking at a front door. He then crawled into the flat. Gardaí later concluded that: 'The change of clothing was an attempt to confuse any descriptions or sightings of him following the shooting.' After spending thirty-two minutes in the flat, clearer CCTV images showed Carroll leaving the property and then cycling to the Liberty Bar in Meath Street. Gardaí later secured the pub's CCTV footage and it showed Carroll inside the bar, making his way to the rear of the premises, where he spoke with an associate of the Kinahan cartel. Former Detective Inspector John Bates said: 'I recall CCTV footage of the pub being examined which showed the suspect conversing with individuals who were associated with the Kinahan and Byrne Organized Crime Group. No evidential value was obtained from this footage.'

Following their brief conversation, Carroll then spoke with another individual outside the pub, with CCTV showing him 'throwing his arms on his head and kicking a shutter'. It was at this point that gardaí believe Carroll was told his mission had been a failure.

Carroll left the bar at 9.27 p.m. and then returned at 10.53 p.m., when he could be seen chatting outside with cartel figure Liam Brannigan. He left at 12.20 a.m. and went back to School Street flats. When examining footage from the bar, gardaí also established that Carroll had been in the pub the night before the shooting, wearing the same runners as the man who was filmed underneath the car and also the gunman. At the time of the bid to kill Hutch, detectives believed that Carroll owed the cartel €40,000 due to his chronic drug addiction.

Satisfied with the CCTV evidence they had gathered, gardaí made their move against Carroll on 27 February 2017. At 6.50 a.m., the Emergency Response Unit stormed into the suspected gunman's home in Bride Street and he was arrested by Detective Sergeant Mark Watters on suspicion of firearms offences on the day John Hutch survived the attempt on his life. Brought to the Bridewell Garda Station for questioning, Carroll was questioned sixteen times by different teams of detectives, which also included specialist interviewers from the Garda National Bureau of Criminal Investigation. To all of the questions put to him, Carroll made no reply. He was released without charge at 9.53 p.m. on 3 March 2017, and the investigation team continued to prepare their file for the DPP.

Even though Carroll had been arrested and was a person of interest to the gardaí and therefore drawing some heat, his cartel paymasters came calling for a second time on Mother's Day, 26 March 2017. On this occasion the Kinahan group's target was Edward Staunton (b. 25 December 1991), a nephew, through marriage, of the Monk's brother Patsy. Growing up, Edward was very close to Patsy's son, Patrick, who was charged over the murder of David Byrne at the Regency Hotel but was acquitted, and was living at the family home in Glasnevin, north Dublin. Edward was unemployed and was regularly seen on the streets of the north inner city and also at the home of his cousin, Derek 'Coakley' Hutch, in Liberty House.

On 26 March 2017, Staunton had spent the day with his friends in the north inner city before cycling to Liberty House to 'use the toilet' at his cousin's place. As he did so, he became suspicious of a silver Ford Focus parked close to the flats complex. When he left the flats he noticed the car was still there, and it began following him. As he cycled on the footpath of James Joyce Street, he was hit by the car at 9.36 p.m. Thrown through the air, he landed on the windscreen, bounced off and hit the ground beside a set of iron railings. Staunton screamed in pain. As he struggled to get to his feet, the driver of the car emerged with a firearm. For some reason, he decided not to fire and turned around and got back into the vehicle. Hurt as he was, Staunton jumped up and ran for his life in the direction of Railway Street.

The gunman made to drive after Staunton again, but the car had been damaged by the force of the impact. The car moved so slowly, he couldn't make any headway. He abandoned it in Seán McDermott Street, leaving a hat in the back of the car in his haste to hunt down his prey.

In the meantime, Staunton had made his way to Peadar Kearney House, a flats complex on Railway Street, where he told a group of onlookers about his injuries. Around eight minutes had passed since he had been catapulted into the air by the car, and he was lying flat out on the ground, awaiting medical help. A man walked up and joined the onlookers, asking if there was 'any gardaí around. He looked down at

Staunton and said: "Is this the young fella hit by the car?"'
When told that it was, the man produced a gun and opened
fire. He fired four shots and hit Staunton twice in the lower
body. Incredibly, and for the second time that night, Staunton managed to get to his feet and run away, seeking refuge
in a nearby house where a family had gathered to celebrate
Mother's Day.

The gunman needed to get away quickly – he turned and
fled down a laneway known locally as Emerald Place. He
took off his jacket in the laneway and dropped it on the
ground as he ran. He continued his escape on foot along
Lower Sheriff Street, where he bumped into a man he knew.
He went on again, but encountered a second man who recognized him from their time in prison together. The second
man had no idea his old cellmate had just shot someone, nor
did he know he was an assassin for the Kinahan cartel, so he
directed the gunman to playing fields at Mayor Square in the
mistaken belief he was being chased by gardaí. The suspect
then made his way to Lombard Street, across the Liffey,
where it's believed he was brought to a safe house by cartel
associates.

Edward Staunton, meanwhile, was rushed to the Mater
Hospital for treatment for his multiple injuries. He was
released from hospital on 7 April and told gardaí he had a
'bad feeling and something was going down' when he saw
the windows of the silver Ford Focus were 'fogged up'. As
he cycled out of Liberty House that day, he said that he knew
the car was 'for him' when it drove towards him and when a
group of local youths shouted, 'Eddie, watch out.' Describing the moment when he was shot at close range, Staunton
told gardaí how he had 'felt an awful burning pain' in his
stomach and believed he had been targeted in a case of

mistaken identity. Detectives included in their investigation the possibility that Staunton's cousin Derek Coakley Hutch was the real target. (Coakley Hutch was subsequently murdered on 20 January 2018.)

During the investigation, gardaí established that the hitman's car was bought from a south Dublin garage that had previously been targeted by the Criminal Assets Bureau (CAB) and was known to have links to cartel associates. The man who bought the Ford Focus provided a false name and address, and detectives were unable to establish his identity.

The CCTV angle of the investigation proved more fruitful. Gardaí identified the silver Focus driving around the north inner city on 21 March. But the really big moment came when detectives searching through CCTV footage were rewarded with a crucial image: the gunman exiting his car and approaching Staunton after the crash. That image was circulated in Garda bulletins and a suspect was quickly nominated: Michael Carroll. As before, the team sought to fully confirm their suspicions by showing the footage to officers who had dealt with Carroll over the years. Eleven officers were shown the footage and asked: 'Do you know that man?' Each of them in turn instantly said Carroll's name. DNA from the hat found in the car also matched Carroll's, and partial DNA found in the jacket discarded by the gunman matched with his. It was him. They had their would-be assassin.

Gardaí now worked on preparing two files on Carroll for the DPP – one for the attempted murder of John Hutch, the other for the attempted murder of Edward Staunton. Before the cases could move to the next stage, however, Carroll fled Ireland and went on the run. Over the next five years he lived in Liverpool and other parts of the north-west of England. The last confirmed sighting of Carroll was two days before the Staunton shooting, when he signed his bail for road traffic offences at Kevin Street Garda Station. Despite disappearing, he was not reported missing by his family, with relatives later telling investigators when they called to his home that he was 'safe and well'.

While Carroll remained at large, both extensive files on the two murder bids were completed and sent to the DPP. However, due to the Covid-19 pandemic and the subsequent closure of the courts, there was a delay in the DPP's decision to charge Carroll in relation to both incidents. The decision finally came in 2021 when the DPP ruled there was enough evidence to charge him and a European Arrest Warrant was issued. In documents examined by lawyers for the DPP, they accepted the Garda belief that there was 'compelling evidence' to justify a prosecution against their prime suspect. Upon examining the Staunton case, the DPP concluded that he had been targeted because of his association with the Hutch family. The role of the cartel was also examined by the DPP, which concluded that criminals were tasked with 'identifying, locating and targeting members of the Hutch family, their relatives and associates. Gardaí are constantly engaged in operations to disrupt and prevent further attempts on lives.'

With the European Arrest Warrant in place, gardaí received intelligence that Carroll was living in and associating with known cartel figures in Liverpool. Tracked down to a flat close to the city centre, the fugitive was finally arrested by UK police in the early hours of 28 April 2022 before being brought immediately to Casement Aerodrome in Baldonnel, County Dublin. Once landed on Irish soil, he was taken to

Dublin District Court, where he was charged with two counts of attempted murder – of Eddie Staunton and of John Hutch. Remanded in custody, Carroll was informed in December of that year that he would go on trial at the Special Criminal Court in March 2023.

When he appeared before the court on 27 March 2023, the career criminal pleaded guilty to the attempted murder of Edward Staunton and to possession of a firearm with intent to endanger life on the same day an attempt was made to kill John Hutch.

The date of 22 May 2023 was set for the sentence hearing. By that time, John Hutch was no longer alive to see his attacker brought to justice – he had died of natural causes after a fall in his home in 2019. It was Vera Hutch who delivered the victim impact statement on behalf of her family. She told the court how the attempt on her husband's life would never leave her mind: 'I get flashbacks, I am paranoid, stopped going to the gym, I am on antibiotics and I don't answer the door without checking who is there. I can't believe how I didn't lose my daughter or husband that day. I think about it all the time. Everything stopped for me that day.'

During the hearing, Carroll's defence barrister, Giollaíosa Ó Lideadha SC, would tell the court how his client had committed the crimes to 'ingratiate' himself with the Kinahan and Byrne crime faction as he was 'under pressure' to repay a 'significant' drugs debt. Remanded in custody once again, Carroll was back before the court on 31 July 2023. He saw the court again sooner than expected when, a week before his scheduled appearance, he was disciplined by the Irish Prison Service after he was caught with heroin, cocaine and ecstasy tablets in Mountjoy Prison.

His barrister told the court that his client would need

'intense help' to address his addiction and read out a letter from Carroll's sister, who described how his addiction to drugs 'broke the family's hearts'. Following the hearing, Carroll was told that he would finally learn his fate on 2 October. Addressing the court that day, presiding judge Mr Justice Tony Hunt described Carroll as a 'ruthless and dangerous criminal with a callous contempt for public safety'. Referring to the botched hit on Staunton, the judge explained that it was a 'deliberate plan to murder a particular target. The CCTV was chilling.'

When he stood before the court again on 2 October, Carroll received a ten-and-a-half-year sentence for the Hutch shooting and a 14-year sentence for the attempted murder of Staunton, with two and a half years suspended to 'allow for rehabilitation'. In an interview with *Irish Sun* reporter Michael Doyle after the sentence, Vera Hutch welcomed the end of the judicial process: 'We're delighted with what he got. We're glad it's over now, thank God. We'll never forget what he's done. It's sad, things will never be the same. All over that scumbag in there. We're told the feud is over. We're trying to move on with our lives now.'

Michael Carroll received one of the longest sentences handed down to cartel assassins. He was just one of a number of men, crippled by drug debt and addiction, the Kinahan cartel exploited to carry out their dirty work.

8. The Innocent Target

(22 December 2016: murder of Noel 'Duck Egg' Kirwan)

'These killers are holding the people of Ireland to ransom and our lives will never be the same again.'
– Noel Kirwan's family statement

When a young father was asked by his friend to meet for a drink in the spring of 2017, he expected he would hear boasts about the callous shooting of an entirely innocent man. The pair often got together to watch football matches, smoke cannabis, drink alcohol and talk about life into the early hours of the morning. On this night, however, the conversation took a more sinister turn. The friend started to talk about the Kinahan and Hutch feud, then brought up the murder of Noel 'Duck Egg' Kirwan. The young father, who cannot be named in order to protect his family, listened intently as his friend began to reveal, in great detail, his role in the killing.

Some months earlier, Noel Kirwan was in good form in the run-up to Christmas 2016 and had bought a new car. The BMW X5 SUV he was driving had been costing too much in tax, so on 10 December he made his way to a Clondalkin dealership and made a deal to trade in the vehicle and purchase a Ford Mondeo, which he collected three days later.

Kirwan was living at St Ronan's Drive in Clondalkin, west

Dublin, with his partner, Bernadette Roe, at the time. The pair had known each other all their lives, their fathers had worked on the docks together, and they had begun a relationship six years before, after Mr Kirwan lost his wife to cancer in 2008. On 22 December 2016, the couple went for a meal with relatives before dropping Ms Roe's daughter, Carolyn Murray, and her granddaughter back to their house and making their way home.

As they pulled into the driveway of their home after 5 p.m., Kirwan was admiring the Christmas lights on their house. Out of nowhere, a lone assassin fired a hail of bullets into the driver's-side window. Ms Roe, in the front passenger seat, initially thought someone had smashed the window, but then Kirwan told her, 'I've been shot.' She pushed open the door and ran from the car. She saw the gunman jump into the side of a white van as it roared off. She screamed for help. Neighbours came out after hearing the commotion and someone called 999 to report a gun attack.

Bernadette Roe rang her daughter, Carolyn, who had been in the car with them just minutes earlier. Bernadette was in hysterics. Carolyn immediately made her way to her mum's home nearby and on the way she saw a white van at a standstill, its driver seeming to be contemplating where to go. Only later did she realize it was the hit team's vehicle. When she reached her mother's house, she saw Noel Kirwan slumped over the gear stick in his car. She got into the car and held his hand, talking to him until an ambulance arrived.

Noel Kirwan, a 62-year-old father of four and grandfather, didn't make it. He had been shot six times, once in the right of the face below his eye, once in the right shoulder and anterior chest, once in the anterior abdomen, two shots in the right arm and once in the right side of his body. The white Peugeot van the killer had emerged from and fled in, with another man driving, was found on fire at the rear of Neilstown Shopping Centre in Clondalkin, less than a minute's drive from the scene. The 9mm Makarov handgun used in the murder was recovered near the scene, in the grass at the end of a row of houses.

A life-long republican, Noel Kirwan had played a role in the anti-drug groups in the 1980s and 1990s, set up to drive dealers out of inner-city communities. He knew Eddie Hutch, the brother of the Monk, as they had gone to school together, but he was not involved in crime, was not a member of the Hutch gang and was not in any way connected to the feud. The only link that could have condemned him was from ten months earlier: on 19 February 2016, Kirwan had attended the funeral of Eddie Hutch after he was shot dead in retaliation for the Regency Hotel attack.

At the funeral, Gerry Hutch had appeared wearing a wig, in what would be his last time on Irish soil for over five years. He happened to be standing by Kirwan when he was photographed. It highlighted the Kinahan cartel's sheer brutality – anyone with any kind of link to the Monk, however tenuous, was a target.

In the days after his murder, Noel Kirwan's family issued a statement to the *Irish Sun*, which told of their devastation while in deep mourning and reiterated that Kirwan was an innocent man:

He was looking forward to spending Christmas with his family, especially his two grandkids, and everyone is just completely heartbroken over this brutal murder. Bernadette has assured his family they had never received any type of warning that he was under threat. If he had been under threat, he would not be visiting his relatives in north Dublin every weekend. The simple fact is that he was killed because he was a soft target. He went to Eddie Hutch's funeral because they went to school together and that's the reason they killed him. What are these people going to do now— murder everyone including the priest who was at the service? Noel wasn't a member of any crime gang and was completely innocent. He wasn't part of Gerry Hutch's gang and only knew him because they went to school together. Noel never socialised with Gerry Hutch or did anything with him. He was targeted because they saw him at the funeral. The only time he would have met Gerry Hutch was if he had bumped into him in the street. These killers are holding the people of Ireland to ransom and our lives will never be the same again.

By this stage the gardaí had already made their first major discovery in the case. Kirwan's new car, the Ford Mondeo, was brought to Ballyfermot Garda Station the day after the murder. When it was examined, a GoTEK tracking device was found on the undercarriage, latched on with strong magnets. The device, in a rubber cover, was removed and sent for analysis as they looked to retrace its movements.

The tracker had quite the story to tell as gardaí delved into its data. It had originated at the GoTEK premises in Calais, France, and was later brought to the the Spy Shop in Leeds, England, on 18 October 2016. Within two days it was 'pinging' from Dublin Port as it arrived in Ireland from Holyhead in Wales. The tracker confirmed the Kinahan cartel's involvement when it appeared at an address in Crumlin, south Dublin, the home of a senior gang member. (This person's identity is known but cannot be revealed for legal reasons.)

By 3 November, it had moved to an apartment at the Beacon South Quarter complex in Sandyford. Five days later it was on St Ronan's Drive after it had been discreetly placed on Mr Kirwan's BMW X5.

Kirwan was completely unaware of its existence, but it was tracking his movements for weeks before he traded in his SUV. The gardaí discussed with family members what journeys Mr Kirwan had taken in that period of time, including one to Gorey in County Wexford, and they matched the movements of the tracker. The gang had also clearly overcome a stumbling block by retrieving the tracker from the SUV after Kirwan traded it in on 13 December. It was placed on to the Ford Mondeo, and they still knew every move he made.

In January 2017, the gardaí raided the Beacon South Quarter apartment where the tracker had appeared on 3 November, and the evidence obtained there revealed that it was the murder squad's headquarters for the assassination operation. Inside, behind a mirror, the instruction manual for the specific tracker on Kirwan's car, identified through a unique serial code number, was discovered. The DNA of the senior gang member – in whose Crumlin house the tracker had turned up – was found on the laptop and its bag, along with his fingerprints on the manual.

There was CCTV at the apartment complex and it gave further insight into this senior gang member's role. He and another associate, who would later be unveiled by the gardaí as a key Kinahan associate, were seen leaving the apartment block at 1.21 a.m. on 8 November 2016, and their movements matched that of the tracker, which travelled with them in a car to St Ronan's Drive, where gardaí found it was 'pinging' from 2.43 a.m., after being placed under the BMW X5.

Gardaí also suspect that this Crumlin figure was in the back of the same associate's car on 14 and 15 December when they were spotted outside the Clondalkin dealership's premises as they were trying to establish the whereabouts of the tracker.

The following day, 16 December, the BMW X5 was passed on from the dealership to Merlin Car Auctions in Naas, County Kildare. Officers retrieved CCTV from that premises and it showed a green Renault Megane turning up on 20 December. The Megane was registered to Jason Keating.

Keating (b. 16 May 1991) was known to gardaí but was far from an intelligent criminal. The father of three had left school with little formal education and was functioning at an almost illiterate level. He had twenty-five convictions at the time for road traffic and public order offences.

The footage showed Keating and a female associate walking around the stockyard at the premises, where cars were on display, before they disappeared from shot for three minutes. They were then seen leaving in the car they had arrived in. Keating had recovered the device during those three minutes and the next day it was attached to Kirwan's Ford Mondeo at St Ronan's Drive.

Further CCTV at the Neilstown Shopping Centre, where the getaway van had been set alight, also showed Keating and another man fleeing from the area on the day of the murder. The van had earlier pulled into St Ronan's Drive at 4.28 p.m., just over thirty minutes before the gunman got out and murdered Kirwan. Gardaí established that Keating was in communication by phone with the Crumlin gang member, who was monitoring Kirwan's movements via the tracker on the laptop and passing the information to the triggerman. The device was programmed to report the movement of Mr

Kirwan's car every four hours, but on his journey home from the restaurant on that day a command was being logged every thirty seconds from the laptop in the apartment.

Keating longed to fit in with the criminal fraternity, and this was his big chance. So he couldn't help talking about it when he met up with his friend, the young father, in the pub in 2017. Breaking the criminal *omertà*, he told the man about his role in the murder in a bragging manner. His pal, who had battled drug addiction over the years, wasn't impressed by the confession. The story he heard that night troubled him, and he approached the gardaí in April to make a statement. By this time, he was only telling detectives what they already knew because they had identified their suspect.

On 2 May, gardaí searched Keating's family home in Drimnagh, Dublin 12, and seized over €3,000 in cash. Officers then raided the house of his former partner in Rush, north County Dublin, and seized his Ford Focus car; he had sold the Renault Megane. Keating was arrested by gardaí on foot of their investigations and six days later, on 8 May 2017, he was charged with the murder of Noel Kirwan.

Keating's friend who went to the gardaí to tell them about what he had been told in the pub tragically took his own life some months later, after losing his battle with addiction. Reflecting on his passing, a relative of Noel Kirwan told the authors: 'This young man's family should be proud of him for deciding to do the right thing. He should never have been put in this situation from Keating and it's clear he knew Noel's killing was completely wrong. The gardaí didn't need his information in the end, but it's reassuring to know he was prepared to help. It also shows the real character of Keating, who was seemingly boasting about the killing of an innocent man. He was nothing more than a wannabe gangster.'

Keating was before the Special Criminal Court in 2018 to stand trial for murder. During the case he entered a guilty plea to the charge of facilitating a criminal organization in carrying out an offence and the first charge, of murder, was dropped. At his sentencing, presiding judge Mr Justice Tony Hunt told how it was 'disturbing' that Kirwan was apparently shot for no other reason than photographs of him in the company of a childhood friend at a funeral. He also noted that providing assistance to the gang was an 'inherently grave matter' and added: 'It is inevitable that it was pre-planned and not spontaneous.' He explained that Keating had been 'clearly instructed' in advance of the tasks he had to carry out and carried them out with a high degree of knowledge and intention.

Referring to the fact that Keating had continued to liaise with those monitoring the tracking device on the day of the murder and had brought the gunman to and from the scene, Mr Justice Hunt said, 'There is no room for any doubt or illusion of the deliberate nature of Mr Keating's conduct or any misapprehension as to the ends.'

Keating was jailed for ten years for his role in the murder.

Bernadette Roe, who is called Bernie by those known to her, had a lucky escape that day, but the events of what happened and the devastation it has caused will never leave her. In her victim impact statement read into court, Bernadette Roe said: 'On the evening of December 22nd 2016, my partner Noel was murdered senselessly and for no good reason. In that moment my whole life as I knew it was horrifically and devastatingly changed forever. It was only by the grace of God, I wasn't murdered also. My Noel, my love, my soulmate, had his life extinguished, all because he was pictured by the press walking into the funeral of a lifelong neighbour – may Noel rest in peace. Noel was a good man, he was very kind and loved to help others in need. He was my best friend and soulmate – we shared everything and we had plans for our future together. I feel very angry and cheated about Noel's senseless murder, he was cheated of the life he had, of the future he wanted and planned. I am very angry that my soulmate was so violently and viciously taken for no good reason and our life and future together is now gone forever. Noel's murder has deeply affected and traumatised every aspect of my life.'

Keating had offered an apology at his sentencing, but Noel Kirwan's daughter Donna said she will never accept one from him. In an interview with one of the authors following the case, she said: 'How would he feel if someone had to tell his three children that he had been murdered? I don't feel anything towards him, but I don't hate him. If he ever tries to apologize to us, we will tell him he can shove it. The people he was working in tandem with have destroyed our lives. He's simply a coward who sat in court smirking and laughing while our lives have been destroyed. My dad was a completely innocent man and, if he had known Keating, he would have told him to never get involved in something like this.'

Gardaí from Ronanstown and Lucan Garda Stations, who followed 650 lines of inquiry in relation to the murder, were supported by specialist investigators from the Garda National Bureau of Criminal Investigation. A spokesman for the bureau revealed how its members played an important role in bringing Keating to justice. He told the authors: 'In particular, the NBCI brought their expertise to bear in the interviewing of witnesses and suspects. The investigation was a team effort. The Family Liaison Officer Colin Sullivan deserves special recognition as he built a strong relationship with the family that was very beneficial for the investigation team and for the family also. CCTV footage in the vicinity of the murder scene proved important in establishing the movements of the persons directly involved in the murder. When other evidence came to light, phone and GPS data from the tracking device, this provided other opportunities to harvest CCTV. Investigators viewed hundreds of hours of footage in which they were able to track Jason Keating's movements in the weeks before the murder and in the immediate aftermath. This evidence proved crucial in securing his conviction.'

The investigation into Kirwan's killing also turned up another name: Martin Aylmer. This low-level criminal had already been dealt with for his role in the murder of Michael Barr (see Chapter 2). Aylmer was a trusted enabler of the cartel, whose members called him 'Casper' because he was so under the radar, like a ghost. However, he made a schoolboy error when he travelled to the UK in October 2016 to collect tracking devices from the Spy Shop in Leeds, one of which was used on Kirwan's car. He booked a ferry ticket in his own name and used his own car before returning to Dublin and passing the trackers on to his associates. Aylmer's decision to buy the trackers would see his name crop up in another major investigation in the future before he would be handed down his punishment over his limited role in Kirwan's murder (see Chapter 12).

Over seven years on from the murder, a senior Kinahan lieutenant's name was read into court in relation to the case. Sean McGovern was shot on the day of the Regency Hotel attack, which claimed the life of his close pal David Byrne. Although a European Arrest Warrant was issued for McGovern for murder in April 2022, the gangster remains in Dubai, where the leadership of the Kinahan cartel are based.

In January 2024, Michael Crotty went on trial accused of facilitating the murder of Noel Kirwan by buying a mobile phone top-up for McGovern. Evidence was heard from Detective Superintendent Dave Gallagher of the Garda National Drugs and Organised Crime Bureau, who told the Special Criminal Court that he had been involved in investigating serious crime and organized criminal groups. Following the Regency attack, he was tasked with investigating the Kinahan and Hutch organizations.

The senior officer outlined how, since 2015, he was involved in prosecuting those in leadership roles in the two organized crime gangs. He explained that the Kinahan group is 'driven by monetary gain, with drug trafficking as the primary source of income'. They are involved at an international level to import drugs and in the distribution at street level, enforcing their control by 'violence, using firearms and murder' and engaging in money laundering.

Detective Superintendent Gallagher described how the gang's structure is complex and well organized. Some of his insight and knowledge came from phone calls, audio recordings and seized mobile phones as well as messages on encrypted platforms that were accessed by Europol in recent years. There was also information from other law agencies abroad which assisted him in building a picture of the gang. He confirmed McGovern's role in the organized crime gang, telling the court: 'He is a significant figure within the organization in a leadership role and is currently based in Dubai.'

McGovern is wanted in relation to the Kirwan murder,

but his role in the killing has never been outlined directly in court as gardaí continue to liaise with authorities in the UAE to organize his extradition to Ireland to face prosecution. The European Arrest Warrant was granted by the District Court and came after the DPP, which examined the evidence the gardaí had built against him, directed that McGovern be charged. It means that if McGovern returns here, he will not face questioning but instead will be arrested and brought straight to court to be charged.

During his trial, Michael Crotty, from Cashel in Tipperary, pleaded guilty to a new charge based on recklessness. His lawyers argued that it was never his intention for the top-up to be used in the endangerment of any person. In May 2024, Crotty was sentenced to two years in prison.

In another statement in court directed at the gang, Donna Kirwan described how she and her family cannot erase the images in their minds: 'You have destroyed our peace, our past and our future. You hadn't got the intelligence between the lot of you to go and do your homework correctly – if you did, you would come to realize that our dad was a completely innocent man. How does it feel knowing you're going to prison for killing an innocent man? You robbed us of a life with our dad – he was all we had as our mam had passed away a couple of years earlier from cancer. You had a tracking device put on to his car and myself and my little boy were in that car while he drove around shopping for Christmas presents. I often wonder, would you have had him killed while we were in the car? How did you decide what time would be best to do it? These are our thoughts every day. We don't get to switch off when we want. I've suffered greatly with my mental health since that day and I absolutely hate that I have allowed you to do this to me – I think you have taken enough. Our dad was an amazing father. He worked two jobs to make sure we never went without. He always drummed it into us to work for everything we wanted. He couldn't bear the thought of us going near drugs or going down the wrong path. None of us did. We all have great jobs and will make sure our children go on to do the same. But because of you, our dad will never get to see his grandchildren grow up – something he was really looking forward to after working so hard all his life.'

The gardaí had been successful in identifying the foot soldiers of the operation and nailing them. But when Noel Kirwan was murdered, another key cartel member was in their sights. This inconspicuous figure was one of the senior gangsters who helped plan and direct but who was never close to the crime scene when it happened. But this man's days working in the shadows were coming to an end as the Garda fightback would see them land a deadly strike.

9. The Quartermaster

(24 January 2017: Kinahan arms cache seizure)

*'The military grade aspects to some of those firearms and the
sheer number of them made it clear that this was the
equivalent of taking out the armoury and the quartermaster
in a terrorist organization.'*
– Former Assistant Commissioner John O'Driscoll

In the wake of the Regency Hotel attack, on the morning of
15 February 2016 the Kinahan cartel paraded their wealth and
power through the streets of Dublin as they mourned the
death of their murdered associate David Byrne. The head of
the cartel, Daniel Kinahan, was among the chief mourners.
He was dressed in black, with a grey tweed flat cap, while his
underlings wore matching designer black suits, black ties and
light blue shirts in an open display of allegiance to the murderous mob. The group of men was made up of well-known
players within the Irish underworld, including the dead man's
brother Liam Byrne, Freddie Thompson and their close
friend Sean McGovern, each standing out prominently in the
crowd of mourners. But towards the back of the funeral cor-
tège outside St Nicholas of Myra Church on Francis Street,
there were also lesser-known faces dressed in the cartel's col-
ours. One of those men had grey hair, appeared stony-faced
and was wearing sunglasses on the brisk February morning.
Garda surveillance teams were watching with interest, taking

discreet pictures of the crowd. Afterwards, they set about identifying the older mourner, which was how they discovered he was the mysterious Declan Brady.

Brady was not known to the seasoned detectives who routinely investigated gangland figures, but then, very few did know of him. On the surface, he was a successful businessman who earned his crust in the haulage business and was living a comfortable life. But when the Kinahan cartel was audaciously attacked in that unprecedented assassination at the Regency, this invisible man stepped on to the stage to take his place among Ireland's most dangerous criminals.

Declan Brady (b. 10 April 1966) grew up in the suburb of Drimnagh in the south of Dublin. His father was a haulier who had an alcohol problem – an issue that ran in the family. By the age of fourteen, Brady had left school and was working in the family business. He later got a truck licence and drove the trucks for years. He married his wife, Deirdre, in 1987 and they bought their first family home in Firhouse with a gift of £10,000 from Deirdre's father. They had a mortgage of £17,000. The couple went on to have three children and moved to Celbridge, County Kildare, in 2001, and were still living in that area in 2016. Brady also did some work in the bouncy-castle business and despite the economic recession in the late 2000s, he seemed to have survived the financial crisis which crippled so many across the nation. Brady had only ever come to the gardaí's attention for seven road traffic convictions, but never for any criminality.

Two months prior to David Byrne's funeral, a Dublin estate agent received an email from a man named 'RC', the Managing Director of Far Logistics, using the email address: farlogisticsltd@yahoo.co.uk. He was making an inquiry into Unit 52 in the Greenogue Industrial Estate, which had been advertised for rent on property website Daft. ie. The email, sent on Monday, 14 December 2015, at 2.34 p.m., read:

> Dear Sirs, we are a Logistics/Transport company based in the UK, and we are in the process of trying to secure a suitable warehouse/office in the Dublin area. We specialize in groupage/consolidation from the UK to Ireland, and it is necessary for us to have a location in Ireland to support our services. My colleague was over in Ireland last week, and he identified a couple of suitable places on the DAFT website, that we would be interested in viewing. In particular we are interested in the UNIT 52, Greenogue Ind Estate. As this is just off the M50, it would be ideal for our needs. I am in Dublin on Tuesday 15th December, and I was wondering if it would be possible to arrange a viewing? We are anxious to find something quickly so that we can hit the ground running in January. I would be grateful for your response. I have included my mobile number below, if you have difficulty with reaching me, it's because I am travelling, however if you send me a mail, I will have intermittent access to same.
>
> Kind Regards,
> 'RC',
> MD,
> Far Logistics Ltd
> Leestone Road,
> Sharston Ind Estate,
> Manchester.

Greenogue Industrial Estate is a business park near Rathcoole, south-west Dublin, close to both the city and the border to County Kildare.

The estate agent replied to this email, confirming the unit was still available, and the next day met with a man after 11 a.m. to conduct a viewing. Afterwards, Mr 'RC' emailed once more, pressing to go ahead with a lease agreement, despite no discussion of rates, and said he was eager to have the unit up and running by January.

The owner of the unit looked up Far Logistics online and was satisfied that it was a legitimate company, therefore gave the estate agent the go-ahead to lease the property. The rent was €1,000 per month, which was considered market value at the time, and the rates were €673.77 per month. Mr RC's colleague met the auctioneer on 18 December 2015 at the unit to exchange the contracts, which were effective from 1 January 2016 for two years.

Within thirty-five days of the lease taking effect, the Regency Hotel attack had ignited a feud and a new level of violence on the streets of Ireland. The identification of Declan Brady at the funeral of David Byrne had intrigued gardaí, and it put him under the scope of the Garda National Drugs and Organized Crime Bureau, which began building intel and a picture of who he really was. The specialist officers soon learned that this man was a character of deception, a 'Mr Nobody' who was living a double life.

By December 2016, Brady had been put under surveillance by gardaí, who established that he had access to three addresses in County Kildare: his home at Wolston Abbey in Celbridge, one at Sallins Bridge in Sallins and one at The Dairy at Rathasker Road. When observed leaving these properties on various mornings and again later in the day, he had often changed from one outfit into another set of clothes. He was cautious driving on the road, too, regularly engaging in countersurveillance manoeuvres as he looped around roundabouts repeatedly and took back-road routes to locations. On 14 December he was observed driving a 141 BMW 5 Series from Celbridge to the Greenogue Industrial Estate, where he entered a unit. Later in the month he was behind the wheel of a red Jaguar bearing the registration LJ63TOV, which was then registered in Ireland under a foreign name and fitted with 141 plates.

Between September 2015 and December 2016, twelve lives had been claimed in the feud, ten of those killed in Ireland. It was clear that the Kinahan cartel had a cohort of people willing to kill on their behalf and unlimited cash reserves to pay them for their services. The bloodshed in such a short period of time highlighted the gang's access to firearms, which were being sourced and accessed from somewhere. The gardaí knew the hitmen couldn't carry out their tasks without guns, so it was a priority to find the location where they were being prepared and stored. Officers were convinced Brady was playing a central role in the back end of the gang's operations, but they knew they had to bide their time to ensure that when they moved on him, it was only when they were confident of nailing him with enough evidence for when the case came to court.

On 21 January 2017, the GNDOCB received a confidential tip-off that Brady had organized a meeting between two men at the Blackchurch pub near Rathcoole in County Dublin. After 3.30 p.m., two detectives in separate unmarked vehicles took up positions in the car park and watched on as a gold-coloured 11-D Volkswagen Passat entered, followed by a grey 141-D Ford Transit van some minutes later. The two men held a meeting in the van and afterwards they went their separate ways. Gardaí followed the van as it travelled to an address at Kerdiff Avenue, Naas, County Kildare. The driver was identified as Jonathan Harding, while the man behind the wheel of the Passat on the day was James Walsh.

Harding (b. 27 April 1972) had two decades of a criminal career behind him and was a close associate of the Kinahan cartel's head of Irish operations, Liam Byrne. He had earned the nickname 'Rocketman' after he was arrested in possession of two loaded rocket launchers in May 2010, but he managed to avoid charges. The deadly weapons were disposable and were discovered in a rented shed on the Clane Road, at Longtown, Straffan, County Kildare. He had served time in prison after being sentenced in 2004 for possession of over €700,000 worth of heroin and cannabis.

Walsh (b. 19 January 1984) was an unknown quantity in terms of gangland crime and only had a number of previous convictions for public order offences.

It was clear something was afoot, even if officers didn't know what it was yet. On the evening of 23 January 2017, Detective Inspector Noel Browne of the GNDOCB received specific information that Brady, Harding and Walsh had access to firearms and ammunition which were to be moved from one location to another the next day. It was suspected that in the run-up to Byrne's first anniversary, the gang was planning Armageddon. From surveillance, gardaí were aware Brady had access to a lock-up in Greenogue Industrial Estate, which they believed was going to be central to the gang's activity, but they did not know which specific one it was. A decision was made to deploy surveillance teams on both Brady and Harding the next day.

On the morning of 24 January 2017, some members were told to position themselves in the vicinity of Greenogue while others were directed into the industrial estate so that if any of the targets arrived, they could pinpoint what exact address in the estate they were using. At 10.08 a.m., Brady appeared on Newcastle Road in the red Jaguar he had already been linked to. At one point, he pulled over, got out and opened the boot of his car, and after around three minutes he got back behind the wheel. The reason for this wasn't apparent, but gardaí thought it might have been his counter-surveillance measures being deployed again.

Brady drove to the Texaco filling station in Newcastle village and parked to the rear of the premises. At 10.21 a.m. he walked into the shop, wearing a baseball cap, navy jacket, white polo shirt and brown shoes. When he got inside the door, followed by two unsuspecting customers, Brady pulled up the back of his blue jeans over his backside then picked up a bottled drink and went up to the cashier. He got mobile phone credit and paid for his goods with €50 in cash before he went back to his car and got into it.

At 10.38 a.m., Harding's Ford Transit van turned into the same filling station and collected Brady. At the same time, Walsh had turned up in the Greenogue Industrial Estate in his Volkswagen Passat, parking on Grant's Drive. Both he and Harding were in the same vehicles they had been in when they met three days beforehand. Harding took a circuitous route, but the surveillance teams were able to track the movements of the van and stay with it. At 10.46 a.m., it arrived at a unit in block 503 of the industrial estate. Brady and Harding got out of the van and walked through the pedestrian entrance of a unit that had its steel roller-shutter raised. The door had the number 52 on it and a small white sign that read 'Far Logistics'. Detective Inspector Browne – who was being updated at every opportunity over radio by gardaí in place – could now seek a search warrant for the premises, having identified its address. Brady and Harding emerged from the unit at 11.06 a.m. and drove back towards the Texaco filling station.

The order was given for the van and its occupants to be searched, while surveillance was maintained at the unit as they worked to get the search warrant over the line. The Ford Transit was followed and when it pulled into the fore-court of the Texaco shop at 11.17 a.m., armed gardaí swarmed their vehicles around the van. Gardaí feared the men could be armed and had their own guns drawn and levelled at the two suspects who got out and identified themselves.

Brady was searched and found to have keys for various cars, ID cards, a photo of a child and a white envelope with car registrations and car models written on it. He also had latex gloves, a black wool glove and a grey work glove and various other documents seized from him. He had four phones in his possession – two Nokia mobiles, one disman-tled, and an Apple iPhone and a BlackBerry – €2,350 in cash and the key to the Jaguar he was driving less than an hour beforehand, which was still parked at the rear of the shop.

When Harding was asked if he had anything in his posses-sion, he replied, 'I have nothing in my pockets.' As detectives searched him, one heard an audible beep. In Harding's front left pocket was a BlackBerry mobile phone. Harding claimed, 'I don't know how that got there.' Both suspects were brought to Clondalkin Garda Station, where their fingerprints, photo-graphs and buccal swabs were taken.

Around thirteen minutes after Brady and Harding were stopped, heavily armed officers stormed Unit 52, Block 503, Grant's Drive, Greenogue Industrial Estate on foot of an emergency search warrant. Walsh was the only person present in the premises and was at the reception desk. He was restrained by gardaí and searched, and the key to his VW Passat, an Apple iPhone, a black Nokia mobile phone and a quantity of cash were seized. The suspect was handcuffed by members of the Special Detective Unit and placed sitting on a chair inside while the search was conducted. He was later removed to Ronanstown Garda Station.

The front door at Unit 52 led into a reception room where there was a desk, chairs and some shelving units. The next room was a small kitchen and in the cupboard under the sink, a silencer for a firearm and a small, empty, black plastic handgun case were found. To the rear, the premises opened up into a large industrial storage facility that was also access-ible through a large roller-shutter door at the front.

Upstairs, there was a smaller loft area and it was there gardaí saw a sheet of flat cardboard in front of a black couch on which were laid five revolver handguns, four of which were fully loaded with suitable ammunition and ready for use. To the left of this room were two cardboard boxes, each of which also contained firearms and ammunition. In one box there was a submachine gun, a Smith & Wesson Model 59 semi-automatic pistol, a .357 Magnum calibre five-shot revolver, a .357 Magnum calibre 'Taurus' six-shot revolver with its serial number erased, a .44 Remington calibre 'Taurus' six-shot revolver and a .32 Auto calibre 'Beretta Model 70' semi-automatic pistol, along with various ammo. In the second box was an assault rifle, a Rossi revolver, a Glock Model 26 semi-automatic pistol, and a Colt 1911 Model 80 MKIV semi-automatic pistol. In all, the team uncovered 15 guns and 1,355 rounds of ammunition, along with a second silencer found in the loft.

On a shelving unit in the same room were two electronic

tracker devices and chargers for them, a radio and a glove. Other items of interest were a motor vehicle licence plate printing machine and a cardboard box containing a Dell laptop and printer.

There was an 08-D Ford Focus van parked on the ground floor, which was discovered to have a concealed compartment in the boot area, behind the driver and passenger seats. It was designed to be accessed by a hinged panel forming part of the boot floor and it had an improvised latch system to keep the panel closed and secure. Inside this compartment were five loose rounds of ammunition. It was a very good day's work – the search team had uncovered a serious cache of weapons, ammunition and surveillance equipment.

John O'Driscoll, retired Assistant Commissioner and former Head of Serious and Organised Crime, told the authors: 'The military grade aspects to some of those firearms and the sheer number of them made it clear that this was the equivalent of taking out the armoury and the quartermaster in a terrorist organization.'

This was a logistics business, but not of the kind it presented itself to be. Behind the empty lever-arch ring-binders on the shelf in the reception area and beyond the cover of two forklifts, there to give the impression of legitimate transport work, what gardaí had uncovered was in fact the arms depot for the Kinahan cartel. And it was clear that those who had been inside the Greenogue unit had been keeping tabs on the ongoing situation from the Garda point of view by reading the work of crime correspondents in the *Irish Sun* and *Herald* newspapers, copies of which were also discovered.

Far Logistics was a legitimate company in the UK, but Brady and his cohorts had cloned the business and used it for their own murderous ends. When gardaí contacted Mr 'RC', he stated that he had not rented this unit and that far-logisticsltd@yahoo.co.uk was not his email address. It was a case of stolen identity to cover the true nature of what was going on in that industrial unit.

The investigators now had three men in custody thanks to their morning's work, and later in the day they turned their attention to Brady's rented home in Sallins Bridge. There, gardaí saw a man emerge from the property and get into a gold-coloured 151-KE Volkswagen Golf. He drove to Naas, where he was approached by an officer in a public car park. The driver was asked for his licence, but he didn't have it. In response to the officer's questions, he said his name was Declan Brady and that he lived at a property in Tallaght, Firhouse, Dublin 24. He had an insurance certificate with matching details, but of course the officer knew it didn't stack up, having already lifted Declan Brady earlier in the day. The man was arrested and the car was seized, as the officer believed the man was not insured on the vehicle.

Once back at Tallaght Garda Station, a prescription belonging to a Michael Brady was discovered in the VW Golf and it matched the address the man had been at earlier that day. This was Michael Brady (b. 9 March 1965), Declan's brother, a fact he eventually admitted to gardaí. In the meantime, the house at Sallins Bridge was raided and two live rounds of 9mm Luger ammunition were discovered in the dining-room area. Michael Brady, who insisted he was just staying at the house to mind the dogs, was released and then rearrested over the new find of the ammunition.

The Sallins Bridge property had been leased by Declan Brady for nearly two years at this stage, but he'd had access to it since 2009. That year, a woman named Erica Lukacs expressed interest in renting it when it came on to the market. Ms Lukacs had come to Ireland from her native Hungary in 2007 and began working in a petrol station. It was during the course of that work that she met Declan Brady and they began a relationship.

Ms Lukacs made contact with the landlord of the property and met him in a pub in Lucan, accompanied by Declan Brady. She later signed a lease and was paying rent of €1,000 per month. In 2015, the landlord noticed that Ms Lukacs was no longer living there. He went to Naas, to a café she had been running, to talk to her about the property. She explained to him that she and Declan Brady had split up and she said that she hadn't lived there for a year. Declan Brady then signed a new contract to rent the house and told the owner that his brother, Michael, would be looking after the property most of the time. Ms Lukacs had moved into The Dairy, Rathasker Road, Naas, County Kildare, in November 2014. Due to the surveillance in place in the months before the guns bust at Greenogue, gardaí were aware that Brady had been staying in both of these rental houses as well as at his own family home, where his wife also resided, at Wolstan Abbey, Celbridge, County Kildare.

In searches of The Dairy on 24 January 2017, gardaí discovered cash to the value of €268,940 in the attic. A safe was found in a wardrobe and, when it was opened, they discovered documents relating to both Brady and his mistress. A passport was found in the name of Charles Lavin, with a date of birth in 1959, but it had Brady's picture on it. At Wolstan Abbey, Mrs Brady was present as gardaí seized money and banking documents. Papers relating to two bank accounts were seized and €140,000 was frozen.

In Harding's residence at Kerdiff Avenue in Naas, County

Kildare, receipts were found for Louis Vuitton items of €945 and €765. Documents relating to the van he was arrested from were also seized. Investigators also searched a unit at Spawell Yard, Templeogue, Dublin 6W, which Harding had been leasing since December 2015. Harding had told the manager of this unit that he wanted to store cars there, but he only visited the location sporadically.

In Walsh's home at Wheatfield Avenue, Ronanstown, Dublin 22, receipts were discovered for building work costing €52,000, a stay in Trim Castle Hotel in County Meath that came to €1,000, various items from Brown Thomas totalling €540, from Louis Vuitton for €475 and from Zara for €228. In a bedroom, a variety of documents was found, including a two-page logistics release. As detectives continued their searches, two large brick-type bundles of cash, totalling €19,000 in €50 notes, were found in a wardrobe.

The raids added to the tranche of evidence against Brady, and there was nothing he could do while he sat in a cell in Clondalkin Garda Station, dwelling on the fact that his double life was on the verge of collapse. Even so, he was determined not to let the act die just yet. At this stage he was totally unaware that he had been under surveillance for nearly two months, and that the gardaí could link him to the three houses he had access to and to Greenogue.

In his first interview with detectives, just hours after being brought into custody, Brady talked away, telling them how he hadn't worked in his haulage contracting business for two years due to an injury he sustained in an accident. He said he had stayed in the Hermitage Clinic after hurting his left shoulder. Asked how he spent his days now, Brady said, 'Exercise, train myself with management skills. I can't drive yet. I also have high blood pressure. I can't drive trucks.' He said that he went walking from Castletown to Leixlip and back and did a 'bit of sparring' in Celbridge.

He and his wife had taken out a €500,000 mortgage on their home, Wolstan Abbey, when they had purchased it and there was around €300,000 left to pay on it, he said. He explained that without income, an insurance policy was paying him until about a year before his arrest. He claimed he was getting €3,800 a month and the policy paid the mortgage of €2,200 per month as well. He said he was paying interest only, adding: 'Some months I don't pay it, it started off at €400, we're trying to catch up on it.' But of late, he explained to detectives, he had begun buying and selling cars. He said, 'I reactivated my VAT number and so did my son. We're going to start trading. I have sold three cars since November.'

Brady said he had access to a silver 2010 Volkswagen Golf registered to his son but owned no transport himself. The red Jaguar belonged to a girl his son knew, he said, and he was going to get the diagnostics done on it because there was an issue with it. He wanted to get it fixed on the basis he could sell it on her behalf and make some money for himself. He knew a man for the job, someone he'd met years ago from the 'haulage game'. Asked what the man's name was, Brady said, 'I think it's John Hardiman.' The detective responded, 'You say you know him years, you must know his name?' Brady said, 'It's Hardiman, I call him Johner.' The man he was referring to was his co-accused, Jonathan Harding. Brady confirmed they had met at the Texaco that morning and were arrested from Harding's van. 'Did you drive out of the Texaco with John?' the detective asked. Brady replied: 'I'd prefer to take my right to silence. I don't want to incriminate anyone.'

By the following day, Brady was feeling the pressure and

had been visited a number of times by a doctor, who prescribed blood pressure and cholesterol medication. On the night of 26 January, his health issues were persisting and Brady was escorted to Tallaght Hospital for treatment, returning back some hours later. He remained respectful to the gardaí who were in charge of caring for him, and his only request was for food, including a tuna salad, a club sandwich with no mayo or butter, and cups of tea with no milk. But he had no answers for the detectives as they laid out the evidence against him in further interviews.

The Automatic Number Plate Recognition at Greenogue established that the Ford Focus van had entered the business park once, the night before the search, and in convoy with James Walsh's car. Harding's Ford Transit van entered or exited ninety-nine times between 25 August 2016 and 24 January 2017. The BMW 520 Brady was linked to in 2016 was on the ANPR system nine times between 5 July and 14 December, while the red Jaguar was captured four times on 14 January 2017. Walsh's VW Passat struck up five hits between 14 and 24 January 2017. The men were also proven to be linked through the calls and texts on the phones seized from them.

Harding's DNA was found on a glove beside the guns laid out on top of the cardboard, but he couldn't explain why. Walsh remained courteous in custody, but he too refused to answer any questions put to him.

The three men were brought before Dublin District Court on Friday, 27 January, were charged under the Firearms Act and remanded in custody. Declan Brady's brother, Michael, had at this stage also been taken to court over two outstanding bench warrants and also brought into prison on remand.

There was more to come, and it would sink the Brady

brothers into a much larger hole than they already found themselves in.

On 28 January, the owner of the Sallins Bridge property arrived to clear it out, along with his sister and nephew. In a downstairs bedroom, they lifted the bed and a box fell out from under it. There were bricks of a substance of some kind wrapped in cling-film and in the mattress they found a rifle wrapped in a red cloth. A shoe box was also found stuffed with brown packets labelled 'king'. They alerted gardaí, who returned to the house they had searched on 24 January. The search had a very different outcome this time: they discovered €1.5 million worth of cocaine, €1.26 million worth of heroin and €1,000 worth of cannabis, as well as seizing a 7.62 × 39mm-calibre VZ 58 assault rifle and a variety of ammunition, some of which was stored in socks.

Both Harding and Walsh later pleaded guilty to the possession of nine revolvers, four pistols, a submachine gun, an assault rifle and various ammunition magazines found at Greenogue. Harding was sentenced to nine years and Walsh to eight years for their role in the 'deadly enterprise'.

In February 2019, Declan Brady, who had widely become known as Mr Nobody to the public, followed his two subordinates in pleading guilty. His sentencing hearing heard how he had been tasked by other senior figures from abroad to ensure 'matters ran smoothly'. Detective Inspector Browne agreed with defence counsel that these were 'serious individuals' and that Brady was not an 'end user' of the weapons. Mr Justice Paul Coffey said Brady 'supervised and was in overall charge' of the 'arsenal' of arms, adding that he was the principal target of the operation as he jailed him for ten and a half years.

Michael Brady also went on trial and was convicted of possessing €1.35 million in heroin after his fingerprints were identified on blocks of the drug at the Sallins Bridge home. The Special Criminal Court found that he was above the drug-mule level, having been trusted to mind the drugs. He was acquitted of charges relating to the drugs and the firearms also discovered at the property but received a sentence of seven years.

Quartermaster Brady had not only involved his brother in organized crime but his wife and mistress, too. When gardaí delved into the trio's financials, it revealed they had money well beyond any legitimate means. In May 2015, Declan Brady and his wife had splashed out €66,301 at Druids Glen Hotel, in Wicklow, for the wedding of a family member, €27,265 of which was paid in cash for bar and room bills.

Brady himself had declared no gross income to Revenue from 2013 to 2017 and yet he had five bank accounts. He admitted to laundering €418,654 and to concealing €268,940 in cash at his mistress's rented home. His wife, described in court as a homemaker, was a grandmother of seven with no income for a time period, yet pleaded guilty to laundering €770,499. She also transferred €140,000 over five years to the Spanish bank account of Thomas 'Bomber' Kavanagh, the Kinahan cartel's No. 2 and her husband's boss. She paid €3,000 a month for her husband's Spanish mortgage for a property in Cala d'Or in Mallorca, amounting to €138,000 between 2014 and 2016. Mrs Brady even unknowingly paid for the rent for property her husband shared with his mistress, who also laundered €196,864.

All three made a settlement with the Criminal Assets Bureau (CAB). The Bradys sold their Wolstan Abbey home in Kildare, another house in Firhouse, Dublin, and an

1 and 2: Gary Hutch (*left*) and his pursuer (*right*). His murder in September 2015 was the trigger for the Kinahan–Hutch feud.

3. Gary Hutch (*above left*) with Paddy Doyle (*middle*) and James Gately (*right*).

4. James Quinn (*right*), found guilty of participating in the murder of Gary Hutch in June 2018.

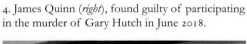

5. Eddie Hutch (*left*) with his son Ross Hutch. Three days after David Byrne's killing at the Regency Hotel, Eddie, brother of Hutch gang leader Gerry Hutch, was shot dead in retaliation. His son, Ross, also became a target.

6. David Byrne's body lies in the lobby of the Regency Hotel, February 2016.

7 and 8: The funeral of Real IRA leader Vincent Ryan (*inset*), March 2016.

9. (*Above left*) The Player's Lounge, Fairview: scene of an audacious gun attack in July 2010 targeting Real IRA leader Alan Ryan. Three innocent people were seriously wounded.

10. (*Above right*) A gunman firing shots during the Player's Lounge attack. In August 2017, Alan Wilson was part of a crew put together by the Kinahans to kill Hutch associate Mr Z. Gardaí who had bugged a car used by the gang heard Wilson admit his involvement in the Player's Lounge attack. They were able to convict Wilson and his associates of conspiracy to murder Mr Z, and also put together a successful case against Wilson for his role in sourcing the firearms and vehicles used in the Player's Lounge attack seven years earlier.

11. (*Left*) Gerry 'the Monk' Hutch outside court in 2023 after he was acquitted of the murder of David Byrne.

12. Michael Barr, shot dead in 2016 at the Sunset House pub, where he was working as a bar manager.

13. A Freddy Krueger style face mask worn by the hitman in the Michael Barr murder. DNA found on the mask was crucial in the Garda investigation.

14. Eamon Cumberton (*left*), hitman in the Michael Barr murder, with Jonathan Keogh (*right*), who gardaí suspected but could not confirm acted as a spotter on the night of the murder. Keogh was later convicted for the murder of Gareth Hutch.

15. Christopher Slator (*far left*), hitman in the Michael Barr murder.

16. CCTV footage (*left*) showing Christopher Slator boarding a flight to Dubai just twenty-four hours after the murder of Michael Barr.

17. Key members of the Kinahan cartel seen at Dublin's 3Arena in 2014, at the WBC world title eliminator between boxers Matthew Macklin and Jorge Sebastian Heiland. *Back, left to right:* Peadar Keating, Sean McGovern. *Front, left to right:* Christopher Kinahan, Daniel Kinahan, Liam Byrne.

18. (*Left*) May 2016 CCTV screen grab showing the moment that Gerry Hutch's nephew Gareth is shot and killed at his car, becoming the ninth victim of the Kinahan–Hutch feud.

19. Gareth Hutch, carrying the coffin at his uncle Eddie's funeral just months before he would also be killed.

20. Regina Keogh, Jonathan Keogh's sister, found guilty of colluding with her brother on the murder of Gareth Hutch.

21. Former IRA man Daithi (David) Douglas (*right*), who was shot dead in Dublin in July 2016.

22. (*Far right*) The bloody scene inside the Shoestown shop on Dublin's Bridgefoot Street after the murder of Daithi Douglas in 2016.

23. CCTV image of Freddie Thompson and friends arriving at a Dublin city centre restaurant the night of the Douglas murder. They were celebrating the successful hit.

24. Senior Kinahan cartel member Freddie Thompson (*right*) with his driver, Lee Canavan (*left*). Both men received life sentences for their involvement in the killing of Daithi Douglas.

25. Innocent victim Trevor O'Neill, who was murdered by a cartel assassin while on a family holiday to Majorca.

26. Innocent victim Martin O'Rourke, who was murdered in 2016 by a bullet that was meant for Hutch gang member Keith Murtagh.

27. Glen Clarke, an up-and-coming Kinahan cartel member at the time of the Martin O'Rourke shooting.

28. John Hutch. There was an attempt on his life in 2016, despite him not being involved in any gangland activity. Gardaí would later discover a tracking device under his car.

29. Michael Carroll, a drug addict working for the Kinahan gang to pay off debt at a bar in the south inner city, where he was seen associating with members of the cartel.

30. Michael Carroll, jailed in 2023 for his attempt to shoot John Hutch and for the attempted murder of Eddie Staunton.

31. Gardaí outside unit 52 in the Greenogue Industrial Estate after a major arms seizure was made by the Garda National Drugs and Organized Crime Bureau.

32. (*Above left*) Noel 'Duck Egg' Kirwan (*left*) at the funeral of Eddie Hutch. Gerry Hutch (*right*) is seen wearing a disguise.

33. (*Above middle*) Noel Kirwan and his son Caine (*left*), a cartel target the following summer.

34. (*Right*) Kinahan lieutenant Sean McGovern leaving a Dublin city centre restaurant.

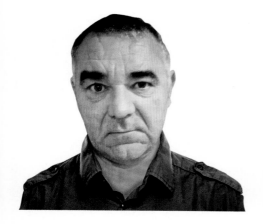

35. Declan 'Mr Nobody' Brady, unknown to gardaí until he attended the funeral of David Byrne.

36. Declan Brady on CCTV at a filling station in Dublin before he was picked up by Jonathan Harding. They made their way to the Greenogue Industrial Estate on the morning of 24 January 2017 and later returned to the same shop, where they were arrested.

37, 38 and 39. Guns, silencers and ammunition seized at Greenogue Industrial Estate.

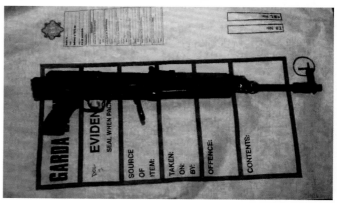

40. (*Above*) Thomas 'Bomber' Kavanagh being questioned by NCA officers, who were waiting for him when he arrived in Birmingham airport after a family holiday to Mexico in 2019.

41. (*Right*) Mugshot of Thomas 'Bomber' Kavanagh. Kavanagh remains the most senior cartel member behind bars.

42. James 'Mago' Gately, targeted by the Kinahan cartel, with his children in Howth before the feud began. The Kinahan gang placed a €250,000 bounty on his head in 2017.

43. (*Above right*) Daniel Kinahan (*left*) training James Gately (*right*) at the MGM gym in 2012. Just a few years later the Kinahan gang would hire assassins to kill Gately.

44. (*Right*) Cartel 'enabler' Douglas Glynn who was tasked with placing a tracking device on James Gately's car.

45. Imre Arakas arriving at Dublin airport. He was contracted by the Kinahan gang to kill James Gately.

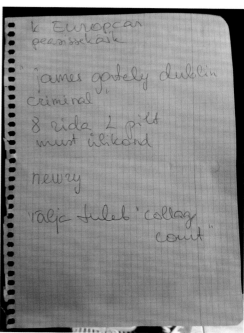

46. The note found in Blakestown Cottages, featuring instructions for the hit on James Gately.

47. Imre Arakas in Estonia.

48. Imre Arakas in January 2024, during an online interview with co-author Stephen Breen.

49 and 50. Gary Gleeson (*left*) and Stephen Dunne (*middle*), both part of the team contracted to kill Michael Frazer.

51. Owen Cummins (*right*), contracted to kill Caine Kirwan, son of Noel Kirwan.

52. Alan Wilson (*above*) convicted as part of the hit team in the plot to kill Mr Z and for his role in Player's Lounge attack.

53. Dean Howe (*above right*), arrested after an attempt on John Hutch's life.

54. Luke Wilson (*right*), cousin of Alan Wilson and hitman for the Kinahan gang.

55. Peadar Keating (*above*), senior Kinahan cartel member. He led the west Dublin Kinahan sub-cell.

56. (*Above right*) Peadar Keating seen on CCTV footage staking out James Gately's apartment.

57. (*Right*) Peadar Keating's phone, showing details of the trackers the gang had placed on cars.

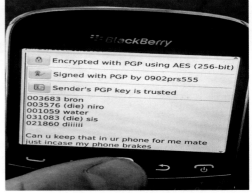

58. (*Left*) Caolan Smyth in the Clonshaugh filling station on the day before he shot James Gately in the forecourt at the same location.

59. (*Below*) CCTV footage showing Caolan Smyth, clearly identifiable by his tattoos.

60. Michael Burns, seen at the Omni Shopping Centre in Santry, where he met Patrick Curtis to discuss their plans to murder Patsy Hutch.

61. Guns found inside the Audi used by Gary Thompson, Glen Thompson and Robert Browne.

62. CCTV footage showing the arrest of brothers Glen and Gary Thompson along with Robert Browne.

63. Patrick and Stephen Curtis. The two brothers were jailed for their involvement in the plot to kill Patsy Hutch.

64. Glen Thompson and his older brother, Gary Thompson, both members of the hit team hired to kill Patsy Hutch.

65. Picture taken in Mountjoy Prison showing, from left to right: Graham Gardner, Trevor Byrne, Glen Thompson and Robert Browne.

66. (*Above left*) Retired Detective Superintendent Paul Scott, now a criminal barrister, was involved in the investigation into Caolan Smyth in 2018.

67. (*Above right*) Senior Investigating Officer Detective Inspector Paul Cleary (now Assistant Commissioner), and Detective Sergeant Adrian Whitelaw (*left*), who both led the investigation into the murder of Daithi Douglas. They also investigated the wider cartel network.

68. (*Left*) Detective Superintendent Colm Murphy, part of the team who led the latter stages of investigations into the murders of Michael Barr and Gareth Hutch.

69. Former Assistant Commissioner Pat Leahy from Store Street station.

70. *Left to right:* Detective Chief Superintendent Seamus Boland; John O'Driscoll, retired Assistant Commissioner and former Head of Serious Crime; Detective Inspector Noel Browne; and Detective Superintendent Dave Gallagher.

REWARD

OF UP TO

$5,000,000.00 USD

FOR INFORMATION LEADING TO THE FINANCIAL DISRUPTION OF THE KINAHAN CRIMINAL ORGANIZATION OR THE ARREST AND/OR CONVICTION OF

Daniel Joseph Kinahan

SUBMIT TIPS VIA E-MAIL TO

KinahanTCOTips@dea.gov

71. Poster showing the $5 million reward issued by the DEA for information leading to the arrest of Daniel Kinahan.

apartment in Portugal to pay over €449,000 to settle their debt with CAB. Their Mallorca property was repossessed by a bank in Spain. Ms Lukacs, who gave birth to Brady's child shortly after his arrest in January 2017, paid CAB €71,327.

Brady was sentenced to a further seven years behind bars while Ms Lukacs walked free with a suspended sentence. Mrs Brady initially received a fully suspended term, but following the state's appeal she served three months of a 1-year sentence in 2023. After she was released, she told *Sunday World* reporter Patrick O'Connell that she had had no choice but to launder money: 'I was told to do it. I'm a housewife. But you have to live the life to understand it and you will never understand it. You'd really have to.' She claimed she had no knowledge that her husband was working for the Kinahan cartel. She added: 'But then my house got raided for firearms and I got the shock of my life when that happened.'

Walsh and Harding also received further sentences for money laundering and likewise their partners pleaded guilty but walked away with suspended terms. There was another man who was pulled into the frame as the investigation dug deeper. Sean Ruth had also attended the funeral of David Byrne wearing the Kinahan 'uniform'. His DNA matched to one of the guns at Greenogue. He was also brought before the courts and received a 3-year sentence.

The Greenogue operation had been well and truly blown apart, and Mr Nobody had been pushed right out into the limelight. But there was still one more shock that would ensure Mr Nobody would never be able to work incognito again.

In January 2024, Declan Brady pleaded guilty at the Special Criminal Court to assisting a criminal organization in the murder of Noel 'Duck Egg' Kirwan on 22 December 2016. It was Brady who drove around the senior Crumlin cartel member around, including when the tracker was placed on Mr Kirwan's car and again as they tried to retrieve it after the victim traded in his BMW X5. He did the same once more the following day when it became clear the two men were trying to figure out the whereabouts of the tracker. Brady's DNA was also found on a toothbrush at the gang's apartment at Beacon South Quarter.

Addressing him in the Special Criminal Court in February 2024, Mr Kirwan's daughter Donna said: 'While the other residents of the apartment block you so calmly walked in and out of were going to work every day – you were planning to kill a 62-year-old innocent grandfather. You did this for weeks and you had plenty of time to change your mind but you chose not to. Can I ask you what did you gain from this? What did they give you? Was it worth it?'

In June 2024, the Special Criminal Court found that while Brady was not on the front-line of Mr Kirwan's murder, he was not on the periphery either. He was jailed for a further nine years.

The extensive Garda investigation had dealt the Kinahan gang a major blow, taking out the quartermaster, who ensured operations had the firepower they needed. It had taken a lot of weaponry out of circulation and out of the hands of would-be assassins. But among all the evidence the searches had uncovered, there was one item that told more than anyone at first realized. The document relating to Far Logistics and a 1,600kg shipment from Romania to Wolverhampton found at James Walsh's home would eventually lead the gardaí and law enforcement to claim their biggest cartel scalp yet.

10. Business as Usual

(12 January 2019: catching crime boss Thomas 'Bomber' Kavanagh and smashing a drug-trafficking network)

'That is the level of impact that convicting someone like Thomas Kavanagh makes – a man who ruled by fear.'
– Detective Chief Superintendent Seamus Boland

Jim Mansfield Jnr was the son of one of Ireland's richest tycoons and fancied himself as a chip off the old block. He joked that even when he was partying, he was making money. He might well laugh, after brokering a deal that saw him handed over €4.5 million in cash stuffed into two suitcases. His intentions, however, differed from those who had made the investment and he would later learn they were not the type you should cross.

His father was the businessman Jim Mansfield Snr, who, from humble beginnings, had built a business empire once worth up to €1.6 billion, owning hotels, apartments, office blocks, a vast amount of land and the Weston aerodrome in Dublin. His son worked in the family businesses, but he also lived a more high-profile life than his father. Mansfield Jnr became a poster boy of the Celtic Tiger era, dating some of Ireland's best-known models, such as Katy French, who tragically died in 2007, and later Ms Universe contestant

Hazel O'Sullivan, as well as throwing lavish parties for social-ites of the time.

But Mansfield Jnr associated with others, too. The day before this extraordinary cash handover, on Good Friday, 10 April 2009, he instructed his head of security, Martin Byrne, that his guests were to be given VIP treatment at Dublin's Citywest Hotel and rooms to stay overnight, if needed.

Who they were became clear later that evening when a group of men, which included Thomas 'Bomber' Kavanagh and Freddie Thompson, arrived. Following those discus-sions with Mansfield Jnr, an agreement was put in place for an investment in four properties at a development in south-west Dublin that Mansfield Jnr was working on, called Saggart Court Lodge. After that, business was set aside and the men drank the night away.

In the early hours of the following morning, security man Byrne was instructed by his boss to open Tassagart House, a Georgian house owned by the Mansfield family, to allow a van to drive on to the property. Two men, who were unknown to Byrne, took two large suitcases out of the van and placed them inside the home.

Later that day, Byrne was with Mansfield Jnr when he opened one of the suitcases. It was filled with bundles of cash. Mansfield explained that the money had been paid by the group of lads in the hotel the night before, telling Byrne that there was €4.5 million inside the cases. Despite the group of men handing the cash over for the four properties, Mans-field Jnr appeared to have other plans for the money, stating to Byrne that it would help him complete a convention centre in Dublin and a housing project in Saudi Arabia. But it wasn't long before the Mansfield empire collapsed, in 2010, and with that their fortunes deteriorated and the deal soured.

'Bomber' and his cousin Gerard 'Hatchet' Kavanagh turned to Celtic Tiger socialite and Irish criminal Lee Cullen – who would later be jailed for over twenty years for importing weapons into the UK – to act on their behalf in the matter. Cullen told Mansfield Jnr that he was under pressure from the Kavanaghs to get keys to a property or to get the cash investment back.

As time passed and no settlement was forthcoming, Thomas Kavanagh began upping the ante and turned his attention to an ailing 72-year-old Jim Mansfield Snr, claiming to have lost all trust in his son. The elderly man received threatening phone calls and was left in a nervous state after them.

A meeting was set up at the Red Cow Hotel in Dublin in January 2012. Mansfield Snr and his other son, PJ, sat in a car and were joined by two associates of 'Bomber'. After a fifteen-minute discussion in the car, a fresh agreement was struck: the Mansfields would stump up three payments of €50,000 to the cartel, along with the keys of a luxury gated house at 10 Coldwater Lakes which would be handed over to 'Bomber' Kavanagh, who was later found to be acting as an agent for Daniel Kinahan. The elder Mansfield had paid a high price for his son's rash decisions, but given the people he was dealing with, it could have been much higher. The Mansfields had got away lightly.

Thomas 'Bomber' Kavanagh was a man who had managed to go under the radar for many years, but his life had been steeped in criminality for over three decades. Born on 10 September 1967, he grew up in Drimnagh, south central Dublin. The detectives who had known him as a young thug described him as 'volatile and violent'. He was first convicted on two burglary charges at the age of eighteen, and by the age of twenty-one he had been in court over two separate assaults on gardaí. His most serious offence in his early years was the possession of a firearm, for which he was handed a hefty sentence of seven years.

Kavanagh was in a relationship with a woman named Joanne Byrne, from Crumlin in Dublin, who he would later marry. Joanne's dad is convicted criminal James 'Jaws' Byrne and she is sister to Liam and David Byrne. Kavanagh was seen as one of the family from the early days of his association with Joanne, and he was loyal to his in-laws: in October 2000 he was involved in an assault on a state witness who had testified against Liam Byrne and he also threatened to kill a garda who was investigating the Crumlin–Drimnagh feud, one side of which was Kinahan-affiliated.

He remained a focus for authorities, who continued to pressure him using the state's new arm, the Criminal Assets Bureau (CAB), which was set up in the wake of the murder of journalist Veronica Guerin in 1996. Kavanagh was among CAB's first targets: he was hit with an unpaid taxes bill of over €125,000 on proceeds of crime and his home on Knocknarea Avenue was seized. He and his wife, Joanne, left Ireland and relocated to the village of Tamworth, just outside Birmingham, where they raised their five children. He appeared to have transformed from a reckless young gun criminal into a successful businessman, running a second-hand motor company called TK Motors.

However, the murder of his brother-in-law David Byrne at the Regency Hotel on 5 February 2016 changed that perception of Kavanagh. The day after the murder he was seen in Crumlin, the homestead of the Byrnes, alongside the Kinahan gang's leader, Daniel Kinahan, and its long-time enforcer Freddie Thompson. The three men were wearing bulletproof vests under their jackets and appeared panicked: Liam Byrne's car was stopped by the gardaí and Kinahan, Thompson and Kavanagh were seen running nearby. Nine days later, at Byrne's funeral, Kavanagh was front and centre with the Byrne family, wearing the same uniform as other gang members as he walked behind the coffin while it was carried out of the church. His appearance at the funeral was significant because it placed Kavanagh at the top tier of the international drugs cartel, a position he had been careful not to betray before now.

Officers from the National Crime Agency (NCA) in the UK had been aware of Kavanagh due to his involvement with one-time close associate and one of the UK's biggest drug dealers, James Mulvey, who was jailed for thirty-two years in 2018 for drug trafficking. Tensions had arisen between the pair when, it was believed, 'Bomber' sanctioned the murder of 'Hatchet' Kavanagh, who was related to both of them, in Spain in 2014.

The issue for police officers was that Kavanagh was thoroughly careful, refusing to talk on the phone, or to meet in buildings or even in cars. Instead, he used public spaces, kids' parties on some occasions, and graveyards to speak to associates. NCA officers had watched as he met Declan Brady, who they did not know at the time, in a cemetery in Birmingham. It was later established that cartel logistics man Brady had travelled to the English Midlands and back to Ireland on the same day just to speak to his boss, as he did on many occasions. Kavanagh also met regularly with senior Kinahan lieutenant Sean McGovern, before McGovern fled to Dubai.

As investigations continued, UK authorities targeted Kavanagh, who also used the alias of Paul Harvey. He was convicted of fraud and intent to defraud the public revenue in January 2017 and fined £83,000, but he avoided jail. That put him back on the map, his first conviction since leaving Ireland nearly twenty years before. This was the same month the cartel's arms depot at Greenogue was uncovered. The Garda intervention undoubtedly delivered a major blow to the cartel and saved lives, but it also provided the NCA with a fresh lead.

A two-page document discovered at James Walsh's home had identified a UK-based freight company and the consignee for shipped goods as a company called Far Logistics, located at 3 Modular Court, Four Ashes Business Park, Wolverhampton. It was dated 12 December 2016 and the consignor was named Emanuel Rosenzweig. Intrigued by the document, the NCA began surveillance and gathering intelligence and soon confirmed their suspicion that this was a drug network connected to the Kinahan gang.

On 2 October 2017 a specific consignment was earmarked by the NCA and customs officials on duty at the Eastern Docks in Dover, south-east England, and it was seized. On board were two large tarmac-removal machines, which custom officials immediately set about examining. They dismantled the casings on both machines and removed a series of 32-millimetre nuts from the sides. They discovered the machines had been specifically altered and stuffed with drugs.

The interior cavity of the first machine held 200 packages of herbal cannabis, with plastic wrappings branded 'Rolex'. The second also held 200 packages of herbal cannabis, with plastic wrappings endorsing 'Manchester United'. There were fifteen green blocks in that machine which contained cocaine and were marked with the number '54'. In all, the 200kg of cannabis hidden in the machines had a wholesale value of £1 million and a street value of £2 million. The 15 kg of cocaine, which had a purity of 75 per cent, was worth £480,000 at wholesale and £1.2 million on the streets. Also discovered in the second tarmac-removal machine was a black box attached by magnet to the inner wall and containing a GPS tracking device.

The following day, the operation continued as officers raided the industrial premises linked to the importation. There were two companies linked to Unit 3, Modular Court, Wolverhampton: Far Logistics and MB Distribution. Another company, RWD Development, was based at Unit 16, Red Mill Trading Estate, in Wednesbury. There was no evidence of legitimate trading businesses under the names of any of these companies at either of the addresses. When surveillance by the NCA led to the interception of the truck at Dover, being driven by a Polish national, they had already identified three men who they believed were behind the major drugs haul: Gary Vickery, Daniel Canning and a Martin Byrne. (This is another Irish national named Martin Byrne, not the former Mansfield business group's head of security, who has no involvement in crime.)

Vickery (b. 3 January 1983) was a car salesman, originally from Dublin. His entrepreneurial success was impressive given that he had left school at the age of fourteen. As well as his home in England, he also owned property in Spain. Vickery and Canning were in-laws as their wives were sisters. Canning (b. 18 September 1978) was a mechanic by trade who owned his own house in Walkinstown, Dublin 12, but it was later repossessed. The third man, Byrne, was also from Ireland. He died of lung cancer on 5 August 2018.

Unit 16 had been leased to Canning since 16 February 2016, the day after David Byrne's murder at the Regency.

When it was searched on 3 October 2017, a wooden crate lay in the corner of the industrial building and it contained a large transformer that had been adapted for internal concealment. Hidden inside it was a large black holdall bag that contained a functioning Smith & Wesson 357 revolver – which had Canning's DNA on it – along with two boxes containing a total of eighty-five rounds of .38 wadcutter ammunition. This confirmed a capability to transport firearms under the radar.

One tracker had been found in the Dover seizure, and now nine other magnetic devices with GPS functions were discovered in Unit 16. Unit 3 was found to be leased to Martin Byrne and, when it was raided, three large wooden packing cases were found, and they were secured with bolts similar to those found on the transformer concealing the firearm seized at Unit 16. The men had used spray paint to conceal alterations made to the machinery and had the specific colour codes which matched the original colour on those machines.

When Canning's home at Gorcott Lane, Dickens Heath, Solihull, in the West Midlands was searched, cash bundles were discovered: £4,500 in the house, £2,000 in his Mercedes car, which he arrived in during the search, and Euro notes amounting to €300. Seven mobile phones were seized as well. At Byrne's home, additional mobiles were recovered.

Vickery's home at Boundary Lane, Shirley, Solihull, West Midlands had cash stuffed into the built-in wardrobe of his bedroom, including British and Scottish sterling notes. Most of the cash was found hidden in bags, wrapped in four bundles, three in black duct tape and one in masking tape, and each containing around €50,000, totalling €198,430. He had six phones and various SIM cards. Significantly, five 25 kg barrels of boric acid, which is used as a cutting agent with cocaine, were recovered from the garage. On an A4 notepad, Vickery had written a list of numbers and letters that matched the markings on the GPS tracking devices recovered at Unit 16 and in the machine seized at Dover. Two of the numbers jotted down were for SIM cards linked to the two tracking devices seized at Greenogue in Dublin.

Evidence retrieved also highlighted the investments Vickery had made recently, including a purchase option contract of an apartment in Lanzarote, another from a Spanish company in the name of Vickery's wife, Nicola O'Connor, for the purchase of a boat dated 28 February 2017, along with a contract sale invoice to her for a white BMW M6.

In custody, the three men denied any involvement in a drugs conspiracy, before being released without charge. Neither Vickery nor Canning had ever been convicted of a crime and did not feature on the list of characters that organized crime investigators kept tabs on. However, officers were well aware that this made the pair typical of the kind of person sought by gangs to work for them on the ground.

The evidence from the surveillance, intel and the drugs seizure itself was likely enough to bring charges against the three men, but following this well-trodden path only plays into the hands of the top-tier criminals. They create these networks beneath precisely to avoid being in the frame for conviction when authorities make such finds. Instead, determined to topple every facet of the gang and end its dealings in Britain, the NCA dug deeper.

The sole use of the trackers was to be placed on shipments to ensure the gang could monitor the movements of the drugs and locate them if shipments went missing or were stolen. It was established that the devices had been purchased by two men in the city of Łódż, Poland, at the request of a native of the country who owned an industrial unit in Barcelona that was used in the conspiracy.

An examination of the tracker seized at Dover revealed the intricate routes it had taken across numerous jurisdictions. It first came online in Poland, before travelling to Dublin and then on to Vickery's address in Birmingham. It later spent eleven days in Unit 16 before it was moved to Dover. The next location was Calais in France. From there it was taken to Belgium, to the Netherlands, back to Belgium, to Germany, and then through Europe before it reached Dover once more and was seized.

Another tracker that was analysed showed how the gang received their drug shipments and extracted them from the altered machines, then stuffed the machines with their cash payment before sending them back to mainland Europe. This particular device had left the same unit and travelled across the continent to an industrial estate located near Barcelona.

It was the phones, however, that gave investigators a way to get to the head of the gang. Vickery's iPhone had Whats-App data that included messages from specific chats with his two co-accused. The team also managed to crack PGP-encrypted BlackBerry devices linked to Canning and Byrne. The Pretty Good Privacy (PGP) system is a way to encrypt email messages so that they can only be read by the relevant receiver, and it was widely used in the criminal underworld at the time. As a result, a number of devices, contact details, telephone numbers, email addresses and nicknames attributed to other suspects in the case were identified. It was the analysis of these messages on the three devices that uncovered the involvement of Thomas 'Bomber' Kavanagh.

The complicated use of their own coded language meant it took time to unravel, but police did manage to break the code. This enabled detectives to identify twenty-three separate importations of cocaine and cannabis from Europe between 28 October 2016 and 2 October 2017 that the gang were behind. The drug loads, estimated to be worth £28.9 million (€35 million) – were all delivered to Unit 3 in Wolverhampton and Unit 16 in Wednesbury.

Kavanagh's phone number was saved by others under the names 'Plasma' and 'Plasma new2' and he was referred to in the communications as 'Gaffer' or 'the gaffer'. Vickery was called 'Jelly', Canning went by 'Smiley', while Byrne was known as 'Scissors' or 'Grumpy'. The communications referred to drugs, money, locations and types of machinery using words such as 'jackets', which were packages of flowering-head cannabis. Kilograms of cocaine were referred to as 'phones', 'tnt' and 'hilfigs', while 'ricky' was also a reference to the drug. In respect of money, 'paper' was cash, and in terms of locations 'the hot' was Spain and 'the flat' was the Netherlands. A tarmac-removal machine, like the ones seized in Dover, was called 'benz'. The transformer from which the revolver gun was recovered was 'aherne'. And 'sist' or 'sister' was another machine used for transportation, but was not among those seized.

Away from the mayhem and murder of the Kinahan–Hutch feud on the streets of Dublin, the UK branch of the gang were quietly marking their successes. On 10 November 2016, the same day as one drug shipment was sent to Wolverhampton, Vickery was in contact with his wife while he was in New York. He sent her a WhatsApp showing a photograph of a group of men, which included himself, Declan 'Mr Nobody' Brady, 'Bomber' Kavanagh and his father-in-law, 'Jaws' Byrne. The NCA noted they were gathered in 'apparent celebrations'. Along with the photo, Vickery wrote to his wife: 'Haha this is worth the money.'

The men regularly used the coded language and often referred to huge amounts of cocaine (120kg on one occasion) and huge amounts of money (one payment referred to was €500,000). Over time, the word 'gaffer' began to be used more frequently. In March 2017, Vickery warned Canning and Byrne: 'make sure yis delete all the messages all the time'. It was May 2017 before Kavanagh first featured in terms of sending messages himself. He asked Vickery: 'Mate have you any euros??' Vickery replied: 'Think Iv about 500/600.' Kavanagh wrote: 'Need about 7000.' Vickery said he'd make a call before informing Kavanagh: 'Have those yoyos mate 7.'

On 26 May 2017, Kavanagh boarded a flight from Birmingham to Dubai. It was the same month cartel leader Daniel Kinahan wed his partner and fellow Dubliner Caoimhe Robinson at the Burj Al Arab Hotel. Some of the world's most notorious crime bosses were in attendance and were spotted by undercover US officers carrying out discreet surveillance, including mafia boss Raffaele Imperiale of Italy's Camorra group, Dutch-Moroccan criminal Ridouan Taghi, Dutch-Chilean trafficker Ricardo 'el Rico' Riquelme Vega, and Balkans mob boss Edin Gačanin.

Significantly, by the end of June 2017, Kavanagh was in direct contact with Emanuel Rosenzweig, the same name mentioned on the paper found in Dublin that was passed on to the NCA. Rosenzweig was in fact a German man by the name of Nikolaj Wall, who was based between his homeland and Belgium and who essentially managed the operation, arranging the transportation of the drug consignments across mainland Europe before their ultimate delivery to the

UK. He was later arrested by German police as part of a separate investigation.

The coded communication also revealed the hierarchy within the gang, with Kavanagh sending Vickery orders, which would then be sent to Canning and Byrne. At one stage, in September 2017, Vickery asked Kavanagh if they were giving Canning money for trips to Spain. He wrote: 'Mate are we throwin Smiley a drink for the 2 times he went hot to give out money and for goin today to sort things.' Kavanagh replied: 'He will b rewarded mate but just leave for now not good time 2 b sort money.'

Kavanagh's commanding and intimidating style of control was also apparent. When Canning was in Spain for work, Kavanagh messaged Vickery in relation to money: 'Dat paper is not 2 b left alone full stop.' Days before the seizure in Dover, a fuming Kavanagh texted Vickery: 'We're having nothing to do wit dis liar after dis 'd hole week just lies lies and more lies.'

In Ireland, CAB had also mounted a successful case against Kavanagh's brother-in-law, Liam Byrne, who decided to move to the West Midlands as a result of the pressure he was under. Detectives categorized Liam as the leader of the Byrne Organized Crime Group, the Irish branch of the Kinahan cartel, and submissions by CAB to the High Court described Byrne as a 'trusted lieutenant of Daniel Kinahan and the Kinahan organized crime group'. It also established that Kavanagh was 'one step above Liam Byrne' in the cartel and had a 'direct role in the directing' of its operations. Like Kavanagh, Byrne had run a car company – Kavanagh's was TK Motors in Birmingham, while Byrne ran LS Active Car Sales in Bluebell, Dublin 12. Both companies were fronts, used as a mechanism to launder money. Associates of

Kavanagh and Byrne often drove vehicles linked with both businesses because if they were stopped by gardaí, the cars couldn't be seized as they were leased, not owned. This allowed the gang to move around freely to conduct their business. Now, both CAB and the gardaí were all over the ploy.

On 12 January 2019, 'Bomber' Kavanagh arrived at Birmingham Airport from a holiday with his family in Mexico. When he walked into the arrivals area, NCA officers were waiting for him. He was handcuffed and he and his suitcase were searched. He had cash in the sums of £500, €340 and $3,414, along with two phones. On the same day, police raided his gated, fortified mansion, which had reinforced doors and bulletproof glass and an €150,000 Audi R8 Spyder parked in the driveway. In a thirteen-hour search, cash was found littered around the house in various denominations, including sterling, Euro and Emirati dirhams. It was stuffed behind a cushion of a couch, in a chest of drawers and in seven handbags, totalling around €40,000 in all. They also found ten mobile phones. The big find was the various weapons scattered about Kavanagh's home at different vantage points, including machetes and shillelaghs, and an illegal pink stun gun, disguised as a torch, on a shelf above the wall units in the kitchen.

This was an open goal for investigators, and Kavanagh was prosecuted for possessing the illegal 10,000-volt stun gun. He accepted the offence of possessing it but denied it was deliberately designed to have the appearance of a flashlight. He told officers that one of his sons bought the stun gun during a school trip and he had confiscated it. A jury at Stoke-on-Trent Crown Court convicted Kavanagh and at his sentencing in September 2019 he was sent down for three years. On that occasion the court heard that Kavanagh had received a threat-to-life warning from police in 2018. Speaking after the sentencing, NCA lead investigator Peter Bellis said: 'Our wider investigation into money laundering, drugs and firearms supply continues.' And so it did.

After being questioned in December 2019 and denying any criminality, Kavanagh, Vickery and Canning were later charged and pleaded guilty. The trio admitted conspiring to import class A and B drugs, and money laundering. Canning also admitted possessing a firearm and ammunition. As 'Bomber' served his stun-gun sentence, the other two men were freed on bail. Canning returned to Dublin for a period before he later entered custody on remand. The repeated delays due to legal argument and Covid-19 were extended when Vickery refused to leave Lanzarote. He was arrested by Spanish police on foot of a warrant and extradited back to the UK in November 2021.

At their sentencing hearing on Friday, 25 March 2022, the full-scale and complicated smuggling operation was laid bare. Riel Karmy-Jones QC, prosecuting, said: 'Kavanagh sat at the top of the operation. Kavanagh's instructions were generally provided to Vickery, who would in turn direct Canning, albeit Kavanagh was fully aware of Canning's identity and role.' She explained that it was clear from the communications obtained that Kavanagh was their superior and that the daily running of the operation by Vickery and Canning was conducted under the directions of Kavanagh. She added: 'The security measures, and general standard of living and cash at his address, also point to him being higher in this chain.'

The following Monday, dad of six Kavanagh blew a kiss to relatives as he was sentenced to twenty-one years in prison.

Vickery got a twenty-year sentence and Canning was jailed for nineteen and a half years. Judge Martyn Levett said the operation was of a 'commercial scale' and that he had 'no doubt that the successful importations would have continued' were it not for the seized shipment at Dover in 2017. Each man will serve half of his sentence in jail before being released on licence, but if they commit a crime while out they will be sent back behind bars to serve the remainder of the sentence. The defendants were also ordered to declare their assets around the world.

At the time of writing, Kavanagh remains the most senior cartel member behind bars. Overseeing both the UK and Ireland operations for the Kinahan cartel, he was actively providing instructions to his murderous subordinates and was suspected of providing vehicles to hit teams. At the same time, it was business as usual for him as he ploughed on with the drug-smuggling operation. But the evidence gardaí had obtained following the Greenogue raid prompted a fresh strategy from the NCA as they targeted 'Bomber' through his subordinates.

Detective Chief Superintendent Seamus Boland of the Garda National Drugs and Organised Crime Bureau, who has been investigating organized crime for thirty-five years, believes Kavanagh's conviction is the most significant he has ever seen: 'It was our assessment that Thomas Kavanagh and his group being brought to justice could impact the threat level in this jurisdiction and the number of murders in this jurisdiction. I don't think it is by pure chance that for the last number of years the level of organized crime murders has dropped dramatically. That is the level of impact that convicting someone like Thomas Kavanagh makes – a man who ruled by fear.'

The following month, the punches continued to land as seven of the cartel's high-ranking members, including Daniel Kinahan, his father, Christy Snr, and Christopher Jnr, joined the ranks of Mexico's lethal Los Zetas crime group, Japan's Yakuza crime syndicate, Italy's Camorra crime clan and the Russian mafia known as 'Thieves in Law' when they were officially sanctioned by the US government.

The multi-agency approach to tackling the mob was highlighted once more when Mansfield Jnr's deal with Kavanagh, acting on behalf of Daniel Kinahan, came to light at the High Court. Lawyers for CAB told the court how the Kinahan gang took control of 10 Coldwater Lakes by the summer of 2014 and the property was fitted with a CCTV system soon after. When CAB raided it in January 2015, Daniel Kinahan's friend, business associate and former professional boxer Matthew Macklin, who has no involvement in crime, was there. While he was courteous with investigators, he refused to give a statement.

Inside, Daniel Kinahan's passport was found and an Aer Lingus baggage sticker with his Marbella address on it. Documentation was also found belonging to James Quinn, who was later convicted over Gary Hutch's murder that year. Further documentation was found relating to a man who was pals with Kinahan and managed his properties for him. One of those properties was on Baggot Street, in Dublin city centre, from which Moroccan thug and long-time associate Naoufal Fassih was arrested by gardaí in April 2016. Fassih was subsequently extradited to Amsterdam, where he was convicted for conspiracy to murder and money laundering. A USB device revealed details of a transaction involving a €10,000 payment to cartel logistics man Declan 'Mr Nobody' Brady in Spain. The High Court heard that all of the evidence pointed towards Daniel

Kinahan owning and controlling the property, and showed it had been acquired through the proceeds of crime, namely drug trafficking. The case was built off the back of statements given by the Mansfield business group's former head of security Martin Byrne, who is now in the state's witness protection programme. The house was officially seized by CAB in 2022.

Since Liam Byrne's arrival in the UK, he had not surfaced on Garda or UK police radars to any great extent. He had formed a friendship with former Liverpool football club captain Steven Gerrard because their children, Lee Byrne and Lilly Gerrard, began dating. Liam later went to Dubai, where the hierarchy of the gang is based, and while he was there the NCA issued a warrant for his arrest. Completely unaware of this, he joined a family holiday and flew into Palma Airport in Spain from Dubai on 26 May 2023. On Sunday, 4 June, he was arrested in Mallorca. It later emerged that his nephew and 'Bomber' Kavanagh's son, Jack, had also been apprehended. Jack Kavanagh, aged twenty-two at the time and from Tamworth, Staffordshire, was swooped on by officers from the Spanish National Police on 30 May at Málaga Airport, while transiting from Dubai to Turkey. The NCA alleged that EncroChat messages showed that Byrne and Kavanagh were believed to be involved in the supply and acquisition of firearms.

In August, 'Bomber' Kavanagh was before Westminster Magistrates' Court in London, albeit remotely through a computer screen from HM Prison Full Sutton. Explosive allegations were read into court, which accused Kavanagh of being behind yet another plot, but this time to get him a reduced sentence for his drug trafficking. The NCA claimed Kavanagh had sourced eleven firearms from prison and, through associates, had them placed in Jetterpass in Armagh.

He then helpfully told police of their location – and the guns were seized in May 2021. He was hit with firearms and ammunition charges along with a charge to pervert the course of justice relating to dates between 9 January 2020 and 3 June 2021.

Liam Byrne, meanwhile, fought his extradition from Spain, but lost. He was flown back to a UK prison in mid-December 2023. He, Kavanagh and two other co-accused will go on trial in September 2024 facing numerous firearms charges. At the time of writing, in May 2024, Jack Kavanagh remains in custody in Spain as he fights his extradition back to the UK, where he would be charged in relation to the same case.

One of the key pieces of evidence in the cases against 'Bomber' Kavanagh and his associates was those encoded messages. The crime gangs are always looking for ways to work under the radar, seeking out the technology that will allow them to communicate without anyone listening in. The use of encrypted devices was pioneered by the Kinahan cartel, who became wholesalers of encrypted PGP phones in the late 2000s. When a security breach compromised PGP, many European drug dealers moved on to a similar system called EncroChat. The EncroChat system was also an encrypted messaging network. It was cracked by law enforcement in 2020, to the detriment of crime gangs everywhere. The thing is, it always works both ways – both the criminals and the police have tracking technology, and what might help you operate under the radar on one day might be the very thing that convicts you another day. By 2023, technology would ensure a place in the dock for 'Bomber' Kavanagh, his son Jack and Liam Byrne. The tables had turned and, for now, business wasn't going as smoothly as usual.

11. The Butcher

(4 April 2017: plot to murder James Gately)

'It could just be one shot to the head and that's it.'
— Imre Arakas, hitman for hire

Detective Sergeant Greg Sheehan (now retired) had no idea how his day would unfold on 3 April 2017. No day was ever the same at the Garda National Drugs and Organised Crime Bureau, but this would be a particularly memorable one. Starting his shift that day at 4 p.m., Sheehan had been on duty for only a few minutes when he was approached by Detective Superintendent Dave Gallagher. Detective Sergeant Sheehan was informed by his colleague that he had information that an Estonian male, Imre Arakas, a suspected hitman for hire who had previous convictions for firearms, was due to land at Dublin Airport on Ryanair flight FR7063 from Alicante, Spain, at 5.05 p.m.

With little time to spare, Detective Sergeant Sheehan, along with four other detectives, made their way to Dublin Airport, as the retired officer explained: 'I recall Dave Gallagher briefing me in the corridor and asking me if I could get some of the lads to the airport as there was an Estonian man coming in who was suspected of being a hitman. We didn't have a photograph because we were in a rush to get to the airport, but we had an excellent description of the suspect. Airport surveillance jobs can be tricky because people can easily walk out the door into crowds of people, hop in a taxi or jump on a bus. The surveillance team had good experience and, in fairness to the lads I was working with, they were brilliant. I didn't know what this fella was coming in for but we knew he was a suspected hitman and we had to be at the top of our game.'

Arriving at the airport just before 5 p.m. that day, the Garda investigation team took up different positions: two of the officers made their way to the gate where the plane was due to land while Detective Sergeant Sheehan and a colleague were heading to the baggage area. The remaining member of the team stationed themselves in the arrivals hall. At 5.25 p.m. the Garda investigators watched as a man matching the description they had been given collected a large rucksack, wrapped in plastic and also containing a ground mat, from the carousel. Sheehan explains: 'As soon as he stepped off the plane the lads identified him and told us he was on his way to us. Once he removed the plastic from his bag, he was on the move. The whole team kept in constant contact on our radios as the surveillance operation was progressing. You have to consider everything on a job like this and we suspected that he would make his way to the city centre.'

Arakas left the airport and boarded the 700 Aircoach bus to Dublin city centre at 5.30 p.m. He did not know that a member of the surveillance team was also on the bus. Detective Sergeant Sheehan said: 'We checked where the bus was due to stop, so we had one of the lads go into the city centre to wait for it, park up close to the Gresham Hotel and then follow him on foot.' As the bus headed towards the heart of the capital, the other members of the surveillance team followed closely behind in other vehicles.

The bus stopped in O'Connell Street at 6.10 p.m. and the suspect got off. He made his way along Henry Street before turning into Moore Street. There, he entered a shop, and one of the surveillance officers who was on foot watched as he bought a wig for €35. Garda eyes were on him at all times. Detective Sergeant Sheehan parked his unmarked car in the nearby Champions Avenue, where Patsy Hutch lived, brother of the Monk and a major Kinahan cartel target.

At 6.50 p.m., the undercover officer watched as Arakas walked past his vehicle, before stopping and looking down Champions Avenue. Detective Sergeant Sheehan was left in no doubt of the reasons behind Arakas's visit to the north inner city: 'I am absolutely convinced that the only reason he was in different areas of the north inner city was for the purpose of identifying targets connected to the Hutch organization. He was walking around with this backpack and it was easy for us to spot in a crowd. It looked to me that he had been given all these locations because why else would someone who had just travelled to Ireland be there? He was acting in a strange manner. To me, he was checking out the area. He looked at two houses definitely connected to the Hutch family.'

The surveillance target spent fifteen minutes walking around the area before heading towards Parnell Street at 7.15 p.m., then spending the next hour in the city centre until he made his way to Gardiner Row. During their observations of the suspect, gardaí noted how he spent a large portion of his time on a BlackBerry phone. When his walk around the city centre finished, he was collected by a white Mercedes van that had the words 'Blakestown Tyres' painted on the side of it. After passing on the van's registration details, the surveillance team was quickly informed that the vehicle was registered to Stephen Fowler (b. 3 August 1959), a long-term friend of Christy 'Dapper Don' Kinahan. The officers were also informed that a tracking device had been recovered from the same van when it was searched on 28 February.

From there, the Garda surveillance team followed the van until it arrived at Fowler's home in Blakestown Cottages, Blanchardstown, west Dublin, shortly before 9 p.m. As Arakas entered the house, the Garda surveillance team's role switched to keeping eyes at the rear and front of the property. Once Fowler and his guest were inside the property, Detective Sergeant Sheehan left his vehicle and walked past the house as part of his ongoing observations. As he did so, he noticed a car in the driveway that looked familiar: 'We were just waiting and engaging with our colleagues to see what the next move would be when I noticed a silver Audi A8 and I thought to myself, "That car looks familiar – that's Ross Browning's car."' A quick check with his colleagues confirmed his suspicions.

At the time, Browning, originally from the north inner city and a former friend of Gary Hutch, was regarded as one of the Kinahan cartel's most senior figures in Ireland.

In a later case taken against him by the Criminal Assets Bureau (CAB), regarding three properties worth €1.4 million, the High Court ruled that 'Ross Browning has had an ongoing significant involvement in organized crime for a number of years and is a senior member of the Kinahan organized crime gang. This transnational gang is involved in importation and distribution of drugs and firearms into Ireland. Ross Browning has associations with Daniel Kinahan and other senior members of the Kinahan organized crime gang. Ross Browning has a long association with Stephen

Fowler, who is a significant criminal. Garda intelligence shows that they are members of the Kinahan gang. Intelligence indicated that Stephen Fowler's son Eric acted as a debt collector for Ross Browning.'

The positive identification of Browning's vehicle convinced gardaí that Arakas was in town on cartel business. As Detective Sergeant Sheehan explained: 'When I saw the car I got on to Dave Gallagher and I told him what we were dealing with and we made the decision to stay there until we would be replaced by another team the following morning. As we were waiting and keeping eyes on the property we learnt more about Arakas's background and also read about him and we knew we were dealing with an extremely dangerous criminal. We didn't know what was going to happen with this guy but we were prepared for any eventuality and all along the preservation of life was our main priority.'

At the time of his visit to Ireland, Arakas (b. 1 December 1958) had been living in Alicante. Prior to his move to Spain's east coast around 2014, he had been living in the Costa del Sol since the late 1990s. He established himself in the region over the years and Spanish police believed he was introduced to members of the Kinahan cartel and other Irish criminals around 2009 due to his close links to Estonian criminals also based in the region. However, his involvement in crime had started in his teenage years when he made a name for himself as an expert car thief. He progressed quickly in the world of crime and in 1979 was arrested for stealing thirteen handguns and hundreds of rounds of ammunition from a shooting club in Tallinn. Authorities believed his associates were going to use the weapons for attacks on officials connected to the Soviet regime. During a court appearance on

18 April 1979, Arakas managed to escape and spent eighty-seven days on the run before he was caught. He received a 15-year sentence after he was convicted of unlawful handling of firearms and hooliganism.

Released from a Soviet military prison after serving ten years, he joined the Estonian Defence League, which was then involved in attacks against Russian officials before the collapse of the Soviet Union. During his time with the Defence League, Arakas was also part of a group called 'weekend warriors' who fought with rival gangs. In the mid-1990s he made his debut in organized crime and is understood to have acted as an enforcer for an Estonian crime gang that was involved in a deadly feud with the Russian mafia. During this period, Estonian authorities had classified him as an 'excellent marksman' and identified him, as one file noted, as 'being suspected for several crimes of manslaughter, murder, illegal drug trafficking, pimping, unlawful handling of firearms and economic crimes'.

The criminal also cheated death on more than one occasion during the mafia war, which left over one hundred people dead. He was convicted in July 1997 of the unlawful handling of firearms and received a probation report. Following his conviction in 1997, and due to the numerous attempts on his life, he made the decision to move his family to Spain. But in 1998 he was tracked down to Marbella by his enemies and was left seriously injured in a failed assassination attempt.

Despite the attempt on his life, Arakas still maintained his links with Estonia over the years, often making return journeys for meetings with his old associates. Before his visit to Ireland, he was also convicted of unlawful handling of firearms in January 2012 but spent only a short time in prison.

In between his involvement in organized crime, he also claimed to be a wrestler and an actor. In his homeland, he was seen by many as a freedom-fighter who fought the Soviets, but to others he was simply 'The Butcher' because of his involvement in organized crime. His involvement in a mafia war in his own country meant he was very experienced and the cartel had no problem in offering him €60,000 to complete his mission in Ireland.

The job in Ireland was not going very well. The plan was thrown into turmoil when members of the Emergency Response Unit stormed into Fowler's home through an unlocked back door at 11.25 a.m. on 4 April. They swept through the house and Arakas was identified standing beside a single bed in the living room. Fowler and another man, who cannot be named for legal reasons, were also arrested on suspicion of assisting Arakas. They were both later released as gardaí prepared files for the DPP.

As the Garda officers searched the room where the contract killer had spent the night, they made a number of startling discoveries. These included a white piece of paper with the name 'James Gately, 8 College Court' written on it and a sentence in Estonian, an encrypted BlackBerry phone, a wig, and €835 and £410 in cash. As Garda Sean O'Neill lifted the phone, he noticed that the device was open and contained a thread of messages. He realized the messages could be wiped remotely at any time and took photographs of the exchanges. It was a quick-thinking response that the gardaí would be very grateful for later.

When he examined the BlackBerry, Garda O'Neill established that Arakas was using the username 'Ow' and was engaging with the usernames 'Knife', 'Bon new' and 'Bon 4'.

In the first message identified, the user 'Knife' sent a message to 'Bon New' providing details on a car and an address: 'Front entrance apartment is King Street. It's right beside Sean Graham bookmakers. The car exits the rear of the building which is College Court from a shutter which opens up and down. Champagne colour Toyota Avensis, his parking space is as soon as the shutter opens directly in front of you. He drives most days he seems to go to Newry and back.' In response, 'Bon New' said: 'Ok, King Street is Belfast main street, is that correct? And where can we see photos of him.' To this query 'Knife' replied: 'For the pictures go into Google write "James Gately Dublin Criminal", go into images – the eight [*sic*] line of pictures it's the second picture in, he has a black suit on and when he clicks on the picture it has "James Gately" wrote under picture. It's a clear picture of him.' Once the messages had been read, gardaí established that they had been forwarded to Arakas's phone from 'Bon 4'.

In response to the messages, the username 'Ow' provided details on the plans to murder Gately, who had a €250,000 price on his head. Outlining his plans, 'Ow' said: 'Well I go to internet soon and have a look. My plan was actually to go there tomorrow for a day or two and see the situation for real. Then perhaps I get a better plan. So far, in case I'm totally alone, it seems it's possible to take him down when he comes out of the car. It's based on google maps pictures. Then there was an open car park behind the house but if they closed it the situation is another.'

The handwriting in Estonian found on the piece of paper was later translated as: 'K Europcar, Front Entrance, James Gately, Dublin Criminal, 8 row 2 picture, black suit, Newry, comes outside College Court.'

Referring to other possible options, the message

continued: 'If not at the car then on his way to the front
door. There were huge advertisements on the way and it
looked like it's possible to hide behind.' Addressing other
issues, the message continued: 'The whole problem is that
there is nowhere to hide – especially you wait for the moment
he comes out of the door. Also silencer would be good. But
especially it is good if the dog [code for gun] is really accur-
ate because if the picture in google is the same that in real life
it could be just one shot to the head from distance and that's
it.' Offering other solutions, the message concluded: 'Also
there is a trick that won't allow him to close the front door
behind him and I could follow him to the corridor. But it
only works when the doors frame is metallic but by the picture it looks plastic but I see there what I can do. Best regards.'

Following the message, 'Bon 4' replied with further solutions to Arakas's mission: 'We have a tracker on his car so my
idea is when he goes out in car we know he is coming back.
We tracks him live when he is heading back to his apt when
he is 10 mins away he get in position and he parks in the
same space always so then you have him.'

Within a few minutes of Garda O'Neill photographing
the messages, they were deleted remotely. They disappeared –
but Garda O'Neill had captured the evidence.

At 2 p.m. on the day of the arrest, Detective Inspector
Noel Browne informed the Police Service of Northern Ireland (PSNI) of an 'imminent threat' to the life of James
Gately. He described the intelligence obtained from Arakas's
device, which suggested a tracker had been placed on the
Toyota Avensis being driven by Gately, who was currently
staying at College Court Central in Belfast's King Street.
Within a half-hour of receiving the information, a team from
the PSNI's Reactive and Organized Crime Department

arrived at the apartment complex only to be told that Gately had left fifteen minutes earlier along with another man. At 3 p.m., Gately was located by the PSNI and his car was seized under the 1989 Police and Criminal Evidence Order because officers believed it contained evidence – the tracking device.

Gately was brought to the Grosvenor Road police station in west Belfast, where he was issued with a formal police 'threat message'. The PSNI outlined how they believed his 'life was under threat' and how 'criminal elements' had fitted a GPS tracker to his vehicle. Once he had been formally warned, Gately was free to leave.

At the same time, a crime scene investigator was examining the Avensis and recovered the tracking device. The following day, the PSNI also dispatched an investigator to Gately's hideout in College Court as part of their efforts to corroborate the information contained within the thread of messages. As they examined the area, they established that a Sean Graham bookmakers was located next door to the complex, that his parking space was in front of the shutter and that there was a Europcar depot opposite the complex's front entrance. It all matched up and confirmed that the gardaí had just saved a man from being gunned down in an assassination.

Following his arrest, Arakas was held for two days before he appeared at Dublin District Court charged with conspiracy to kill James Gately. During his nine interviews with gardaí, Arakas said that he was 'under financial pressure' and at times insisted that he was in Ireland as part of 'an act'. He replied 'No comment' to other questions about the messages found on his device.

The device was still telling tales on him, however. Gardaí

had now established that he had been communicating on the Kinahan cartel's exclusive encrypted network – secretblackmars.com. This encrypted network channel had been established by the cartel leaders as a platform for its members and associates to communicate privately, with each member receiving a unique code to allow them access to the platform. Gardaí also received confirmation that Arakas's DNA was on the BlackBerry phone and his fingerprints were on the note featuring Gately's name.

Arakas was charged with conspiracy to murder and held on remand before being brought to the Special Criminal Court on 12 November 2018. One month before his court appearance he suffered a stroke in Portlaoise Prison and had a monitor fitted to his heart. As he stood in the dock, he was asked how he intended to plead. He replied: 'Guilty.' Remanded once again, he returned to the court on 30 November as the facts of the case were outlined by Detective Superintendent Dave Gallagher. After that, he was back in court on 12 December to learn his fate.

Addressing the court that day, Mr Justice Tony Hunt outlined how the defendant was 'ready, willing and able in this dedicated role'. The judge said: 'This murder was planned in a very sophisticated manner and in the context of an ongoing feud involving surveillance and the deployment of significant technology and resources. He agreed to the vital role of pulling the trigger for financial gain or for it to be set off against a larger sum he owed. Without his involvement the planning would have been useless. This offence was not carried out in the end because of the excellent work from Gardaí, who had prevented another execution-style murder. I would like to compliment the quick-thinking actions of Garda Sean O'Neill, who retrieved text messages from a phone seized during the arrest and without whom the prosecution of this offence would have been more difficult.'

Judge Hunt sentenced Imre Arakas to six years in prison for conspiracy to murder.

Speaking to the media outside the court, Detective Chief Superintendent Seamus Boland outlined how the conviction was part of An Garda Síochána's 'continued relentless pursuit' of those who were willing to target others for assassination: 'I'd like to take this opportunity to thank our colleagues in Europol and our colleagues in the Police Service of Northern Ireland and also the members of An Garda Síochána without whose commitment and dedication this murderous conspiracy would have succeeded. An Garda Síochána will continue to invest the necessary resources to ensure others who are involved in this conspiracy are brought before justice in the Irish courts and that our communities are kept safe from people who are willing to target for murder for financial gain.'

Arakas was brought back to Portlaoise Prison. There, he received news on 22 December of the murder of Eric Fowler, the man who had recruited him for the Kinahan cartel. Fowler was shot dead at his family home, where Imre Arakas had spent his only night in Ireland as a free man. At the time of writing, the investigation into the killing of Fowler is ongoing and appears to be linked to a feud among local criminals in the Blanchardstown area.

Arakas had started serving his time in his cell in Portlaoise, but it wouldn't be long before he had other legal issues to contend with. Two years later, on 7 July 2020, he appeared before the High Court in Dublin as part of his efforts to halt his extradition to Lithuania. Shortly after his conviction over the conspiracy to kill Gately, a European Arrest Warrant had been issued for his arrest because the Lithuanian authorities wanted to charge him in connection with the murder of gangster Deimantas 'the Diamond' Bugavičius, who was shot dead in front of his pop-star lover Vita Jakutienė on 6 November 2015.

Appearing in court on 20 July 2020, Arakas was determined to fight his extradition. Following a series of court hearings, however, the professional hitman was informed on 7 November 2022 at the High Court that the request to extradite him had been accepted by the state. On 4 January 2023 the former Estonian separatist was extradited to Lithuania by members of the Garda National Bureau of Criminal Investigation's extradition unit. Since then he has been held at a high-security prison in Vilnius as he waits to hear the specific charges he will face over the 2015 murder.

Shortly before Christmas 2023, Imre Arakas decided to speak and give his side of the story. The professional hitman gave his first ever interview to an Irish journalist, speaking with co-author Stephen Breen in a video call from his prison cell. He had grown a beard and looked frail and mentioned that he had experienced some health problems.

During the bizarre interview, Arakas, who had previously pleaded guilty, now insisted that he had no intention of killing Gately. He also claimed that he had once enjoyed drinks with the man he was sent to Ireland to kill: 'If I wanted to clip Gately, there was no need to ask for a picture because I know what he looks like in real life. The two of us were held in the same police station after some fight, but it was some time ago. We were never charged but I had met him in Spain. Why did I want a picture of him if I knew him? I also saw him in some nightclubs in Spain, but I won't be saying sorry to him. I wasn't going to shoot him. I was going to Ireland for a camping holiday. They say there were messages written by me, blah, blah, blah, about where Gately lives, but how could I write them if I was arrested?'

When asked about his relationship with cartel boss Daniel Kinahan, he replied: 'If he was brought to the court, I would testify, but on his side. I have read *The Cartel* and other articles about Daniel Kinahan, but it doesn't mean we have worked together or killed people together. They say I am "The Butcher" but it's bullshit.'

At the time of this interview, an extensive investigation file on Daniel Kinahan remained with the DPP. The massive file – compiled by the Garda National Drugs and Organised Crime Bureau – was sent to the DPP over a year after an international press conference at Dublin's City Hall in 2022, attended by America's Drug Enforcement Administration (DEA), Europol and the UK's National Crime Agency, which outlined details of $5 million rewards for information leading to the arrests of Daniel, his younger sibling Christopher and their father, Christy. Daniel Kinahan also featured in the investigation file into the murder of Eddie Hutch, with detectives hoping to charge him in relation to that murder. At the press conference, details were also released of a European Arrest Warrant for Sean McGovern, which sought to charge him with the murder of Noel 'Duck Egg' Kirwan and with directing the activities of the gang involved in the plot to murder James Gately.

In another extraordinary claim, Arakas insisted that investigators in Lithuania were determined to link the Kinahan gang to the killing of cage-fighter Remigijus Morkevičius in Kaunas, Lithuania, in 2016. In return for testifying against Daniel Kinahan, he maintained he would get to keep the

$5 million bounty: 'They are pushing to bring the Kinahans into this. They want the legal reasons to bring them to Lithuania. They tell me to confess and I get ten years, which means I will be eligible for release soon. I'm told the offer is still on the table but the situation is abnormal. The boxer was murdered in Lithuania and people wrote that I am an excellent marksman but he was shot ten times, including in the arse and the shoulder. It is a strange situation. They want to pin this on me and other things. They know I was in Spain, they have all records from Spain. I have no involvement in the fighter and the killing of Bugavičius.'

When asked if Daniel Kinahan was 'Bon' and if Sean McGovern was the name 'Knife' on his BlackBerry phone recovered during his arrest in Dublin, he replied: 'I don't know. I don't know Daniel Kinahan personally. The Kinahan guys were helpful when I was in Ireland. They were helpful because I was connected to them. I have seen pictures of Sean McGovern but I don't know him.'

When asked if he had ever killed people, he replied: 'No. I should not be known as The Butcher. I am not involved in organized crime.' The same could not be said of his associates, who would also be arrested over the plot to kill James Gately.

12. Border Patrols

(2017: logistical support in the plot to kill James Gately)

*'The Kinahan Organized Crime Group have in effect a
private army with the financial ability to make things happen.'*
— Detective Superintendent Dave Gallagher

The WBC world title eliminator between boxers Matthew
Macklin and Jorge Sebastian Heiland at Dublin's 3Arena on
15 November 2014 was a sell-out event. Boxing fans gathered at the famous venue in the hope of seeing 'Mack the
Knife', whose parents were originally from Ireland, storm to
a historic victory. At the time of the fight, Macklin, who has
no involvement in crime, was running the MGM gym in
Marbella with his business partner and best friend, Daniel
Kinahan.

As Macklin geared up for one of the biggest fights of his
career, he was joined in Dublin by his legions of fans from
across Ireland and the UK, including Kinahan, his younger
sibling Christopher and two other members of their inner
circle, Liam Byrne and Sean McGovern. Alongside them in
the ringside seats were David Byrne, his father, James 'Jaws'
Byrne, and their UK associate Maurice Sines. There was
another individual standing next to Christopher Kinahan,
and when gardaí later analysed CCTV footage from the
event as part of their ongoing work to gather intelligence on
Daniel Kinahan and his inner circle, they were interested to

find out who he was. That man was identified as Peadar Keating.

Keating (b. 29 March 1981) was from the Ronanstown area of Dublin and was a brother-in-law of cartel money-launderer Jason Carroll, who had been murdered by a rival gang outside his home in Clondalkin on 29 August 2013. At the time of the boxing match, Keating was well known in the west Dublin area due to his involvement with Collinstown Football Club. Although he portrayed himself as a pillar of the community, the reality was very different. Keating first came to the attention of gardaí on 7 May 2003 when he was stopped as he travelled as a passenger in a taxi on Wheatfield Park and was found to have €23,000 in cash on him. Gardaí believed that he had forged a close bond with Thomas 'Bomber' Kavanagh and noted him as one of Kavanagh's associates. Before losing the cash, his only other encounters with gardaí were in November 2000, when he received a €215.86 fine for driving with no insurance and probation for breach of the peace.

When the cash sum of €23,000 was seized, Keating was in receipt of a weekly disability allowance of €410.50 that dated back to an accident in August 2000, when he fell from a horse after a passing motorist beeped their horn. Keating suffered a leg injury in the fall that forced him to walk with a limp, in the process earning him the nickname 'Leg'. In 2005 he received a two years and three months suspended sentence and was banned from driving for five years for dangerous driving. He then received an additional 2-year driving ban on 9 May 2005 when he defied the driving ban and was arrested for careless driving.

In 2006, Keating took an action against the Motor Insurers Bureau of Ireland, resulting in him receiving a €215,855 compensation package. He later used the cash to buy a property in Rowlagh Green, Clondalkin, which included a huge extension, bulletproof windows, a non-breach door and a CCTV system. In the years that followed, Keating cemented his position within the cartel due to his close links to 'Bomber' Kavanagh and was the leader of the gang's drugs distribution network in west Dublin. As the money flowed from his drug-dealing network, his love for the good life was evident in the five family holidays he enjoyed each year. His next appearance before a court came in 2009 when he was fined €900 for his involvement in a 'tumultuous brawl' in Benidorm.

Even though he was not a household name when he attended Macklin's fight, it was no surprise to gardaí who viewed the CCTV footage of Macklin's defeat at the 3 Arena to see him standing shoulder to shoulder with the top tier leadership of the cartel, as one investigator explained: 'Keating was the Kinahan group's director of operations in west Dublin and the fact he was sitting alongside the top tier members of this gang shows just how respected and trusted he was. Only those who are in the inner circle and who have been connected to their drug-trafficking operations for many years would get to sit so closely with the leaders.'

In the months that followed the fight, Keating's association with the gang grew stronger, especially his relationship with 'Bomber' Kavanagh, who remained the CEO of the group's UK branch. Before the killing of Gary Hutch in 2015, Keating was a regular visitor to Kavanagh's base in the West Midlands, often flying in for a brief visit before returning the same day once business had been concluded. Given that Keating's loyalty was never in doubt, it was no surprise to see the cartel call on him for its war with Gerry Hutch and his associates. His senior position within the transnational gang was also confirmed to gardaí when they discovered that Keating, who was still in receipt of social welfare and had never registered as a director of any company, had spent five weeks on the Spanish island of Mallorca at the start of the summer in 2016. During his stay, he was joined by Liam Byrne and 'Bomber' Kavanagh as their onslaught against anyone even remotely connected to the Hutch clan raged at home. Investigators believed their meetings in the sun were 'war summits', in which they identified potential targets.

Upon his return to Ireland, Keating continued to have responsibility for the gang's drug-trafficking network in west Dublin. However, in January 2017, just a few weeks after the killing of Noel 'Duck Egg' Kirwan, Keating's main role within the gang changed. This time, his long-standing expertise in organized crime would prove useful to the cartel's killing machine. His job, along with the individual using the name 'Knife' on Imre Arakas's phone (see Chapter 11), was to put together a hit team to kill one of the cartel's prize targets – James 'Mago' Gately. The gardaí didn't know it at the time, but Keating's team included loyal servants Stephen Fowler, who was released from prison in June 2016 after serving time for possessing €450,000 worth of cannabis; Douglas 'Doggie' Glynn, a native of north inner-city Dublin who had remained loyal to the cartel; David 'Blinky' Duffy; and Martin 'Casper' Aylmer, who had already proved his worth in his logistical support for the hit teams behind the killings of Noel Kirwan and Michael Barr.

Even though gardaí had by now identified Keating as one of the cartel's leaders, they would not know the full extent of his involvement in the cartel's war until March of that year.

But before that, they were left in no doubt of the cartel's determination to continue their murderous blitz given the events of 27 February 2017. That morning, gardaí received confidential information that the cartel had placed a tracking device on the car of long-term Hutch associate Jason Bonney, who would go on to receive an eight-and-a-half-year sentence in April 2023 after being found guilty of acting as a getaway driver during Byrne's murder at the Regency. On foot of this tip-off, the gardaí launched an immediate investigation and recovered a tracker close to Bonney's north Dublin home. The device had been accidentally placed on the car of an innocent neighbour of Bonney's. On the same day, gardaí established that Gately was also being actively targeted when two tracking devices were recovered from the car owned by his partner, Charlene Lam.

Investigators later established that the tracker found on the innocent neighbour's car had arrived in Ireland on 9 December from the UK. Analysis of the trackers from Lam's car confirmed that they had arrived in Ireland on 12 January. Detectives were able to ascertain the tracker's movements by examining the GPS coordinates from its unique IMEI number. They concluded that the device had travelled from Solihull in the West Midlands before arriving into Dublin Airport at 9 a.m. on Ryanair flight FR663. The investigation team further discovered that 'Bomber' Kavanagh's sidekick, Daniel Canning, was on board the same flight.

The following day, they received yet more proof of the cartel's intentions when Stephen Fowler was stopped by Detective Garda Jonathan O'Leary and Detective Garda Declan Moloney in the Tyrellstown area driving the same van he would use a few months later to collect Arakas from Dublin city centre. The two gardaí searched Fowler's van and recovered a tracker and charging mat. Hauled in for questioning, Fowler was later released without charge, but Garda investigations continued.

In the meantime, the tracker device found in Fowler's van was analysed by senior crime and policing analyst Dr Orla Dempsey, who discovered that it too had arrived into Ireland on 9 December. In another breakthrough, data obtained from the device showed that it had been placed on the undercarriage of the car of a female relative of Gately's on 17 January, before being removed on 28 January. The investigation team also established that the tracker had been deployed to Gately's relative's car when they were parked close to the Gately family home in Portland Row, in Dublin's north inner city.

Following the discovery of the tracking devices, gardaí remained on high alert. One month after the discovery of the tracker in Fowler's van, Detective Superintendent Dave Gallagher received confidential information that a van parked at the short-term car park at Dublin Airport was to be used by members of the Kinahan cartel as part of their continuing efforts to target the Hutch gang. In response to this intelligence, a Garda surveillance team was dispatched to the airport. They conducted random checks on vehicles in the car park and in the afternoon they came across a VW Caddy van located on Level 1. When checked against the list of vehicles being used by senior cartel figures, it was quickly confirmed that the vehicle, which had a bicycle in the back, was registered to Peader Keating.

The Garda team kept a watch on the vehicle, and at 5.40 p.m. Keating arrived. He moved the VW from the space and a waiting blue Peugeot Partner van moved into the space and parked. The driver of the Peugeot got out and walked to

Keating's van and got into the passenger seat. The van drove off. The undercover team watching all this immediately identified the passenger, who cannot be named for legal reasons, as one of the Kinahan organization's most senior members.

The Garda team continued to keep the Peugeot under observation and looked on as Keating arrived back at the airport in his van at 8.10 p.m., this time with close associate David 'Blinky' Duffy as his passenger. Keating again left the airport and the undercover officers maintained their surveillance operation on the Peugeot, now being driven by Duffy, as it made its way to the Clarion Hotel in Liffey Valley shopping centre, arriving at 8.32 p.m. Five minutes later, Keating arrived to collect his friend and they drove off.

The Peugeot remained the focus of the undercover operation until it moved again on the morning of 30 March. Leaving the hotel, the van headed north on the M1, making its way towards Northern Ireland. As it approached the border at Newry, the surveillance team was unable to follow their target out of the jurisdiction, but they remained along the border in anticipation of its return. As the team waited, they noticed the Peugeot van now coming towards them, being driven towards Dublin, and they jumped on its tail again.

The Peugeot arrived into the Ashtown area of north Dublin at 1.38 p.m. that day. The surveillance team watched as the driver parked and left the vehicle. They took photos of their target as he waited for a taxi and quickly realized they had identified Douglas Glynn, a close associate of Ross Browning from the north inner city.

At 1.50 p.m., Keating was identified parking the Peugeot at the Clarion Hotel before walking to his Volkswagen Caddy and meeting with the senior Kinahan figure, who cannot be named for legal reasons. The pair then drove to the Crumlin area, where Keating's companion left him and cycled home. However, their cartel business for that day was by no means completed.

Later that evening, the Garda surveillance operation continued as investigators suspected Keating himself was monitoring and tracking the movements of an individual, who was not identified, in the Fairview area of north Dublin. At 9.15 p.m., a GNDOCB surveillance team identified Keating's Volkswagen Caddy parked across the road from the Tesco store in Fairview. Keating, who had a child in the passenger seat, was monitored talking on his mobile phone before he left the area at 9.40 p.m. and returned home.

The following day, 31 March, the gardaí established that Gately had attended the Criminal Courts of Justice in Parkgate Street earlier that day and had left at 2.15 p.m. on a motorbike and returned to his family home in Portland Row. Aware that Gately was not in Belfast but now back in the capital, Detective Sergeant Greg Sheehan and his team were tasked with monitoring the man who might be a murder target. They found out that a Toyota Avensis he was using was parked in Strandville Avenue on North Strand. They observed Gately returning to his car later, unaware that a cartel sub-cell was busy trying to discover his location, and heading off to drive north.

When Imre Arakas was arrested a few days later on 4 April (see Chapter 11), Gately became very aware of the lengths the cartel were willing to go to in their efforts to kill him. Once regarded as a friend, Gately was now seen as an archenemy to be eliminated. The truth of this became clear when the PSNI examined CCTV footage from Gately's Belfast hideout. Footage from the days before the Arakas arrest showed Keating walking outside the apartment block. The Peugeot van was parked nearby and it was believed the cartel leader was sitting in the back of it as Keating embarked on his scouting mission on 28 March. During that day, the cartel hit team had spent around thirty minutes outside the complex before driving off.

The footage had more to reveal. Images obtained from the apartment block's CCTV system on 30 March captured the moment when 'Doggie' Glynn attempted to place the tracking device on Gately's Avensis at 10.27 a.m., before he was disturbed by a security guard. Forced to leave the complex, Glynn, who used the codename 'Oscar', returned to the Peugeot to await his next opportunity. It arrived at 11.12 a.m. when Glynn gained access to the car park as another vehicle was exiting. The hit team moved quickly and parked their van at the entrance, preventing the shutter from closing. Glynn got out and calmly walked to Gately's vehicle and placed the tracker underneath as Keating looked on.

Alongside the discovery of the hit team in Belfast, gardaí also obtained footage of Keating's crew at Dublin Airport. CCTV from the airport in the days before 28 March showed how Keating and the cartel leader, who cannot be named for legal reasons, had travelled on Aer Lingus flight EI3264 to Birmingham before returning later that same evening. Investigators believed the flight was arranged to finalize plans for the transport of the Peugeot van to Ireland. Other images examined included CCTV footage of Keating driving to Dundalk Retail Park on his travels north, where his associate went in and bought a Garmin satnav. Investigators believed the device was to be used by the gang when travelling north.

The arrest of Arakas left the cartel plot against Gately in ruins, and the investigation team was gathering information quickly. Gardaí established that the Peugeot had remained at the Clarion Hotel between 30 March and 4 April. On 5 April, it was collected by a car wash and valet company, when it was stopped by gardaí and seized. Examination of the van turned up a booking form in the name of a UK national, nicknamed 'Chunk', who was suspected of being a member of 'Bomber' Kavanagh's UK outfit, as well as a Garmin satnav. It showed a location labelled as 'Home' – it was Gately's apartment in Belfast. The device had been in and around Gately's apartment before returning to Dublin.

Examining the booking form for the Peugeot van, investigators established that the van had arrived into Dublin Port from Holyhead at 5.55 a.m., arriving at Dublin Airport at 6.23 a.m. Once parked, 'Bomber' Kavanagh's associate returned to the UK on Ryanair flight F4534. As gardaí had suspected, the cartel's UK branch was also at the heart of the conspiracy.

Arakas was charged over the cartel conspiracy on 6 April, and on 12 April investigators made their next move, swooping on the homes of Keating, Glynn, Duffy and the cartel leader who had accompanied Keating on their trips north. This part of the operation did not focus on arrests. Instead, the strategy was to recover evidence linked to Arakas, the trackers, the CCTV evidence, electronic devices and any documents linked to the Peugeot.

The raid on Keating's family home recovered a Nokia mobile phone, four iPhones, two laptops, four iPad devices and an encrypted PGP BlackBerry. When examining the BlackBerry, investigators recovered the image of a message sent to another encrypted device. The image provided details of the numbers of five trackers, four of which were used in the plan to target Gately. But also within the image was a message: 'Can you keep that in ur phone for me mate just in case my phone breaks.' It was clear that Keating was determined to keep a record of the trackers being used by his hit squad. The message also showed that Keating had given names to the individual trackers, with the one placed on Gately's car labelled '(diiiiii)'. For the investigating gardaí, the name was a clear indication that this was the tracker placed on Gately's car that would ultimately lead to his killing. The phone also revealed that it was pinging off a mast close to Parkgate Street on the day Gately was in court and was pinging off a mast in the Fairview area on the night he was being watched by gardaí.

While Keating's home was being raided, a Garda team was searching the north inner-city home of Glynn. They recovered five BlackBerry devices and a Nokia phone.

It was a similar story in the raid on Duffy's home, where a BlackBerry, three GSM tracking devices and meteor SIM cards were recovered. Duffy's BlackBerry showed that his phone had been pinging off a mast in the Clontarf area of north Dublin on 31 March and in the Blanchardstown area at the time Arakas was arrested.

In the days following the raids, investigators also established that the tracker recovered from Gately's car had been moved from the New Seskin Court apartment complex in Dublin, which was the home of cartel fixer Martin Aylmer, at 6.15 a.m. on 30 March. The device then travelled to Glynn's home before it eventually found its way to Gately's home. The investigating team had enough evidence to prove there was a plot to kill Gately – and who was involved in it.

The entire hit team went to ground – Stephen Fowler, Douglas Glynn, David Duffy and Peadar Keating – after the dramatic developments that April, having seen Imre Arakas take the heat for the murder plot. But they couldn't hide for ever. At the same time, Martin Aylmer was being held on remand over his involvement in the Barr killing.

On 27 August 2017, Keating stepped off a plane from the UK at Dublin Airport and was met by gardaí, who arrested him. The senior cartel leader, who cannot be named, was held for questioning for two days before being released without charge. The Garda team continued to work on their comprehensive files for the DPP. As they put together their book of evidence, investigators discovered that the junior member of the hit team had booked the flights for Arakas to travel to Spain.

Following extensive analysis and examination of the evidence gathered, the DPP made the decision to bring charges against Keating and Fowler. Appearing at the Special Criminal Court on 1 July 2020, Keating was charged with directing the activities of a criminal organization and enhancing the ability of a criminal organization to commit the murder of Gately between 7 December 2016 and 4 April 2017.

Stephen Fowler, Christy Kinahan Snr's lifelong friend, was also charged with enhancing the cartel's ability to kill Gately.

Sixteen days later, Glynn and Duffy were before the court, charged with enhancing the cartel's capability to murder.

Aylmer was brought to the court from Mountjoy Prison, where he was being held for his involvement in the Barr and Kirwan killings.

When all four men were charged – Keating, Duffy, Glynn and Fowler – Keating was the only one remanded in custody until the cases came to trial.

In March 2021, Keating was brought before the court and pleaded guilty to directing the activities of an organized crime gang. Detective Sergeant David Carolan agreed with Keating's defence barrister, Hugh Hartnett SC, that his client had been 'taking directions' from others. At his sentencing hearing on 2 September, Keating was put away for eleven years, ending his pivotal role in the gang. In his address to the court, Mr Justice Tony Hunt said Keating was a 'senior figure for the Kinahan Organized Crime Group, which is a well-organized, complex, sinister and dangerous organization' and that 'His role went over and above the role of direction and he was a senior frontline member. He was a significant part of the surveillance of James Gately and his family regarding the proposed murder. The failed attempt was not due to any reluctance on the part of Keating but was due to Garda intervention. He was a repository of trust and confidence.'

Speaking after the sentencing, Detective Chief Superintendent Seamus Boland referred to the Garda strategy when he said: 'The sentence is a significant development for An Garda Síochána's strategy to disrupt and dismantle organized crime groups participating in violence, which is the scourge of communities. This investigation also identified the transnational outreach of organized crime, where such groups and people involved in this activity do not recognize law or respect our borders. We would like to take this opportunity to thank our own investigation team and our international partners and, in particular, the PSNI, the NCA and Europol.'

Twelve days after Keating's sentencing, Fowler was the next to plead guilty to his involvement in the plot. He received a 6-year sentence on 4 October that year for his 'logistical' involvement. Mr Justice Tony Hunt outlined how Fowler had also been 'operating under the direction of others' and had been involved in the plot as a 'favour'. The veteran criminal did not take the news of his 6-year jail stint too well, telling the court that the gardaí were: 'Scumbags – everything they said was lies.' He told a court reporter to 'fucking write that'.

The following month, it was the turn of Glynn to receive his sentence, six and a half years, on Valentine's Day, 2022. He had been found guilty the previous October. Mr Justice Hunt explained that Glynn's involvement in placing the tracker on Gately's car put him 'higher' in the criminal organization.

On 15 April 2021, Duffy was brought for his day in court. Seconds after entering the dock, Duffy replied 'Guilty' when asked about his plea. He was remanded in custody and brought back before the court on 21 June for facts in the case to be outlined. Addressing the court that day, Detective Garda Tony Kennedy described how the criminals who had attempted to murder Gately believed he was 'a suspect in that murder at the Regency Hotel', before adding that Duffy had provided 'logistical' support to the gang. On 30 July, Duffy was given a 5-year sentence. Mr Justice Tony Hunt outlined how Duffy had aided an organized crime group of the 'most serious variety in the commission of serious crime' with the 'forestalling of the attempt on Mr Gately's life only made possible by Gardaí'.

On 17 November 2021, fellow gang member Aylmer found himself taking his turn before the court, also charged with providing support to the gang. He too pleaded guilty to participating in the plot to kill Gately. On 29 July 2022, Aylmer was handed down an 8-year sentence for his role in Noel Kirwan's murder (see Chapter 8) and for his role in the attempted killing of Gately. Mr Justice Hunt described how Aylmer had made a 'schoolboy error' by using his own name and car to import tracking devices into the country, before adding that he was a 'reliable, trusted source of assistance who was plainly not in a position of higher involvement but his assistance was important if not absolutely essential to carry out a planned execution'. Speaking after this second sentence for cartel activity, Detective Superintendent Gallagher said: 'Today's convictions of Martin Aylmer at the Special Criminal Court are significant in bringing to account a trusted enabler, without whose support and assistance a violent criminal organization could not operate a campaign of murder and violence which impacted immensely on families and local communities.'

By the time Aylmer was sentenced in 2022, five members of Keating's hit team were in prison: Imre Arakas, Peadar Keating, Douglas Glynn, Stephen Fowler and David Duffy. But it wasn't the last court appearance for Glynn and Keating. On 16 March 2023, Glynn received an additional 8-year sentence after he was convicted of overseeing the 'industrial scale' storage of €1.4 million worth of drugs, and also ammunition. Detective Garda John O'Leary told the Special Criminal Court how a breakthrough in encryption-cracking technology led gardaí to Glynn after they recovered an encrypted device during a raid. Mr Justice Hunt described Glynn as a 'trusted manager over a significant period for a high level criminal organization' with responsibility for the 'day to day running of the warehouse'. Mr Justice Hunt also said that Glynn was involved in the distribution of ammunition to 'protect profits' made by the organization before outlining how the case was a 'good example of those higher up in the organization being able to insulate themselves by using lower- and mid-level coal face operatives who are regarded as dispensable cannon fodder. Society is entitled to a long period of silence from Mr Glynn. He is facing the consequences of his involvement through free choice with a dangerous and destructive criminal organisation.'

Unfortunately for the hit team, the technology keeps on talking and its evidence is compelling. Just over two years into his sentence, on 8 January 2024 the High Court in Dublin heard that Keating was wanted by the UK's National Crime Agency on charges of possessing firearms and ammunition between 1 January 2020 – when he was under investigation for the plot to kill Gately – and 3 June 2021. The same case also saw charges brought against Liam Byrne and 'Bomber' Kavanagh's son, Jack Kavanagh. The case stemmed from investigators gaining access to the men's encrypted messages on the EncroChat network. Yet again, the tables had been turned and the technology the cartel had relied on to shield them from the law was being used to shed a glaring light on their activities. If convicted of this offence, Keating could face a 20-year stretch in a UK prison.

Incredibly, Gately had survived a well-planned attempt on his life, including one which would have been carried out by an expert sniper who undoubtedly would not have missed. He had a lot to thank the gardaí and the PSNI for, as it was only their interventions that had kept him alive. But the danger hadn't passed. This feud was personal, which made it all the more lethal, and the cartel was not giving up on killing Gately. Unknown to everyone, they were already busy lining up yet another contract killer.

13. 'Five World Cups and I'll be out'

(10 May 2017: second assassination attempt on James Gately)

'He was like an empty vessel. He was detached and had a sociopath mindset.'
— Senior Garda investigator

On 6 May 2017, a 999 call was answered by an employee at the Garda control centre at 9.05 p.m. At the other end of the line was a man with a thick north Dublin accent who used the pseudonym 'Stephen'. He was calling to raise concerns about suspicious activity and he specifically named James Gately.

Call taker:	Hello, Gardaí in Dublin.
Caller (male):	Yeah, howiya, I just wanted to report something. I seen something very suspicious. I'm around Coolock, there was a lad sitting in a black Lexus car, he has a red top on him, but I heard him talking to somebody, something about a fella called James or Gately or something and told he had a handgun in his car and is waiting on his road, he's after getting out of his car. I don't know, there's something suspicious going on there.

Call taker:	What road?
Caller:	I think it's Clonshaugh, the Glin.
Call taker:	Sorry?
Caller:	The Glin road or something.
Call taker:	Yeah, sure, we'll get someone down there.
Caller:	It's a black Lexus car. I heard him saying that he is gonna walk back to the car in a minute, I think he has the gun in the car.
Call taker:	And your name is?
Caller:	If somebody wants to wait at the car.
Call taker:	What's your name?
Caller:	Stephen, sorry.
Call taker:	Stephen, we'll get somebody up there.
Caller:	The car is there, the black car is there.
Call taker:	Have you the reg of the car?
Caller:	I don't know. I didn't see it. It's sitting there outside your man's gaff, ya know.
Call taker:	No problem. Do you know the address of the house?

CALL ENDED

Within sixteen minutes, the same man rang again. This time, in a conversation that lasted sixty-two seconds, 'Stephen' provided some extra detail about the clothes the man was wearing, specifying a red jacket and a baseball cap. He claimed that the man was staking out Gately's home. He said he was in an i250 model of a black Lexus and that the man was headed to Santry but was going to return.

Gardaí responded soon after the second call was made and went to Glin Drive in Coolock, north Dublin, where Gately lived. Due to the nature of the call, a full patrol was carried out of the wider area, but nothing suspicious was uncovered and the call was deemed a hoax. It was just over a month since Imre Arakas had been flown into Ireland to take out Gately and had his plan dismantled by specialist officers from the Garda National Drugs and Organised Crime Bureau. The gardaí had already officially warned Gately that his life was under threat, but no one knew the level of danger posed against him more than Gately himself.

The murder target had returned to his home in Coolock – which he had in 2013 bought for €125,000 before adding a significant extension on to it – by May 2017, after spending time in Belfast. He had continued about his day-to-day life, but tried to stay under the radar and took precautions. Wednesday, 10 May 2017, was no different. Four days after that strange hoax call to Garda control, Gately emerged from his home at 1.10 p.m. wearing a jacket over a Kevlar bulletproof vest. He could not have had any knowledge of what was about to happen, but he was prepared for the eventuality.

He got into a black Volkswagen Golf that was being driven by an associate. He was taken to a nearby location to pick up his wine-coloured Ford Mondeo, registration PJZ810. He got into the vehicle alone and drove towards the local Topaz Service station, on the outskirts of the Clonshaugh area. The filling station is a seven-minute drive from Gately's home, a distance of 2.7km. It was always very busy there due to its location near the motorway intersection of the M1 and M50 as well as other secondary roads.

At 1.29 p.m. Gately pulled into the forecourt of the Topaz and parked his Mondeo on the left-hand side of the shop, close to its entrance. He got out and walked in, re-emerged four minutes later and sat back into the driver's seat of his car. Around him, some people were filling up their vehicles with fuel while others sat in the cars, eating lunch or taking a break from work. Within seconds of Gately sitting into his car a black Lexus pulled up on the right-hand side of the Mondeo, with its front passenger window open. A lone male was in the car, sitting in the driver's seat. He had made no attempt to disguise himself. He pointed a pistol in the direction of Gately and pulled the trigger. He struck his target but also hit an advertising hoarding 20 feet away, which was in direct line with Gately's vehicle. The place fell silent after the loud burst of gunfire, and the assassin performed a U-turn and sped off.

James 'Mago' Gately had spent the previous fifteen months avoiding a bullet, but now he had been riddled with them. Gately managed to get out of the car, with blood pouring from his neck and chest, and collapsed on to the ground. The incident happened so quickly that many witnesses did not realize a shooting had just taken place. Those who did notice rushed to the aid of Gately, while others rang 999.

Four minutes later, the first responding gardaí arrived at the scene. The maimed victim was still conscious and as gardaí stepped in to tend to him, he fumed: 'Are youse going to get me a fucking ambulance or what?'

For the second time, Gately seemed to have cheated death. His bulletproof vest had done its job, although one bullet had lodged in his jaw. After being treated at the scene, Gately was brought to Beaumont Hospital in an ambulance, escorted by the Armed Support Unit. Once there, he underwent emergency surgery.

By that evening it was clear that Gately was going to live. The bullet had entered his head and neck region before it travelled to its end point in his jaw. He was struck five times, but four of the shots hit his protective vest. Following the procedure, Gately was admitted to an Intensive Care Unit at the hospital. He remained under armed protection before he discharged himself on 26 May 2017, against medical advice. Soon after, gardaí learned that he had left the country.

Just over an hour after the shooting, gardaí received a call about a car engulfed in flames at a remote location in Newrath, four miles from the town of Castlebellingham, County Louth. It was completely burnt out and could only be identified from its Vehicle Identification Number, which confirmed that it was a black Lexus bearing the reg 08-D-51984.

In the immediate aftermath of the shooting gardaí did not know who the gunman was, but they were in no doubt that this was another attempt to kill on behalf of the Kinahan cartel. The gang were willing to pay a hefty price for the hit, with senior gardaí believing there was a €250,000 bounty on Gately's head, which made it a lucrative gig.

Little usable evidence was gained from the crime scenes in Dublin and Louth and no weapon was recovered. Gardaí examined the CCTV footage from the filling station, which had picked up a side-profile image of the shooter. He was wearing reflector sunglasses as he approached Gately's vehicle. The newly upgraded CCTV system also had Automatic Number Plate Recognition technology, and through this it was established that the reg of the gunman's car matched that of the vehicle found burnt out in Louth.

They soon discovered that the Lexus had been there prior to the shooting, specifically on the day beforehand, 9 May, at 3.33 p.m. Its driver, who could be clearly seen in the high-quality video of that day, wore a plain white T-shirt, navy tracksuit bottoms, cream runners, and a gold watch and had reflector sunglasses on his head. He put €20 of diesel into his car and held the pump in his right hand, with his distinctive tattoos clearly visible on the same arm. In another shot, he entered the shop and paid for the fuel and an air-freshener with cash before leaving. It was from this CCTV footage that, just two days after the shooting, gardaí were able to identify the man as Caolan Smyth of Cuileann Court, Donore, County Meath.

The investigation team was based in Santry Garda Station and led by Detective Inspector Eddie Carroll and Detective Superintendent Colm Fox. When Detective Superintendent Fox passed away in February 2018, Detective Superintendent Paul Scott joined the team. In files prepared for the DPP, gardaí noted about Caolan Smyth: 'Until early 2017 he was only known to Gardaí for involvement in stealing high-end vehicles in burglaries. Reports also indicated that he became involved in the sale and supply of drugs in recent times. It is suspected that he is now operating as a "hitman for hire".'

The attempted murder of Gately marked a real step-up in the level of violence Smyth was capable of and involved in. Smyth (b. 22 November 1991) was the middle child, with an older sister and a young brother and had lived in Coolock, north Dublin, before relocating with his family to various addresses in counties Meath and Louth. He was a promising young boxer, becoming an all-Ireland boxing champion at the age of twelve. But following his parents's split, he left school after Junior Cert and by the time he had turned eighteen his attention was anywhere but the ring or the athletes who graced it. Instead he now aspired to emulate the likes of slain drugs boss Eamon 'the Don' Dunne, whose picture he used to carry in his wallet.

In his early interactions with gardaí in 2011, Smyth regularly gave a false name when stopped. He was caught attempting to steal diesel from a parked car at Millrace in Duleek, County Meath, on 9 December 2011. He managed to avoid a conviction over the incident when it came to court, but his own solicitor described it as a 'Laurel and Hardy' act because Smyth was driving a petrol car.

By 2012, he had his first criminal conviction under his belt at the age of twenty and he featured on the Garda radar more frequently over the following years. Smyth began associating with various different criminal groupings, something that would become a trend in his career. One of the gangs was based in north Dublin and he became active in the burglary of high-end vehicles with them. On one occasion in 2015, Smyth was suspected of fishing car keys through a letterbox to steal a top-of-the-range vehicle. At the same time, he was supplementing his income by working for a security company and manning the doors of some of Dublin's best-known pubs. But his court dates began to stack up as he faced numerous charges in relation to possession of weapons, knives, stolen property, unauthorized taking of a vehicle, driving with no insurance and drugs possession.

Nothing was deterring Smyth, though, who was only becoming more engrossed in the business of crime. Standing at 6 feet 2 inches, the meticulously groomed athlete with a boxing pedigree began working for gangs as an enforcer. Less than two months before the Gately hit, Smyth was arrested, suspected of carrying out a terrifying attack on a home in Drogheda. In the early hours of one morning in March 2017, a woman heard a series of bangs and noises at the front of her house while she was upstairs. He was later released from custody.

By then, Smyth had spread his tentacles to the Finglas area of north-west Dublin, where he struck up a working relationship with the group who called themselves the Gucci Gang. The group marked the new breed of criminals who had stepped into the gangland scene. Many of them were in their twenties, made a living from selling drugs, and made no effort to conceal that fact. Their approach was to openly flaunt the spoils of their work, wearing the most expensive designer clothes, going on trips around the globe and regularly posting it all on social media. Clean-cut Smyth fitted in and appeared alongside them more often. This gang had connections to the Kinahan cartel, and gardaí believe this created the link for Smyth to take on the task of killing Gately. Not only was the money too good to turn down, it is also suspected that Smyth saw it as an opportunity to cement his place at the top tier of organized crime.

Detective Superintendent Paul Scott, who has since retired and is now a criminal barrister, told the authors: 'Money is the attraction together with the bonus of establishing personal power within their peer group. It's a toxic mix which comes at a price. It's a world where actions speak far louder than words. Smyth was still viewed in the criminal fraternity as a bit of a loose cannon. For him, killing Gately would have firmly established his position as a force to be reckoned with.'

Gardaí established that the black Lexus had been purchased for €3,700 from a man in Dunboyne, County Meath, on 17 April 2017. The car, which had previously been owned by the Pakistan embassy and had a diplomatic licence plate, was then parked in a residential area in Tallaght for a period. CCTV revealed how a black Lexus had parked up repeatedly in the vicinity of the target's house. The footage from 9 May was telling: Smyth was seen at the Topaz with the Lexus and then spotted lurking around the location of Gately's house at six different times between 3.43 p.m. and 5.30 p.m. that day.

On 10 May, footage showed that Smyth left his apartment in Donore, Co Meath, at 9.34 a.m. wearing the same shoes as those seen at the garage the day before. The black Lexus was then seen in the Clonshaugh area from 10.05 a.m., lying in wait for Gately to move from his home. It parked up at three different times for periods on Clonshaugh Avenue. Once Gately was on the move, the car followed him to the shop and watched on from the nearby Clayton Hotel. When Gately went into the shop, the gunman's car could be seen entering the forecourt and parking at the truck stop. When Gately emerged and sat into his car, the trigger man pulled up and struck.

Separately, gardaí in Ardee were tasked with following up on the burning out of the car used in the hit and they canvassed the general Castlebellingham area for CCTV. Officers found that the black Lexus had met up with a white Fiat Scudo van outside the Gort Nua estate in Castlebellingham at 2.29 p.m. on the day of the murder attempt and that both vehicles had then travelled in convoy to the site where the Lexus was set alight. Tracking the movements of the white van, footage was obtained from a local petrol station that showed it pulling in there at 2.07 p.m. An older man purchased €3 of petrol in a red container and put €20 of diesel in his van. He then met with the Lexus and drove to the burn-out site before returning to his home in Gort Nua at 2.38 p.m. From the footage, gardaí were able to identify that man as Gary McAreavey.

Little was known about McAreavey (b. 29 October 1967), who was originally from Lurgan in County Armagh. McAreavey had been claiming disability benefit from the state since 2000 and had only four convictions at the time, with his most recent coming at Dundalk Circuit Court in June 2013 when he received community service for the reckless discharge of a firearm. He was a father of three and his youngest child had a significant disability. He worked as a painter-decorator but couldn't do it full time because of an injury. He had no links to any organized crime gang at the time.

When gardaí raided McAreavey's home on 25 May, they made the next breakthrough. They seized his phone and on it was a o85 phone number under the name 'Q New', which had been saved after receiving a text from the same digits saying 'Smitzer New'. The number previously stored on McAreavey's phone under the name 'Q New' was Smyth's. Investigators were able to find that out because Smyth had given it to Social Welfare when he'd filled in a claim form in February of that year. But gardaí suspected Smyth was forced to change and update his number when he was arrested over the shooting in Drogheda in March. Further proof for the officers that the new number belonged to Smyth was that records showed it had been in contact with his father on 442 occasions between 30 March and 17 May that year and with his brother 410 times in that period. Gardaí matched the number, via telecommunications masts, to the movements of the black Lexus the day before and the day of the shooting. This showed Smyth's new number was in regular contact with McAreavey after the shooting had been carried out.

Focus returned to the two 999 calls made four days prior to the attempted murder from another o85 number, which was different from the numbers identified for Smyth and McAreavey. This other phone number was bought at a Meteor phone shop in Blanchardstown, west Dublin, on

5 April 2017. When CCTV was examined, it showed that Smyth had purchased it.

After call data records were retrieved and statements taken from three people, gardaí identified the man using the number as one of Smyth's close allies. Analysis of phone records showed the man had been in contact with Smyth before and after the first of his 999 calls on 6 May. But this man had also spoken to gardaí in the days after the shooting. He told a garda at Coolock Garda Station that he had seen Smyth in a fancy Lexus at Northside Shopping Centre the day before the incident. He said he'd heard about the shooting and that a Lexus car was burnt out down the country. He said he was informing gardaí because it was 'all wrong'.

But once established as the 999 caller, he refused to cooperate. In files later reviewed by the DPP, the gardaí stated: 'The most likely conclusion is that he had some allegiance to Gately's side of the dispute and was trying to prevent the shooting and get Smyth caught.'

In the weeks after the murder bid, Smyth bolted to Northern Ireland, but he came to the attention of the PSNI when he was arrested in Belfast in a stolen Toyota Auris on 4 July 2017. Later that month, he was back to Dublin. On 25 July, gardaí from the Divisional Task Force at Santry Garda Station were carrying out a checkpoint on Dublin's Griffith Avenue when they stopped two men in a beige 06-registered Skoda Octavia. The men gave their names as Graham Gardner and Oisin Smyth. Gardner was an established Kinahan OCG figure.

The two men were detained for a drugs search and brought to Ballymun Garda Station. Officers carried out inquiries in the meantime and established that the second man was, in fact, Caolan Smyth. He had given the name of his younger brother. Smyth was released at 1.14 p.m. but rearrested six minutes later outside the station for the unlawful possession of firearms with intent to endanger life in relation to the Gately hit. He was hauled back inside the building.

Smyth refused to answer any questions or comment on evidence put to him over the course of six interviews. At 11.50 p.m. on 27 July 2017 he was released without charge, but then rearrested once more over an outstanding bench warrant. He was brought to Dublin District Court, where he was remanded in custody the following day. Officers were later warned that Smyth had access to firearms and to exercise caution when dealing with him.

By August 2018, Smyth had moved in with his girlfriend, Ciara Byrne, at the Pearse House flats in Dublin's south inner city. Ms Byrne had no involvement in crime but she had come to the attention of gardaí before. On 26 October 2007, when she was in her early twenties, she was involved in a row outside Tramco Nightclub on Lower Rathmines Road. Using a scissors, she stabbed three men who played for St Mary's College rugby team. One of the injured parties was Jonathan Sexton, who went on to have a glittering career with Leinster, Racing 92 and Ireland, with 119 caps for his country before his retirement after the 2023 Rugby World Cup. Ms Byrne had pleaded guilty to three counts of assault causing harm and got a 3-year suspended sentence at Dublin Circuit Court.

Now Caolan Smyth was living with her, and the gardaí in Pearse Street became concerned by his presence. The chief suspect in a major gangland hit, he was on their patch in the busiest policing hub in the capital. Such was the nature of the business Smyth was involved in, it was an all too likely possibility that he would also become a target.

Joe Gannon, who was Superintendent at Pearse Street Garda Station before his retirement in 2021, told the authors: 'It was for the greater public interest that we didn't want these gangland individuals who were targets coming into town to live, for them to be targeted and for bullets to start flying, because of the density of the population in that part of the city – it's the main hub in the city for the night-time economy, discos, pubs, restaurants. And there would be a much greater probability that there would be widespread collateral carnage. So really that was the focus of our intensity in terms of keeping an eye on Caolan Smyth.'

Superintendent Gannon tasked his team, led by Detective Sergeant Patrick Traynor, to collate every cough and spit on Smyth, searching him at every opportunity, taking down the names of people he was associating with, recording what cars he had access to, what areas he was in and what outfits he was wearing.

For his part, Smyth had soon put his stamp on the flat, installing reinforced bulletproof doors and windows as well as paying for a state-of-the-art camera surveillance system. In his small bedroom he had a huge TV screen at the end of his bed, where he lay for hours just watching the CCTV footage. Youngsters in the area began looking up to him. Gardaí noted how they were 'in awe of Smyth' and would 'try to impress' him, so much so that he often got them to walk his English bulldog for him. On a number of occasions the county council cameras were damaged on top of the building and gardaí suspected it was done on the orders of Smyth.

Pearse House provided Smyth a safe haven where it was very difficult for any rivals to get to him, but his character was different from those who lived there. Superintendent Gannon told the authors: 'Pearse House has a great tradition going way back, they had all been dockers, hard workers, so the locals wouldn't tolerate the likes of Smyth. They are very proud of their complexes down there and they despise gangland coming in or even internal home-grown people who become involved in that sort of activity. None of us wanted Caolan Smyth there.'

Smyth had maintained his links with members of the Finglas Gucci Gang, but it was his fresh association with one man that alerted the gardaí. In October 2018, an 07-registered Audi Q7 jeep linked to Smyth was observed outside the home of Ger Mackin in Limerick over two days. Mackin was a notorious enforcer for the Kinahan cartel. He was a member of the Continuity IRA and the INLA and had a long-standing reputation of being a dangerous individual who was reportedly contracted by the Kinahan OCG to take out Gerry 'the Monk' Hutch.

In December, Smyth, who was wearing a bulletproof vest regularly at this stage, visited Mackin again. Then on 30 December, gardaí in Dublin stopped Mackin in a 141 Audi car with Smyth sitting in the front passenger seat. Mackin had €1,400 in cash on him while Smyth had €600 and three mobile phones. The driver claimed he knew Smyth from prison and said he was staying in the Red Cow Hotel. Officers seized the car under the Road Traffic Act.

Mackin also paid flying visits to Smyth's flat in Pearse House, where he stayed some weekends. Another man who visited was Iranian asylum-seeker and suspected hitman Hamid Sanambar, another dangerous emerging gangster, who often stayed at Pearse House with Smyth.

In 2019, Smyth was relaxed in interactions with gardaí, joking on one occasion that he wanted to get away but he could only afford a trip to Kerry. This persona didn't fool anyone, however. A senior investigator based in the capital told the authors: 'He was strange, there was never aggression in him. He always cooperated with gardaí . . . but he was like an empty vessel. He was detached and had a sociopath mindset.'

Smyth became a father for the third time that year, but he did not see his daughter for at least the first seven weeks after she was born. He was preoccupied with a dangerous dispute and it took precedence.

The Coolock feud had kicked off in January 2019, and its first life claimed was barber and drug dealer Zach Parker, who was shot dead in Swords. Smyth was close friends with Parker and was at the scene in the immediate aftermath of the shooting before being stopped at a checkpoint on his way back into Pearse House.

The second victim of the feud was Sean Little, a 22-year-old man who was shot dead and left in a burning car off the M1, near Walshestown in north Dublin, on 21 May 2019. Blame was aimed at Smyth's close pal, Hamid Sanambar. Just seven days later Sanambar was shot dead in the driveway of Little's home. The blame now shifted towards Smyth, but he protested his innocence. Smyth flew to the UK and took a lie detector test; it indicated that he had no involvement in Little's killing. However, Little's father wasn't satisfied. On 14 September, officers from the Garda National Drugs and Organized Crime Bureau arrested Stephen Little before he could carry out a hit on Smyth. Little Snr fumed at the gardaí: 'Had you given me another hour, I would have killed the bastard that killed him.' He was later jailed for six years for firearms possession.

Eleven days after Smyth was subject to that murder bid, gardaí called to him at his flat in Pearse House and served him with a Garda Information Message. By the following month he had moved to Artane in north Dublin – welcome news to his neighbours in Pearse House. He was keeping a low profile and insisted to gardaí that he had nothing to worry about, yet when they called into him while visiting his father's home in Bettystown, County Meath, they saw Smyth was wearing a bulletproof vest sitting inside the house. Some days later when he was stopped while in the back of a taxi in Finglas, he was wearing the protective top again, but said it was to stop him getting cold. When the gardaí asked about his current feud, he said: 'Why would I be afraid of a fat fella?' The gardaí believed this was a reference to Little Snr. Smyth added that he was not fighting with anyone and had no enemies.

On the evening of 16 October 2019, Smyth went to Raheny Garda Station to sign on in relation to bail conditions and was met by a detective based in Santry. There, he was arrested for the Gately hit over two years earlier. He was then brought to Coolock Garda Station. The following morning, McAreavey was arrested at his home in Castlebellingham, County Louth, and brought to Ballymun Garda Station. While detained, Smyth was interviewed six times but answered 'No comment' to everything. McAreavey was quizzed five times and gave the same answer.

The pair were charged separately before a judge in courtroom no. 4 at the Criminal Courts of Justice that afternoon, 17 October. Smyth was remanded in custody; McAreavey had his bail set and later took it up.

Following a trial at the Special Criminal Court, Smyth and McAreavey were found guilty. The prosecution relied on CCTV and mobile phone evidence to track the movements of the pair. Mr Justice Tony Hunt said Smyth was a 'ruthless and dangerous' man who worked in 'tandem' with others. Smyth was jailed for twenty years for the attempted murder of James Gately, while McAreavey received a 3-year term for his assistance.* As Smyth was led from the courtroom, he turned to his family in the gallery and said: 'Five World Cups and I'll be out.' Given the enemies he had made, his conviction may well have saved his life.

James Gately has lived to tell the tale, but while he had seen off two Kinahan hit teams, he has since become embroiled in another fight, this time with the Criminal Assets Bureau, as they pursue him in a legal battle that is ongoing at the time of writing in 2024. In an affidavit submitted to the High Court, CAB alleges that Gately is a leading member of the Hutch organized crime gang, which is involved in armed robberies and the importation of drugs. It said he once had a strong association with Daniel Kinahan, but that ceased when his close friend Gary Hutch was gunned down. It claimed that he was linked to a number of armed robberies and to three murders, Aidan Byrne and Eamon 'the Don' Dunne in 2010, while he is being investigated over the murder of David Byrne at the Regency Hotel. The Bureau is pursuing the home he shares with his partner, Charlene Lam, which was remodelled for up to €440,000, a car and a watch, all of which CAB says are the proceeds of the crime.

The Kinahan cartel had been sorely thwarted in their bids to kill Gately, but there were other targets on the list and plans were in motion to get them.

---

* McAreavey's conviction was quashed in June 2024 following an appeal. The Supreme Court found that the prosecution in the original case failed to establish that McAreavey 'knew or believed' that Smyth had carried out a serious offence when he helped him burn the getaway car.

14. Disposable Assets

(July and August 2017: hit teams target Michael Frazer and Caine Kirwan)

'Aim for the head, yeah? Have to get him in the head. Head shots or we won't get fucking paid.'
— Gary Gleeson, career criminal

Long before the Kinahan–Hutch feud erupted, back on 10 February 2004, gardaí at Sundrive Road in Dublin received information that Michael Frazer was being actively targeted by Brian 'King Ratt' Rattigan's gang. They delivered a Garda Information Message to Frazer, advising him that his life was under threat and that he should take necessary security precautions.

The following day, Frazer attended the busy Garda station and received crime prevention advice, but he refused to acknowledge his associations with any gangland figures in the south inner-city area of Dublin. But during his brief conversation with gardaí there, Frazer did admit that if 'anything were to happen to him', it would be 'because of my former friendship with Freddie Thompson and Brian Rattigan'.

At that time, Michael Frazer was identified as one of twenty-seven 'core associates' of 'Fat' Freddie Thompson. Others on that list included Sean McGovern, Liam Byrne, Liam Brannigan, Dean Howe and David Byrne. Another list, this time featuring the names of thirty-one individuals classified as 'associates', included James 'Jaws' Byrne and James Quinn. These lists had been compiled under Operation Anvil, drawn up by gardaí in Crumlin, Kevin Street and Kilmainham stations as they fought to keep the Thompson and Rattigan factions from killing each other in what had become known as the Crumlin–Drimnagh feud. By 2015, sixteen men would have lost their lives in the dispute, which was kicked off by the killing of Freddie Thompson's best friend, Declan Gavin, in 2001 by Brian Rattigan.

In February 2004, there was a spate of murders, pipe bombings, shootings and arson attacks as both factions fought for control of the drugs turf. In an echo of the later Kinahan–Hutch feud, anyone even remotely connected to either faction was considered 'fair game'. Detectives suspected that Frazer was being targeted because of his decision to maintain his friendship with Thompson. After being interviewed, Frazer refused to sign any statement and worked to keep a low profile – until another threat emerged on 2 April 2005.

On that occasion, gardaí received intelligence that an innocent female relative of Frazer was being targeted simply because of his loyalty to Thompson. After receiving a 999 call to alert them that members of Frazer's family were being followed by two men in a Volkswagen Bora, gardaí stopped the car and identified two associates of Rattigan, both wearing bulletproof vests, before recovering a concealed bowie knife.

The incident prompted Frazer to distance himself from Thompson even further, and he continued to maintain a low profile over the subsequent years. Even though the pair had maintained their childhood friendship throughout the bloody Crumlin–Drimnagh feud, their relationship broke down in early 2014 after Thompson, without a shred of evidence, accused Frazer of betrayal. He accused Frazer of making advances towards his long-term partner, Vicky Dempsey, and of continuing his friendship with members of the Rattigan faction. In the underworld, betrayal is the worst crime and demands a deadly punishment.

Despite his full-time role in the cartel, Thomson had to seek permission from his paymasters to kill his old friend. Permission was granted at the beginning of March 2014. The first hitman-for-hire to accept the offer was James 'Nellie' Walsh, from west Dublin. He put his plan into action on 26 March that year when he targeted Frazer in the car park of the Church of the Transfiguration in Clondalkin. That time, detectives believed Frazer was lured to the area on the basis of a meeting with a known and trusted associate. But when he turned up, Walsh emerged from a car and shot him in the neck. The bungling hitman also managed to shoot himself in the leg as he ran from the scene.

Badly injured, Frazer managed to scramble back into his car and drove to Clondalkin Garda Station, where he told officers: 'I've been shot – it's to do with Crumlin and Drimnagh.' When interviewed by detectives, he refused to make any complaint. Walsh, who would later be involved in a feud with other senior cartel figures, would eventually receive a 10-year sentence for the attempted hit on Frazer after spent bullets were recovered from a car linked to him.

In the weeks after the attempt on his life, Frazer moved to Turkey, sure in the knowledge that Thompson would continue to hunt him. In spite of this, he made the decision to return to Dublin and was back in the capital by the end of July.

On 1 August 2014, Frazer cheated death for a second time

when a gunman pointed a gun at his head in Firhouse, west Dublin, but it jammed and didn't go off. Just as in the first attempt on his life, Frazer refused to cooperate with the Garda investigation. Left in no doubt of Thompson's intentions to have him killed, Frazer kept on the move, staying in different safe houses across Ireland.

The third and final attempt on Frazer's life that year happened on 1 November when two hitmen fired eight shots at him as he sat in his car in the Islandbridge Court area of Kilmainham. Miraculously, none of the shots managed to hit the target and he escaped by ramming his vehicle into the hit team's car. Over the next three years, Frazer spent time in England and in Turkey. He had earned the nickname 'Mickey Nine Lives' due to his ability to avoid being killed by an assassin's bullet. By July 2017, he was back living in Dublin, often sleeping in his van, and was classified by gardaí as 'homeless'.

When Thompson was being held on remand for the Douglas murder, Frazer might have been tempted to believe he had more pressing problems to attend to – but he would have been wrong. Despite being held on remand in prison, Daniel Kinahan's enforcer was as determined as ever to settle old scores. Just as in 2014, Thompson had once again received the green light to target Frazer for a fourth time.

This time, the assassins who offered their services were Gary Gleeson (b. 26 October 1983) from Ballyfermot and Stephen Dunne (b. 3 June 1979) from Lucan. Gleeson was classified by gardaí in west Dublin as an 'extremely volatile and violent man' who had used knives during previous confrontations. He had links to organized criminal gangs from the Ballyfermot and Clondalkin areas throughout his lengthy criminal career and was connected to the Kinahan organization through their associates operating in west Dublin.

Despite having convictions for possession of drugs with intent to supply, Dunne was not regarded as a major gang-land player, but was recognized to be a close associate of Gleeson. In his private life, he battled drug addiction and suffered from severe depression.

As the two contract killers laid their plans for killing Frazer, they did not know that investigators from the Garda National Drugs and Organized Crime Bureau had received confidential information on 28 July that Kinahan cartel assassins were actively targeting an unknown individual in the Drimnagh area with 'murderous intent'. At the same time, investigators became aware that a Fiat Doblo van was to be used in the murder plot. The same day, 28 July, gardaí had the van under surveillance and noticed it driving in the Lissadell Avenue area of Drimnagh. At 9.21 a.m., the van left south Dublin and drove to the nearby O'Donoghue Street, where it stopped beside a silver Honda Civic, with both occupants recorded pointing at the vehicle. The van then drove off and arrived at the Park West Business Park at 9.43 a.m. The two men parked the van there and walked over to a grey Volkswagen Golf. They then returned to the van and drove off.

As the Garda investigation continued, detectives quickly discovered that the registration of the Fiat was false, as was its registered address in Seville Place. The brand name 'Anthony Kelly Electrical' on the side of the van was also fake. Detective Garda William Saunderson, from the Stolen Motor Vehicle Investigations Unit, also confirmed that the Honda Civic had been stolen from a property in the West Bromwich area of England on 4 July 2016 and fitted with false plates. However, the biggest breakthrough came when gardaí established that the Volkswagen Golf was registered to Stephen Dunne. Over the following days, all of the vehicles were kept under surveillance. Gardaí had by now identified Gleeson as well and had concluded that Frazer was the intended target because of the pair's frequent visits to Lissadell Avenue, the location of Frazer's family home.

Determined to prevent the hit team from completing their mission, gardaí obtained a warrant to place listening devices inside the pair's Fiat Doblo based on concerns they were conducting their own surveillance on their target. The Garda devices became active on 7 August and the gardaí listening to the pair's conversations were left in no doubt this was to be the day when they made their move. Frazer was about to face the fourth attempt on his life.

When they got into the van that evening, Gleeson and Dunne started their mission by taking cocaine. Gardaí listened as Dunne asked for instructions: 'What do you want me to do, Gar?' Gleeson replied: 'Plug him. Just pull out then when you see him coming. Plug him there when you see him coming, like. Get that out of the way.' Dunne, clearly irritated and feeling the pressure, replied: 'Relax there. For fuck's sake. You're pressurizing me, relax would ye?' Dunne then said: 'I haven't got faith in this gun, that's being honest with you, right. I'm going to have to get him proper, Gar, you know what I mean, I haven't got good eyesight, man.'

As the pair continued to prepare for the murder, gardaí listened intently as Dunne appeared to have a change of heart regarding his role as the shooter, suggesting to Gleeson: 'You shoot him. Thought you were fucking shooting him, you're bleedin' driving, you mad thing.' With tensions mounting between the pair, Gleeson replied: 'I'm driving.

What are you snapping at me for? I asked you the other day did you want me to do it and you said, "no I want to do it." What do you want me to do?' In response, Dunne said: 'Are you for fucking real? Then I'll do it, for fuck's sake. Relax, will ya, for fuck's sake. I'm just saying, Gar, I can't afford to miss him. Do you not get me?'

Gardaí heard the 'sound of snorting' as Gleeson continued: 'As soon as you get out, go up and do it. Tap the shite, he's going to have nothing behind him.' They moved on to discuss the location of the murder, with Dunne again voicing his concerns: 'I think we're mad stopping here on the Naas Road, yeah? If you move it down a bit, yeah, when you see him coming in your mirror give me the yoke [gun], yeah. It better not jam, Gary. What will I do if it jams?' Gleeson instructed Dunne to hold the weapon in a particular way to prevent it from jamming. The pair then talked about the road being 'too wide' before Dunne suggested 'blocking' him in his van.

Gleeson sighed and then Dunne said: 'I don't give a fuck. I have to get him proper, I can't afford, I can't afford to get him on the limb – it's my face he's going to see. What if it jams, man, talk to me, will ya?' Gleeson replied: 'Chill out. Give it up, Stephen.' Dunne replied: 'I need glasses, you know what I mean.'

Seconds later, gardaí's suspicions about the hit team surveilling Frazer were confirmed when Dunne asked: 'Is he coming down this way?' and Gleeson replied: 'Says he's at Newlands Cross doing six miles an hour.' Back to requesting instructions now that Frazer's arrival was imminent, Dunne said: 'Right, tell me what to do. Will I get ready, will I?' Gleeson replied: 'Yeah.'

Dunne again expressed concerns about the gun, about the

magazine being upside-down, before asking: 'Safety's on it. Just pull it back and it's ready to go, innit?' Dunne's next gripe related to his gloves: 'Right. This stupid poxy glove. I asked you to get extra-large ones.' Gleeson replied: 'They are extra large, Stephen.' Dunne continued to sound unsettled and anxious: 'I think we're jumping the gun here, you know what I mean? We're only fucking finding out he's moving. We don't even know if the police are watching him, you know what I mean? If I jump out, I'll get fucking riddled. This is going to be loud, Gar. I'll just keep pulling the trigger, yeah?' A fed-up Gleeson replied, 'Ah stop,' before telling him: 'Aim for the head, yeah? Have to get him in the head. Head shots or we won't get fucking paid.'

Dunne still needed reassurance from his fellow assassin, saying to Gleeson: 'As soon as we block him, I'm going to let a shot off in the van, yeah? Once I get him a bit I'll keep walking towards him, yeah, right up to the windscreen, and I just keep shooting then and around to the side and I keep shooting him, yeah?' Gleeson agreed to Dunne's plan with two chilling words: 'Riddle him.'

Dunne's preoccupation with the gun continued: 'I think we should have tested it, Gar, that's being honest with you. We didn't even test it.' Gleeson must have been watching Frazer's journey as he now said: 'Get it out there, have it ready.'

Dunne laughed at Gleeson's orders: 'Oh Jesus, you're mad.' Gleeson then checked the weapon and said: 'It's ready to rock, safety is off. You touch and it's going to go, you know what I mean?' Dunne's nervousness increased: 'Relax, will ya. Please don't put me under pressure, will ya. Don't drive off on me. I can't run.' Gleeson responded: 'I'm not going to fucking drive off on you.'

Dunne said: 'I don't feel happy about it here. I don't even feel happy doing it now. I'd rather test this, that's being honest. Can't do him here, Gar, he could see us. Whatever you think, Gar, use your head, Gar. You are more of a criminal than I am, you know what I mean?' Referring to their target, Dunne also said: 'Five fucking times he's been tried to be killed, do you know what I mean?'

They continued to monitor Frazer on the tracking device as they sat parked on the Naas Road, and now Dunne sounded excited: 'There he is there, look, it is, Gary, see that white van. Ah that's a refrigerated one, isn't it?' His disappointment was short-lived: 'There's another one coming down, see it? That's him there, Gary. There is he over there, see him? See him over there, look. He's stopped, he's stopped. What's he doing out of the transit?' Unsure of the individual they had identified, Gleeson replied: 'That's not him. I'll tell you now in a moment.'

By that stage, gardaí had seen and heard enough. Armed officers from the Emergency Response Unit surrounded the vehicle at 7.50 p.m. The attempted assassination was dead in the water.

Gardaí seized the van and recovered a fully loaded 9mm Taurus handgun from under the handbrake. Gleeson and Dunne were hauled in for questioning. In the meantime, detectives also recovered a tracking device from Frazer's Ford Transit van.

Frazer's would-be killers were held until 12 August, when they were both charged with conspiracy to murder. Before being charged, Dunne's DNA had been recovered from the handle and hammer of the pistol, from the SIM card installed inside the tracking device and from the latex gloves. Gleeson's fingerprints were recovered by the glove box of the stolen Honda. CCTV footage of Gleeson buying a top-up for the tracking device's SIM card was also recovered.

All of this evidence alongside the audio recordings made it a slam-dunk case for the Garda investigation team. When the pair's trial got under way on 21 June 2018, it was no surprise that they both pleaded guilty to possession of a semi-automatic pistol and ten rounds of ammunition with intent to endanger life. The DPP had dropped the conspiracy to murder charges. The following day, the court heard the facts of the case, during which Detective Superintendent Dave Gallagher said: 'The plan was to attack this Mr Frazer with murderous intent. Mr Frazer was targeted by senior figures in the organized crime group for internal matters and the two men were contracted and paid to carry out the attack.'

Remanded in custody, the pair were returned to the Special Criminal Court on 30 July 2018. Gleeson received a 12-year sentence with one year suspended, while Dunne received the same but with two years suspended. Addressing the court, Mr Justice Tony Hunt described their criminal enterprise as 'shambolic, confused and ill-prepared'. Referring to the transcript of the audio recordings, Mr Justice Hunt described it as a 'disturbing document' which included a 'graphic description' of their plans. The court also heard of Gleeson's €80,000 drug debt and how he had written a letter of apology to Frazer. Dunne's heroin addiction was also used in mitigation. Following the sentencing, Detective Superintendent Dave Gallagher told the waiting media how the convictions were the end result of a strategy that involved the 'relentless targeting of individuals who attempt to target individuals for assassination'.

In another part of Mr Justice's Hunt summary, he also referred to the plot to kill Frazer as a 'dangerous and outrageous escapade'. In that summer of 2017, it wasn't the only one.

There was another murder being planned out when Gleeson and Dunne were plotting their killing of Frazer. The next target was Caine Kirwan, whose father Noel 'Duck Egg' Kirwan had already been murdered by Kinahan assassins (Chapter 8). For this deadly mission, the cartel recruited drug addict Andrew O'Keefe (b. 20 April 1989) and his associate Owen Cummins (b. 1 September 1978). At the time, O'Keefe was a chronic heroin user, but that didn't deter the cartel from putting a gun in his hands.

The contract killers chose 6 September as the day Kirwan's life would end. Once again, there were things the gardaí knew that the hit team didn't realize they knew. Detective Superintendent Dave Gallagher had received information that there was a 'hit team aligned to the Kinahan Organized Crime Group in place in the Ballyfermot area of Dublin with the intent of murdering a person', and that the cartel hit team was using a white van. This intelligence was just one of many tip-offs the gardaí received at that time as the hunt for the cartel assassins gathered pace.

Based on this information, the senior investigator and his team initiated a huge operation to prevent further loss of life. The operation involved members of the GNDOCB and the Special Crime Task Force swamping the area of Ballyfermot and searching for any suspicious white vans as part of their efforts to identify the hit team. Unlike the previous case, there would be no time to place listening devices in any vehicle. This time, any positive sightings of suspicious vehicles would require immediate interception.

As efforts to locate the white van continued after

lunchtime that day, Garda Stephen Gillespie, Garda Eoghan Byrne and Garda Wes Kenny were part of a Special Crime Task Force (SCTF) patrol that drove into the Raheen Park area at 2.50 p.m. As they did so, they noticed a white Citroën Berlingo van with its rear windows blacked out and a man, wearing a fluorescent jacket, sitting in the driver's seat. Keeping a watchful eye on the van, the team were in the process of obtaining the vehicle's registration details when it suddenly sped off. In an instant, the SCTF team activated their blue lights and siren and gave chase.

The van drove through a red light at the junction of Le Fanu Road and Kylemore Avenue, narrowly missing another vehicle as it headed towards the Kylemore Road area. It continued to drive at speed, often on the wrong side of the road, before it turned into Kylemore Way. As the Garda team sped after it in pursuit, they saw a brown plastic bag being thrown from the passenger side of the van at the entrance to Kylemore Business Park. The van driver continued to speed along Kylemore Way, seemingly unaware that the end of the road was a dead-end, with a set of bollards blocking the route to Jamestown Road.

The driver realized it too late. The speeding van screeched to a halt just inches before the bollards. As it did, the Garda team rammed into the rear passenger side of the van as the driver and a passenger, who had not been previously identified in the earlier observation, ran from the vehicle. Garda Gillespie ran after the passenger, who was over six foot tall, yelling: 'Armed gardaí, stop, armed gardaí, stop.' The suspect continued running, on to the Jamestown Road.

Garda Gillespie finally caught up with the suspect as he ran towards a Hyundai Tuscan.

At the same time, the driver of the van was also sprinting

away and he managed to jump into the Tuscan, lock the doors and start it up. Outside, Garda Kenny and Garda Byrne, also yelling, 'Armed gardaí!' frantically tried to smash the driver's side window, but without any success. They continued to hammer on the window as the driver reversed the vehicle, smashed into a parked vehicle behind it and narrowly missed Garda Byrne, who was beside the jeep.

As this was going on, Garda Gillespie and the passenger from the van continued to struggle on the road. Fearful for his life and concerned there could be another firearm inside the vehicle, Garda Byrne fired a shot at the jeep, hitting the front windscreen. Garda Gillespie, fearing that his life and that of the other suspect could also be in danger, opened fire, too, again hitting the jeep's windscreen.

Despite the shots being fired, the driver drove the Tuscan towards the Garda team before crashing into a Volkswagen Passat on the opposite side of the road. He then reversed again, before Garda Byrne fired another two shots as part of his efforts to prevent him getting away. When the driver failed to stop, Garda Kenny also discharged three shots at the vehicle. The driver kept going nonetheless and made his escape along the Jamestown Road before eventually abandoning the Tuscan in Tyrconnel Park. By that stage, the passenger, who had been identified as Andrew O'Keefe, had been restrained and arrested. Garda Kenny went back to retrieve the bag that had been thrown from the vehicle minutes earlier. Inside the bag, Garda Kenny identified a Beretta handgun fitted with a silencer.

Over the course of the next two days of questioning, O'Keefe answered 'No comment' to all of the allegations put to him. He was eventually charged with possessing a firearm in suspicious circumstances. By that stage, gardaí had recovered O'Keefe's DNA from a neck warmer, gloves, a waistband from tracksuit bottoms, Adidas runners and a baseball cap found inside the van. The case against him was also made stronger after a partial fingerprint was found on the bag used to discard the firearm.

O'Keefe was safely in detention, so attention over the next few months turned to the driver of the vehicle. Gardaí focused their efforts on examining 148 hours of CCTV footage. Their strategy involved tracking the movements of the Tuscan before it was abandoned, which included CCTV footage of it arriving in Ballyfermot around 2.17 p.m. that day. One piece of footage showed a man matching the driver's description removing his jacket on Tyrconnell Road. This man was then tracked on different cameras walking into Inchicore Village and entering the Black Lion pub. Other footage showed the man leaving the pub at 2.55 p.m. and getting into a taxi. The taxi was tracked across the city to its destination at Saint Attracta Road in Cabra, where it arrived at 3.13 p.m. These clear images of the man suspected to have been driving the van were shared with officers in Mountjoy, Coolock and Finglas stations, and it wasn't long before the driver of the Tuscan was identified as Owen Cummins.

While gardaí hunted for Cummins, the investigation team made good progress when they established that the Citroën Berlingo had been bought on the website DoneDeal on 31 August by a man named as 'John Molloy'. This 'John Molloy' was using a mobile phone number also used by Owen Cummins. It was clear that 'John Molloy' was a bogus name used by Cummins.

Cummins was still on the run, but by now gardaí had discovered that the intended target was Noel Kirwan's son, Caine. At the time, the family of Caine Kirwan's partner was living close to the spot where the hit team's van had been parked. Investigators suspected that O'Keefe and Cummins had been planning to kill Caine Kirwan, the second member of his family to be targeted, when he brought his young son to the nearby Raheen Green area to ride his quad bike. Kirwan, who arrived in the area at 1.40 p.m. that day, would have had to walk past the van en route to the park.

Luckily for Kirwan, something unforeseen happened. There had been a problem with his son's bike, so father and son played in the front garden instead and didn't head to the park. That decision likely saved his life.

At the time, gardaí believed that Kirwan was targeted because the Kinahan cartel had identified him as a 'threat'. But in an interview with one of the authors, a relative of Kirwan's dismissed this assumption: 'Caine did not believe that he was under any threat because he was not part of the Hutch faction – his only link to the feud was because his father was killed. If he thought he was in danger, he wouldn't have been in Dublin. They must have assumed he would have been a threat to them and that's why it was easy for them to have him killed. Once again, it was a case of them targeting someone who didn't have anything to do with the feud.'

Kirwan's luck eventually ran out. The cartel had failed to murder Kirwan in September, but on 2 December the 24-year-old's body was found in a field in Walterstown, County Meath. Investigators believed he was lured to the area on the premise of a business deal by a major west Dublin criminal before being shot dead. At the time of writing in early 2024, the west Dublin hit team suspected of being recruited for the murder have not been charged.

*

Four days after the discovery of Kirwan's body, gardaí made their move against Cummins. He was arrested in the Fassaugh Avenue area of Cabra. His time on the run had been spent staying in safe houses across Ireland, and it was also suspected that he spent time in the UK and Spain. Arrested and hauled in for questioning, Cummins was released without charge at 11.55 a.m. on 8 December as gardaí prepared their file for the DPP. Cummins realized it was only a matter of time before the DPP brought charges against him, so he went to ground for a second time. In January 2018 he headed for southern Spain, where he was supported by cartel associates.

Cummins was still in Spain when O'Keefe returned to the Special Criminal Court on 24 June 2018 and pleaded guilty to possession of a firearm in suspicious circumstances. He was back before the court on 30 July 2018, when he received an 8-year sentence for his role in the criminal enterprise. Mr Justice Tony Hunt remarked: 'For a young man, you have a shocking record and it is high time you got your act together as otherwise you are facing a lifetime of this.' O'Keefe would get his opportunity to rehabilitate when he was released from Mountjoy Prison in November 2023. What he makes of that opportunity remains to be seen.

Cummins remained in the Costa del Sol area before his homesickness got the better of him and he returned to north Dublin. He was arrested on 27 May 2019 and brought before the Special Criminal Court to answer the same charge as O'Keefe. Remanded in custody, Cummins was back before the court on 19 November when he too pleaded guilty to possession of the firearm in suspicious circumstances. The heroin addict was remanded in custody once again ahead of his sentencing. He suffered a personal loss when his son,

Ryan Bond, was killed in a motorbike accident on 6 December that year.

Cummins returned to the court on 3 March 2020 and received an 8-year sentence. As Mr Justice Hunt remarked: 'His participation was at the lowest part of the pyramid and he had been persuaded by those higher up to act as a driver of the van and had been exploited.' Cummins's barrister, Michael O'Higgins SC, told the court that his client was 'drug free' and that there was another person who was 'extremely insulated from any form of detection and who was pulling the strings'. In conclusion, the barrister said that his client had only agreed to participate in the murder plot because of a drug debt – a theme similar to many of those who offered their services to the Kinahan cartel.

15. 'They're gonna get killed'

(6 November 2017: conspiracy to murder Mr Z)

'You tell me, look, he's at the door and I'll slip out and kill him.'
— Alan Wilson, hitman for hire

The year of 2017 was huge in terms of the gardaí's fight against the Kinahan cartel and they were now having a real impact on its extermination project. The Garda National Drugs and Organised Crime Bureau's (GNDOCB) raid of the gang's arms depot at the Greenogue industrial estate and the arrest of its quartermaster Declan 'Mr Nobody' Brady was significant, removing the gang's arsenal of weapons and the main logistics man. Key figures were also being taken out as gardaí had success in on-the-ground murder investigations associated with the feud, while they were also regularly intervening in plots to kill.

John O'Driscoll, former Assistant Commissioner, told the authors: 'However relentless they were, that's what we were – we were relentless. No matter how many times that they attempted murder over a period of time, we were there. On other occasions, you might take out somebody with a firearm, you know they have it for a purpose which is to kill, but you're not quite sure who it is they're going to kill and you mightn't be in a position to put in the resources. So we were taking out a lot of other people along the way.'

Alan Wilson was one of those people. He received jail

time for his involvement in a Kinahan cartel murder plot, yet within months of his incarceration he believed the same gang were trying to kill him. Wilson claimed he had been the victim of a barrage of threats that he would be got at behind bars. An attack in June 2018 in Mountjoy Prison saw him slashed with a blade that left him with permanent scarring and a broken nose.

Wilson made his allegations in pursuit of €75,000 in damages as he sued the Irish Prison Service for failing to keep him safe. In submissions to the High Court in 2023, documents stated: 'The plaintiff indicated that he had a €100,000 bounty placed upon him for death. The plaintiff indicated the bounty had been created by the Kinahan drug cartel for the harm or unlawful killing of the plaintiff. There was a high number of prisoners in Mountjoy Prison with associations and/or connections and/or loyalties toward the Kinahan drug cartel. There was a failure to ensure the protection of the plaintiff despite having a knowledge of inflammatory graffiti in Mountjoy Prison concerning the plaintiff.'

He, however, had offered his services to the cartel after he walked from his previous stint in jail six years earlier.

Alan Wilson was a nephew of crime lord Martin 'the General' Cahill, who was assassinated in 1994. Wilson (b. 24 February 1979) is a father of four from Dublin's south inner city. He first came into the public eye when he was charged with the murder of 18-year-old Marioara Rostas, a Romanian woman who disappeared from Dublin city centre in 2008. Her body was discovered four years later in a shallow grave in the Wicklow Mountains. Following a trial in 2014, a jury acquitted Alan Wilson of the crime.

Alan's cousin Eric 'Lucky' Wilson is serving a 23-year sentence in Spain for shooting English criminal 'Tall Dan' Smith at a Costa del Sol bar in June 2010. Eric's brother, Keith, is also doing life for the contract slaying of Daniel Gaynor in Finglas in August 2010. Their brother John was shot dead at his Ballyfermot home in September 2012. The Wilsons were deadly and feared, and relished their role in the underworld as violent hitmen for hire.

When Alan Wilson beat the Marioara Rostas murder rap in 2014, he was serving a 7-year sentence handed down for a meat cleaver attack in Blanchardstown, west Dublin. However, the Supreme Court later quashed that conviction and he was free for the first time in six years. Unlike his Wilson relatives, he had no significant convictions to date, but it was only a matter of weeks after his release in August 2017 before he was on the Garda radar.

Once he got out of Mountjoy, Wilson went to see Liam Brannigan in search of work. Brannigan was a key figure for the Kinahan cartel over the years and had been involved in the logistical end of the Crumlin–Drimnagh feud. Recently, Daniel Kinahan had turned to his close friend once more to put together a team for the gang's latest venture. Brannigan (b. 30 March 1982) was to head the sub-cell unit, making him the only point of contact for the gang, based at headquarters in Dubai, responsible for issuing specific tasks to those below him. Also from the south inner city, Brannigan is a cousin of Freddie Thompson and Liam Byrne. He had only one serious conviction on his record, dating back to 2007, for drugs possession and for which he had received a suspended sentence at Dublin Circuit Criminal Court. While he was busy in his latest role of identifying targets to kill in the ongoing feud, the dad of two was combining that with studying for a degree in archaeology and history at University College Dublin.

Brannigan recruited long-time pal and associate Dean Howe to come on board. Howe had also been involved in the Crumlin–Drimnagh feud. He was the chief suspect for masterminding the attempt to whack Martin 'the Viper' Foley in 2008 on the orders of godfather Christy 'Dapper Don' Kinahan. Foley, a notorious criminal himself and uncle of cartel enforcer James Quinn, miraculously survived the hit despite being shot four times. Howe was also arrested following the attempt on John Hutch's life (see Chapter 7).

Although in its infancy at the time, the GNDOCB was on to the group nearly immediately. Detective Superintendant Dave Gallagher received information specifying that a navy-/grey-coloured Seat Leon, with false 08-D registration plates, had been parked up in Inchicore, south Dublin. It was believed to have been placed there by members of the Kinahan Organized Crime Group. The Seat had come from Birmingham and it was suspected that it had been provided by Thomas 'Bomber' Kavanagh, who ran a car business as a front in the West Midlands.

Within days, the investigation team had established that heroin addict Joseph Kelly, who had sixty-four previous convictions, and Alan Wilson both had access to the Seat. The GNDOCB identified Brannigan and Howe as suspects and were also interested in four other cars linked to the group: a Nissan Primastar van, a BMW 3 Series estate, a Renault Laguna and a Mazda 6. The Mazda had also come from Birmingham.

Gardaí began a surveillance operation on the men, but armed with the specified information and, most importantly, the belief that the ultimate aim was to murder, they went to the District Court and sought audio surveillance on the vehicles. On 9 September the audio surveillance was approved and teams from the National Surveillance Unit and Crime and Security teams bugged the vehicles over the coming days. Before the authorization was made, Joseph Kelly bought another vehicle, a Volkswagen Caddy van, from the website DoneDeal for €2,700.

While the gardaí had identified the persons and vehicles involved, that was all they knew. The target had not been identified, nor had the location of where the hit was going to take place. That information would have to come from the gangsters' own mouths.

Oblivious to the fact that the gardaí were now listening in, on 11 September 2017 Kelly collected Wilson in the Nissan Primastar and they travelled to Stephen's Lane, located between Mount Street Upper and Lower in Dublin 2. This was one of the possible 'switch' locations, where a hit team would drive to after committing their crime, burn that cart and get into another vehicle left parked for them. But as they headed into the north inner city, Wilson began pointing out other possible spots that might serve well. Later, Kelly drove the van to Fairview in north Dublin and then drove back in towards the city on a route Wilson instructed him to take.

The next day, Kelly collected Wilson at 5.12 a.m. and Wilson got into the rear of the van. As they discussed various elements of the murder plot, one point of conversation gave the first alarming insight. Wilson began talking about two people sitting upstairs in a pub, though he did not mention which pub it was, and said: 'I'm just gonna fly upstairs with the machine gun, point it at the two of them, shoot them, get out back and into the back seat of the car and drive off, heading this route.' Kelly asked should he also go inside the pub with him, but Wilson was happy to do it himself. Kelly said, 'You don't want any hero bastards,' seeming to refer to others possibly inter-vening. Wilson replied: 'That's gonna be a problem. That's why I'm gonna point at the two of them, pull the trigger.'

On 13 September at 10.03 p.m., the men set off again in the Primastar. As they drove, Wilson suggested involving another associate of his to draw the target out of a house party to the front garden of an unidentified property, where the gang would strike. The gangster he was referring to was a former member of the Westies gang who is a dangerous, hostile criminal and a suspect in a number of shootings.

The need for an extra driver came up repeatedly in their conversation, but both men agreed that if a new member of the team came on board, they would have to be paid less than them. Wilson insisted that if they were paid €100,000, it was not going in three equal ways, that he and Kelly would share the majority. They inspected Fairview again, discussed the pub again and the possibility of including Wilson's pal, but the gardaí believed the actual murder location had yet to be established.

They took the following day off but were back out on 15 September. At 11.40 a.m. Wilson was seen going into the 74 Talbot Street pub, the first solid indication of the premises he had been speaking about. He went inside and had a look upstairs. Earlier that morning Liam Brannigan and Dean Howe were observed making their way into the Phoenix Park on foot after 9.15 a.m. and going to the Wellington monument. Around twenty-five minutes later an unidenti-fied man, who had driven to the same spot in a Toyota Avensis, was seen getting out of the car and speaking to Brannigan, who gardaí, watching on, could see was holding a device in his hand and speaking to the man.

The gardaí suspected the device in Brannigan's hand might

be a tracker, and this was confirmed two days later when the GNDOCB got a tip-off that proved to be a major break-through. The tracker had been fitted to a white Range Rover that was being driven by the partner of criminal Mr Z (who cannot be named for legal reasons). Following a meeting of the investigation team, two detectives went out in search of the jeep and found it parked in the Whitehall area of north Dublin. Under the vehicle, two magnetic trackers were dis-covered and a decision was made to remove them. The devices were examined and it was established they had been activated in the south inner city before being transported to the Phoenix Park, where Brannigan and Howe had met the unidentified man. They were switched off there and reactivated that morn-ing at 4 a.m. as they were being fitted to the Range Rover.

Mr Z was considered a Hutch associate by the cartel. He was friends with Jason 'Buda' Molyneux, who was a suspect in the murder of Michael Keogh, the brother of Kinahan associate Jonathan Keogh, on 31 May 2017 (see Chapter 3) before he himself was slain in 2018.

Mr Z had an extremely violent background from an early age and had been detained both in juvenile and adult prisons. Now he was cropping up on gardaí radars again but this time he might be the victim. Following the discovery of the tracker on his girlfriend's Range Rover, gardaí informed Mr Z of the threat to his life. He refused to sign the Garda Information Message form or to acknowledge it.

On the evening of 25 September, Kelly was accompanied in the Nissan Primastar by Dean Howe for the first time. Howe was angry at his subordinate, who had failed to show up for work one day because he was in court after getting a summons. Howe, who was operating as one of the leaders alongside Brannigan, was aggressive as he asserted his power:

'We had to do your job' cause we couldn't get you. Why do we have to do your job?' Kelly replied: 'I'm saying I've no way of getting in contact.' Howe fumed at him: 'That's bollix, pal, that's bollix, Joey. The day you went to court you fucked up. Look, we all fuck up. Just don't let it happen again, pal. When you have a job to do, you need to do the job.'

Kelly was back working with Wilson four days later when he picked him up outside his Dublin 8 address in the van. Wilson directed his accomplice to a northside location and for the first time the target was named: 'This is where your man is, you know [Mr Z], yeah?' Kelly said he did know Mr Z, but only through an associate. Wilson added: 'So the same route we're going to use on the pub, we're going to use on [Mr Z], yeah?' In a casual jump of subjects, Wilson went on to tell Kelly how he had spent the previous day in bed after taking cocaine for the first time in seven years on the Wednesday night. He told Kelly it was 'very strong' and added, 'I didn't actually like it.' Back to business then as Wilson instructed: 'These want this done as quick as possible.'

Wilson had got information that Mr Z would be at a particular location at 5 p.m.: 'If we get him at five o'clock, the inward-bound traffic is actually free-flowing.' As they drove by the target's house at 2.49 p.m., Wilson said: 'That door won't go in, that's a security door he has. I was told the windows are bulletproof as well, like you can see them as well.' Wilson and Kelly knew the risks at play and didn't want to be in the van with a firearm for too long. Wilson said: 'We watch in the van, right, go out and do what we have to do, kill him and we jump straight into another car, drive off and someone else is going to drive off in the van.' This was a big moment: investigators now knew that the men were planning to kill Mr Z and they were going to do it at his home.

Kelly and Wilson returned to the area two days later, on 1 October, for more surveillance. The operation was building up now. Brannigan and Howe drove out in the Primastar to survey the area the day after.

Over the phone, Brannigan informed Wilson that he had an extra driver for them. He wanted progress to be made now and he told Wilson to get back out and pick a spot that night. Later on in the evening, after 8 p.m., Kelly and Wilson were back in the van, which had a small, square hole cut out in the blacked-out windows and a chair in the back for the purpose of surveillance. After his phone call with Brannigan, Wilson was feeling the pressure to pick the spot where they would wait before carrying out the hit. Kelly was told there was some-one else who was going to keep watch and call them when Mr Z emerged. Wilson said: 'We both need a spot where we can park. Me in the back seat, you sitting in the driver's seat, say an hour, the driver's sitting at the house, then we get a call on the mobile, he's at the door, then we drive around. You tell me, look, he's at the door and I'll slip out and kill him.'

On 5 October, Howe and Brannigan were out near Mr Z's home, to oversee Kelly moving the car that was to be used as the getaway vehicle. They weren't alone – the gardaí were overseeing things as well, and they observed Kelly driving and attempting to park the Seat Leon but failing at his first attempt. He drove around the corner, where he did manage to park, but not to the standard of his bosses. Howe was driving the Laguna, with Brannigan as a passenger and Kelly in the back seat, as they drove by the Seat.

Wearing thin on patience, Brannigan sarcastically said: 'We're having a great time here.' He quickly snapped into a different tone as he continued: 'Buddy, I just have to say, mate, it seems to me that I always have to keep saying things to ya. Like, I may as well be doing this myself, here now. Mate, I could be doing this myself. I don't know what you're in for.' Brannigan left then and Howe stayed to watch over Kelly moving the vehicles in the area of Mr Z's home.

At this stage, there had never been any mention of who was instructing Brannigan, but that indication came on 6 October. While chatting with Howe in a bugged vehicle, Brannigan began to refer to 'D', which was how cartel gang members referred to the boss man, Daniel Kinahan. Gardaí also suspect that is who they were speaking about. A chirpy Brannigan said: 'I had a bit of craic with D last night. He was saying, "how are you?" and I says, "what's the story, pal, how are things?" I was telling him, this is where we're at. He goes, "Mate, relax yourself. Don't push it. It'll happen, don't push it. As long as everyone stays safe, I don't give a fuck how long it takes, ya know what I mean . . ." So he says, "how are ya anyway, what's the craic?" I said, "Ah mate, still doin' a bit, a good bit of running, a bit of hot yoga, flat out. Bleedin' feeling great," I said. He says, "I keep meaning to go back next week." So I said, "how are you, mate, how's you doing, how's married life post wedding?"' Howe intervened and said: 'The honeymoon period is over, yeah.'

Kinahan wed his partner, Caoimhe Robinson, in May 2017 at the Burj Al Arab hotel in Dubai.

Brannigan continued: 'I said, "the training, bla, bla, goin' back and all next week and still haven't managed to get back into it." "Fuckin' hell," he said, "my bird is seven months pregnant, baby before the Christmas, I'm going mad for something strange. But she thinks I'm ridin' everything. She thinks I'm riding everything, I'm not ridin' anything. I'm mad to ride something." He said, "ah yeah, I'm havin' a great time."' Howe erupted in laughter as Brannigan told him of the conversation with 'D'.

Sometime later, Brannigan referred to his cousin, Freddie Thompson, who was in prison on remand for Daithi Douglas's murder. He said: 'He couldn't get bail for an assault, never mind a murder.'

Kelly's incompetence had frustrated both Brannigan and Howe, who called him 'Joker', and so they took on much of the surveillance work over the coming weeks as the Primastar van and the Laguna car were moved on to Mr Z's street. Kelly was the topic of discussion for a while as they sat in the back of the van on 26 October. Howe branded him the 'worst driver ever', adding: 'Jesus Christ, he can't drive nails, fucking hell.' The men were chatting as they sat outside Mr Z's house for two hours from 5.45 a.m.

The Primastar had been the sub-cell's main vehicle until now, but the next day Kelly and an unidentified associate were in it as they drove past Mr Z's house while the target was standing in his front garden. Their drive-by was captured on Mr Z's home CCTV. The mystery man was concerned that Mr Z had spotted them, but Kelly attempted to turn it into a positive: 'That's a good thing, that is a very good fucking thing, do ya know what, see that drive by there, that was better than a week's wait if you ask me.' However, clearly concerned that the Primastar could put their weeks of work at risk, the gang had it burnt out on 30 October in the city.

Gardaí noted that this was when the 07-TS Volkswagen Caddy came into significant use by the gang. Although it was first identified as being in the possession of those involved in this conspiracy on 2 October, it didn't become involved in direct surveillance until 2 November, and then it too was bugged. That same day, Luke Wilson stepped forward into the gang.

Luke Wilson (b. 19 September 1994), another member of the notorious Wilson clan, was unemployed and lived with his grandmother in Ballyfermot at the time. When he was eighteen years old, he was shot by his pal Patrick McCann in a botched murder attempt and Wilson lost his right eye from the attack, and now has a prosthetic one. He also had a dire cocaine addiction, which was immediately clear when he stepped into the back of the Caddy and straightaway asked driver Kelly: 'Do you wanna whiff?' Kelly replied: 'Quick, before we leave . . . to wake us up.' The two men set off to the northside at around 6.45 a.m.

Until this point, Alan Wilson was the designated shooter, but now the plan appeared to have shifted and his cousin Luke was going to be the hitman. He had evidently been brought up to speed by his relative. Despite Kelly repeatedly being the cause of serious annoyance to his bosses, he was retained as the getaway driver. Alan Wilson took a step away from direct involvement and was now in the role of organizer, although he had not been seen by the gardaí in some weeks.

On the journey north across the city, Kelly told Luke Wilson: 'This fella is a paranoid cunt. This fella takes precautions big time. This fella won't leave his gaff, like.' Wilson told Kelly that he had a few ideas, including sitting in the back of the van and simply waiting for Mr Z to come out before pouncing. But Kelly, taking on a self-appointed more senior role, advised Wilson that Mr Z might not appear at all and that there was no way to get in through his reinforced door. After further discussion, and opting against trying to get in the door with crowbars, Wilson settled on staking him out from the vehicle: 'I have no problem camping in the back of the van and waiting for my opportunity to get him, because he is going to step out at some stage.'

Wilson was determined to kill Mr Z and nothing was going to stop him – even if he was holding his baby. He stunned gardaí when he was heard saying: 'Baby, no baby, I don't give a fuck.' Wilson, who continued to snort cocaine along the journey, returned to the scenario where he managed to get into Mr Z's household, declaring that no one was safe if he did. He told Kelly: 'For instance, if we get through the door, yeah? There's gonna be his missus there, there's gonna be a child there. If they get in the way, they're gonna be killed . . . I'm not fucking giving them, I'm not, like, she's obviously gonna try and get in the way, there's a child gonna be there.' Even for Kelly it was a bridge too far: 'Ah no, c'mere, listen, the way it is, like, under strict orders no birds have to be hit.' After getting lost, despite being there on many occasions, Kelly finally found Mr Z's home. The men proceeded to rant about the lack of preparation and 'homework' done on the job. Cocaine-erratic Wilson rambled: 'I'm not in this game to be fuckin' caught. We want fucking money, not jail.'

The following day, Alan Wilson was back, picked up by Kelly in the Caddy at 6.24 a.m. Wilson proceeded to tell Kelly: 'Jesus, tell ya what happened to me two weeks ago? Awh, drank a bottle of whiskey, took a load of pure coke. I took a fit, right, so I went on a walk to calm down, I opened the bag again and took more coke. I sat at the top of a set of steps and tumbled down head first, was knocked out cold. Took another fit then and I ended up in hospital.' Wilson laughed as he continued: 'Only got out of hospital there two days ago, brain scan and all. Signed meself out, I said I'm not staying here any further . . . back in bits, can't fucking move here, still in a bad way.' Despite his troubles, Wilson had plans with his girlfriend that night, as he told Kelly: 'Going to get a litre of vodka, twelve cans of Red Bull, few DVDs, an eighth of coke, two Viagras and stay up drinking and taking coke til about three in the morning. We can either do that, or we could go see a film or go for dinner. Viagra and coke don't work together, I get paranoid on coke.'

Although it had taken a bizarre turn, the conversation explained why Wilson had been absent. As they talked on, it became clear that, like his cousin, Wilson had no issue in taking out anyone if it meant that they got Mr Z: 'If she came out and he came out there with the baby, I'd slip open the door. Duck down there and fly straight over, be in that garden in fucking seconds. He wouldn't know what's happening.'

On 6 November the scheme had reached its pressure point. Brannigan rang Alan Wilson and said, 'Buddy, you're bleedin' breaking my fuckin' heart, ya are, man. I'm getting it up the arse off my man, ya know? He's giving me death, ya know what I mean?' Patience was running thin and the squeeze was on as Wilson was told to set things in motion.

Kelly and Alan Wilson were observed later that evening driving the Seat in Dublin 2 Leon and the VW Caddy in convoy. Kelly parked the Seat and left the key in the arch of the wheel. Kelly got into the Caddy with Wilson and at 7.24 p.m., Luke Wilson was collected in Rialto. His uncle Alan's phone rang and he spoke to Brannigan at the other end and asked about the 'toy', a reference to the gun. After Alan Wilson passed on instructions to Luke Wilson and Kelly, he got out of the van in Dublin 8 and left the area on foot.

Kelly and Luke Wilson made the trip to Glasnevin in the Caddy and parked outside the Lidl across from the cemetery. They waited. They collected a backpack from a man on a bike. Luke Wilson looked inside the backpack and saw the gun. The men's anticipation was building. Wilson was confident of the task at hand and said: 'Just leather him out of it in the chest, then he's getting it in the crust of the head.' Wilson felt it was easier to get the job 'out of the fucking way' to get paid in the run-up to Christmas: 'Kids to be worrying about.' As they got to the area where Mr Z lived, Kelly said: 'Silencer is what's going to be perfect.' Luke Wilson then prepared the weapon and told Kelly: 'She's fully clipped, all right. No, we're laughing with this, we're laughing.'

They parked near Mr Z's home at 8.08 p.m. The firearm and the men were now in place for the hit.

The gardaí didn't need to hear any more. It was time.

The order was given and members of the Special Tactics and Operations Command swarmed the vehicle and surrounded it, guns drawn and at the ready. Kelly wailed, 'Old Bill, Old Bill, we're set up!' as a garda pointed his gun at him and roared, 'Armed gardaí, show me your hands!' Wilson was wearing gloves and had a ski mask in his pocket and he cried out, 'Aw no, aw no.' Gardaí recovered the Adidas backpack, which was found to contain a 9mm Luger Beretta handgun and 'improvised sound suppressor' along with fifteen rounds of ammo and three petrol cans.

Ironically, Mr Z came out of his home when he heard and saw the commotion outside. Gardaí immediately told him to get back inside.

Alan Wilson was stopped in a car at 8.24 p.m. on the Crumlin Road in south Dublin by members of the GNDOCB and arrested. At the same time, members of the Armed Support Unit breached the gates of Liam Brannigan's apartment block in Hanover Court in the south inner city. He was walking towards the building at the time and fled on foot before an officer tackled him. Brannigan threw his phone away, but it was later recovered by a search team.

Dean Howe was the last man standing, but gardaí could not trace his whereabouts. Eventually, they established that he was at a Little Mix concert with his kids at the 3Arena. By the time a team of officers got there, he had been tipped off and done a runner.

The gardaí had four of the five-man gang in custody. An examination of the various burner phones recovered from them proved they had been in contact with each other and had each other's numbers saved under different names. The gardaí had all the evidence they could possibly need to prove their case.

On 13 November, the four appeared in court, charged with conspiracy to murder Mr Z between 15 September and 6 November.

Luke Wilson was the first to hand in a guilty plea – to conspiring to murder Mr Z and possession of a Beretta handgun. He was jailed by the Special Criminal Court for eleven years in November 2018, with Mr Justice Tony Hunt noting that: 'Very serious harm was intended and it was only prevented by good police work.'

Dean Howe spent nearly eighteen months on the run, mostly in the UK's Midlands with the help of Thomas 'Bomber' Kavanagh. He made contact with investigators through his solicitor in April 2019, after which he was arrested by appointment and charged the following month. After pleading guilty, Howe was handed down a 6-year sentence in 2020.

Joseph Kelly pleaded guilty and was jailed for six years for his part in the plot to kill Mr Z and for twelve years for the possession of the Beretta pistol, with both sentences running concurrently.

Alan Wilson admitted his role too and was put behind bars for six years.

Brannigan got an 8-year sentence for being at the 'centre of the wheel' of the murder conspiracy after he was found guilty following a trial in 2020.

The audio surveillance by the gardaí had caused more significant issues for Alan Wilson, however. During the operation he was heard admitting that he had carried out an attack at the Player's Lounge, Fairview, in July 2010 (see Chapter 1). In that attack, three men were shot – although all miraculously survived. Wilson's defence later claimed that what he said on the recording was 'bravado' and said he was acting on behalf of one faction of republican dissidents involved in a feud but was not himself a member of the group. On foot of the evidence, he pleaded guilty to conspiracy to murder, admitting he sourced the firearms and vehicles used in the shooting. He further pleaded guilty to possession of a .38-calibre Smith & Wesson revolver and a .32-calibre Zastava semi-automatic pistol. He was sentenced to another ten years behind bars.

The operation to save Mr Z's life was successful, but it was also lengthy and costly, running on twenty-four hours a day, seven days a week, and believed to have cost over €1 million. Retired Assistant Commissioner John O'Driscoll admitted the costs involved have posed an issue, telling the authors: 'We had to convince everyone that this was a worthwhile project. And that if you were successful in taking out the particular hit team involved, that it would not alone result in preventing the specific murder that was planned on that occasion, it would prevent those people from murdering into the future.' It was the economics of murder and murder prevention, and the gardaí were fully invested.

16. Following Orders

(February 2018: planning to murder Patsy Hutch)

*'Whatever yas do, ya see this fucker, just make
sure and toast him.'*
– Michael Burns, member of hit team

There had been no sighting of Gerry 'the Monk' Hutch since 19 February 2016. He was last seen at the funeral of his brother Eddie, the fourth victim of the feud. His other brother, Patsy Hutch, continued to live in Dublin's north inner city at his home on Champions Avenue. Patsy was defiant, refusing to give in to the gang that had murdered his son, Gary, and so many of his relatives. His defiance was understandable and, some would say, brave, but it also made him the cartel's prime target. Despite bankrolling the ongoing massacre of the Hutch family, the cartel had failed in at least four attempts on Patsy's life – as far as the gardaí were aware.

On one occasion, in the months after John Hutch was targeted by Michael Carroll (see Chapter 7), the Garda National Drugs and Organised Crime Bureau got a tip-off about yet another murder plot. When a feud is personal, as this one was, it's more savage, no-holds-barred, and that was certainly the case with this plan – the cartel hit team were planning to kill Patsy Hutch as he visited his son's grave in Glasnevin cemetery.

In an interview with the authors, Detective Sergeant Greg

Sheehan (now retired) recalled the encounter: 'My colleagues across the entire Garda organization were doing everything they could to preserve life and when intelligence came in to us, we acted on it. I recall one occasion when we were on active patrols as part of the strategy to disrupt the Kinahan group from moving weapons and targeting people when we received a call around lunchtime just a few months after they had tried to kill John Hutch. This time the call related to concerns around Patsy Hutch and the intelligence was that two gunmen from the Finglas area were planning to kill Patsy Hutch as he visited Glasnevin cemetery. Once we received the information, my colleague and I made our way to the cemetery and we were told he had made his way there from a friend's house on his motorbike.

'When we got there, we went into the graveyard, had a look around before we spotted him a short distance away. My colleague went to check the rest of the cemetery while I made the decision to approach Patsy Hutch. He didn't know me and when I approached him I could see he was a bit apprehensive, but when I showed him my ID he listened to what I had to say. I told him we had concerns for his safety in the graveyard and he told me he would be on his way. But when we were watching him we noticed him going to another part of the cemetery, to his son's grave. We kept an eye on him while my colleagues remained outside different parts of the cemetery and then he was away on the motorbike. It didn't surprise us that they would try and kill someone at a cemetery. It was a very challenging time for the Gardaí and we were just thankful that the threat against him on this occasion did not succeed.'

The operation to save Mr Z's life at the end of 2017 had changed the landscape once more. The Kinahan cartel were running out of options for on-the-ground hit teams and managers. Liam Brannigan was in jail on remand, as was his cousin 'Fat' Freddie Thompson. But, on the other hand, Daniel Kinahan's lust for vengeance remained as strong as ever and he was not ready to bring things to a halt just yet. In early February 2018, the GNDOCB received confidential information that the Kinahans were out for blood once more.

The intelligence focused on Michael Burns (b. 27 November 1976). Burns, a father of four, had left school at the age of fourteen to become an apprentice welder but fell into drug addiction. He had been involved in assaults and was caught in possession of narcotics. He had his mental health troubles, too, and had done a stint in the psychiatric unit at Tallaght Hospital. Now, he was put under surveillance by officers, who noted that he had access to an 08-KE silver Mercedes car. Given that there might be a fresh murder plot under way, permission was sought from the District Court for audio surveillance authorization on Burns's car. This was granted and a listening device was planted inside the Mercedes.

Eavesdropping on Burns's conversations soon allowed the gardaí to build a picture of the structure of the north inner-city sub-cell of the Kinahan gang in which Burns was involved. Gardaí established that the cartel had turned to Patrick Curtis to be its on-the-ground controller, to ensure directions from the most senior members of the group were carried out.

Curtis (b. 18 September 1981) had grown up at Seville Place in the Hutch stronghold of Dublin's north inner city. He had experience of gangland violence, having been in the pay of slain Dublin gang boss Eamon 'the Don' Dunne when he worked as an enforcer for him. Curtis had deep, underlying psychological issues that stretched back to the age of seven, when he got locked into a car and broke his fingernails trying to get out. Ever since, he had lived with a debilitating fear of confined spaces and of being alone and suffered crippling panic attacks. On the exterior he was a hard gangster, but behind the facade was an anxiety-ridden man who had now been handed the reins of an operation to ensure someone else would die in the feud.

Curtis was first spotted in the company of Burns, who was being watched by gardaí, on 7 February 2018. But while later listening to Burns's conversations, after the bugging device was planted, officers established that within the sub-cell Curtis was senior to Burns, who was the on-the-ground supervisor but had to take on the tasks set out by Curtis.

On 18 February, Burns made a phone call to an unidentified man and asked: 'Here, do you know anyone that can get a proper silencer, do ya? A mate of mine is looking for one.' Four days later, Burns rang Mobiletime, a phone shop, and spoke about the 'small Nokias' he had previously bought from the store, telling the clerk that he was on his way over to get more. He and Curtis spoke a number of times that day and Curtis also received a text from another man, named Mohammed Smew.

Burns was in two separate relationships at the time, but on 23 February he was seen with a third woman who lived at a complex in Dublin 1. Gardaí soon learned that he was now in a relationship with her too, which meant he had access to three different properties across the capital. The next day, Curtis and Burns met at the Omni Shopping Centre in Santry, which would become the headquarters for their discussions. Afterwards they headed out to Cardiffsbridge Road, where they met Mark Capper.

Capper and Smew were known to each other and to gardaí but, unlike the members of the cartel murder team in November 2017, they were not professional hitmen. Capper (b. 11 November 1988) was no stranger to a criminal court room though, with sixty-five previous convictions, but he was a local criminal with no big ambitions. He had learning difficulties and had struggled in school. He was diagnosed with ADHD and had an IQ of 63 when he was thirteen years of age. He became a student at a school for children with learning disabilities before falling into drug addiction in later life. He had no work history and had been claiming disability allowance since 2004.

Capper and Smew knew freelance gunman Caolan Smyth (see Chapter 13), but they weren't cut from the same cloth. Smew, however, had come from a different background that should at least have given him better prospects in life. He was born in Ireland on 23 July 1992, the son of immigrants from Libya, both of whom are doctors. He began a law degree at Griffith College in Dublin, but following a motorcycle accident his life took a turn. He had convictions for burglary, drugs and road traffic matters and had also never worked a day in his life. This was the crack team that was going to plan and execute a murder.

The surveillance continued. On 25 February, Burns was seen driving an 08-D Yamaha motorcycle, which had been bought on DoneDeal and was falsely registered. He and Smew bought a tarpaulin to cover it and then stored it at the house of an associate of Burns.

The following afternoon Burns was back in his Mercedes, and he collected Smew at the Green Isle Hotel after 2 p.m. and they made their way to Omni Shopping Centre in

Santry, and into Costa Coffee. Curtis had collected Capper, and those two walked into the coffee shop soon after. Looking on, gardaí saw the men in deep conversation. At 4.26 p.m. Burns left, with Capper and Smew tagging along with him in his Mercedes. Burns drove into Dublin's north inner city and it soon became clear to detectives that this was a reconnaissance trip. The car was seen near the home of Patsy Hutch and later near where Patsy's daughter lived, before travelling to an underground car park at Belmont apartment complex on Gardiner Street.

The conversation developed into discussion of Capper and Smew's roles, and it became apparent that they were set to be the hit team. The gardaí believed the strategy had been set out and discussed at their meeting in the coffee shop, but it seemed Capper had some ideas of his own that he wished to put forward. He said: 'Do you know what be good? Even if we had a decent, big enough van down the road and we could just drive the bike into the back of it and then jump from the back and close the doors. One of us jump into the front and just drive off then. The other fella sitting in the back with the bike, do you get me? They looking for the bike and the bike just after going around two or three corners and into the back of the van.' Burns rebuffed this suggestion, claiming the Garda helicopter had the use of thermal camera systems.

At 4.46 p.m. the silver Mercedes was observed travelling along Summerhill towards the junction of Gardiner Street and Parnell Street. To the right on Gardiner Street is the Belmont apartment complex, which has large black gates at the entrance to its underground car park, and Burns pulled in at the junction. After Capper and Smew discussed the type of motorcycle Patsy Hutch would be driving, Burns turned the conversation to the use of the car park: 'Up to the right is where you're going to be sitting in like this waiting. So what I'm saying, when you get the phone call, you're gonna come out on the yoke, yeah, you're gonna come out there and down there. Now take your time because not this turn, the next one, which is just there. That's where he is going to come out, right.'

Capper interrupted: 'So up there and go left, that's where his gaff is, yeah?' Burns predicted the route Patsy would take from his home on the day, and responded, 'Yeah, he's going to come out of there, yeah, he's going to come this way. I reckon he's going to go straight, straight through, right.' Capper replied: 'That's where I wanted to be up here, see, the likes of one of these roads.' Burns had clearly gone through every minute detail in his head: 'When you get the phone call he's going to be, he'll be taking the cover off his yoke and all, so what I'm saying here this will be the crucial part here. Once you get the call, come out of there, sort of get in between this junction and the next junction. Pull into the left and, you know, the usual, just tap away. Leave the pocket open for that thing to go onto your pocket there. Once you get sight on it, that's it.'

At this point, gardaí were able to put together some elements of the plan through the audio surveillance. The underground car park at the Belmont apartments was set to be used as a staging point for the hit team. Once Patsy appeared, they would get a call from a watcher informing them that he was out on his motorbike.

Burns informed Capper that he knew where Patsy was going to go. 'Why don't we just get him there?' Capper asked. Burns said: 'That's up to you, pal.' Armed with the new information, Capper believed there was no point coming from the car park, but instead reckoned it would be best to wait for Patsy near where they planned to kill him. He said: 'You didn't say ya knew where he's going, ya mad thing. That's one hundred percent. We will sit there the fucking night before it, that's much better, pal. Isn't it, [Smew]?'

Burns drove past Champions Avenue and to the gates of the murder spot at 4.51 p.m. and said: 'See them gates, he's going to stop at them. So what I'd advise you to do is pull up right behind him. Do what you have to do straight down here.'

Capper's inquisitive behaviour developed into nervous chat, and he picked holes in what Burns had planned. 'If he sees us on a bike, he's gone, pal,' Capper claimed. 'No he won't, he won't,' Burns scoffed. 'There's couriers up and down here all the time.' Capper didn't see the need to use the nearby car park at all: 'I think we should just park here, pal, if he's guaranteed to come here, there's no point in following him.' Burns warned: 'No you need to listen to me, that road there is on fire. I'm telling ya straight out. Like every time I pull into there, I get stopped.' Capper snapped back: 'How the fuck am I going to get in there, then, if it's on fire?'

The place where they were planning to assassinate Patsy was the gateway to an apartment block his daughter lived in. Burns knew the place well as his third girlfriend – who was innocent and had no idea what he was planning – lived there and he was in and out of the building. In fact, officers believed he had struck up the relationship solely for the purpose of this hit.

As they drove on, Burns told them he'd get the details on Patsy's motorcycle before telling the men: 'I'd personally wait till he gets to the gate.' Capper repeated his reservation, however, saying: 'I know a million for fact, boys, when he sees this bike and there's two of us on a bike, he's going to take off. He's not going to pull up at a gate 'cause he'd be a thick if he did, he wouldn't be still alive. There's no point in following where he's going. Just come around the corner two seconds later.' Supervisor Burns said: 'Listen, listen, when he pulls out of that gate, yeah, just pull in behind him. Who- ever's doing that, jump off, off you go, back onto the thing and gone. Just floor it straight in behind him and do what you have to do because he'll be facing in and you know your- self by the time he turns that it'll be game over.'

At 5.01 p.m. they passed the planned murder scene once more as Burns said: 'So when he pulls in facing that, that's your chance. That's the only chance you're gonna get, pal, that's it. If you fail it there, you might as well just drive on.'

Following the second lap of the north inner city, Burns drove out to Stoney Road in Dublin 3, which can be accessed through a pedestrian archway, the other side of which a car would be in place for them to make their getaway. Capper's anxiety over the job was growing. He moaned: 'The only thing that I'm thinking of, pal, is the meantime before I even get the chance to get to the cunt, do ya get me, about getting grabbed, that's the only thing that I'm thinking of.'

Burns ignored Capper, instead issuing further instructions about going through the pedestrian archway, which would also provide cover if the gardaí attempted to track any of the hit team with a helicopter. 'You're gonna go straight down the end, here look I'll just show ya, come all the way down here, pal, straight through that, ya get me? Straight through there you're gonna go, coz just fucking imagine something did come on top, do ya know what I mean, there's nothing gonna get through after ya there, do ya get me? So I'm gonna show you where that leads you out, pal, yeah? And I'll show you where I'll leave the other yoke for you then. You won't find a better route than that, lads, in fairness, coz you see under the arch, once you have that copped, you're free, you're gone.'

The men then discussed the key component of the plan, which was to damage Patsy's daughter's car so that he would leave his house and rush around to help her. 'That's where he's [Patsy] going coz her car is in that underground where my bird lives,' Burns explained. He then asked: 'So when do yous plan on sorting this out?' A nervy Capper responded: 'I don't know, we're going to have to keep getting our bearings on him. I'm going to have to notice him and watch him myself, do ya get me, all these phone calls.'

Burns was well aware that Patsy had been shrewd enough to avoid being plugged despite the best efforts of the cartel over the previous twenty-four months. He said: 'This is the thing, pal, you're not going to be able to watch him, you have more of a chance of standing on that, screaming from the roof with the Lotto numbers for Ireland. You're not gonna get a sighting on him. This has to be drawn out, do ya get me? You can be sitting there for the next six years, pal, and you're still not gonna get a visual of him, and trust me when I say that. So what you need to do is, you think about a day and let us know and we'll draw him out then.'

Burns then drove out to the residential area of Collinswood estate in Dublin 9. When they arrived, a white 07-KK Ford Connect van was already parked up. 'There she is there. There's a blow-out on the front wheel. That was proper stabbed, man,' Burns said. This was another vehicle involved in the plan, which had also been fitted with false plates. Once identified, gardaí obtained a warrant that night to bug it.

Burns drove back to the Omni Shopping Centre and on the journey Capper asked Smew, 'Mohammed, have you a lend of fifty euro?' Smew replied: 'Haven't got it, Mick tell him the situation I'm in ... literally, serious on me bollix.' Capper was in the same boat: 'I wouldn't be sitting in the back of this car if I wasn't on me bollix either, pal.' Capper and Smew were by no means the professional hitmen the Kinahan cartel had once had the option of employing. It was clear to the gardaí that the cartel were now drafting in men who were on their uppers and desperate for cash. It could only make a bad situation worse.

Later that evening, Burns and Curtis went back out to Collinswood and attempted to fix the spare tyre on the Ford Connect, but failed. Curtis informed Burns he would give him €500 to cover some expenses, but it was their discussion of other financial figures that caught the gardaí's attention. A female associate of Curtis had accompanied the two men on the trip and he revealed to her the type of money being made available by the cartel. Curtis told her: 'They have so much money that they could buy half of them Hutches to kill their own half. That's the way it's gone. People are getting money for a hit, people are getting money they used to get for a hit, people are getting money for setting them up now.' In further conversation, he continued: 'People are getting twenty grand and all for setting somebody up, ya used to get that for doing the hit, not even, ya know.' It was no wonder the desperate saw it as 'easy money'.

The next day, 27 February 2018, Burns collected Smew at the Green Isle Hotel at 7.41 a.m. and headed to Abbotstown Avenue in Finglas, where Mark Capper was to be picked up.

He arrived late, and questions were raised about his commitment to the job:

Capper:	What time is this, man?
Burns:	It's the time I told ya.
Capper:	Anytime, boys, I won't be rushing into this for nobody, do ya hear me, like?
Burns:	What do ya mean?
Capper:	I'm getting pressure, boys, running and outta this, this has to be done on my time, like.
Smew:	Don't do it then, man, know what I mean?
Capper:	Yeah, I know, boys, but this is cowboys . . . I'm just gonna go in here and pick something up and just go in the morning like, what do you think that's gonna happen?
Smew:	Pick something what like? This is work, two or three days.
Capper:	Shut the fuck up, I'm prepared to do it already, I'm just not jumping into something.
Burns:	I told ya yesterday, mate, that I was gonna collect you in the morning.
Capper:	One million percent. I'll do it, yeah.
Burns:	So you're prepared to do it in the morning?
Capper:	No, I'm not prepared to do it in the morning, ya mad cunt, is that what you think?
Burns:	That's what the other fella told ya yesterday.

Capper:	No, I'm not prepared to go in the morning at all, pal, have to look out, suss it out, do ya get me?
Burns:	I'm gonna have to tell him then.
Capper:	I told him that meself, like.
Burns:	When ya tell him that?
Capper:	On the phone yesterday, this is a big job, pal, he knows this himself. It's a very big task, like, if I go in here, this is all down to me, if I fuck up going round one corner, then do ya get me, he's on the back of me as well, like this is an awful lot coming onto me, like.
Burns:	Well we showed it to you yesterday and then today, like, ya know?
Capper:	No, one million percent I'll do it, pal, yah. I have balls.
Burns:	This is the only time we're gonna get a fix on this fella. I understand what you're saying, pal, that this has be done on your time, but the timeframe is tomorrow. This is the only time we're gonna get this fella out, yeah, there's a reason there for getting him out and the limit on it is tomorrow, like.

In the eyes of the on-the-ground supervisor and his superiors, the job had to be done early the next day. Burns drove the men back into the north inner city for one last run-over of the plan. The conversation dovetailed off to the motorcycle to be used for the job, which Burns said would be ready that evening, before attention turned to what time Patsy would be lured out. Burns explained: 'We're gonna try have him out for, say, yous will be in there for, say seven, we're gonna try have him out for say eight, half-eight. Ya can't miss there, yiz are gonna be sitting waiting.' Capper wanted extra firepower, to be sure: 'Well ninety percent. I'll be asking for two yokes anyways, pal, because I'll be on the front of him and he'll be behind me coz we'll be pulling up behind him and I'll whip one out meself. Not going on this and we end up missing a person, fuck that. It's not nice going home empty-handed.' Burns replied: 'It's just that there's something wrong if yous miss this fella, like I said, from here to the back of that yoke, that's how close you're gonna be.' Capper asked Smew, who was nicknamed 'Bin Laden', how good his aim was. Smew replied: 'In the back of his head, mate.'

At 8.44 a.m. the Mercedes pulled in at Glasnevin and Smew went into the shop. Burns turned to Capper and said: 'Whatever yas do, ya see this fucker, just make sure and toast him.' Conversations up until this point had all indicated that Smew was the more prepared party in the two-man hit team, but now Capper questioned his capabilities. Burns was having none of it. 'He's well prepared for it,' he insisted.

Capper spoke about the possibility of ditching the getaway route and fleeing Dublin altogether: 'As soon as he gets whacked onto the back of that yoke, my mind will probably change to a totally different way, do ya get me? I'll probably be down in fucking Bettystown.' He also referenced the fact that officers were permanently in place outside Patsy's home. A Garda post had been in place since the early stages of the feud due to concerns for the target's well-being and Capper saw it as another in a growing list of concerns he had.

By now, final preparations were being made, with Burns

reporting to Curtis over the phone. At 3.20 p.m. Curtis sent Burns a message regarding firearms. Burns later called Curtis and told him: 'I have the two bleedin' instruments there for you. They're full of diesel as well, so all good with them.' Burns had collected loaded guns from an unidentified person at Liffey Valley Shopping Centre and he was keeping Curtis up to date with the latest on what had been done and what was left to do.

That night, a second Ford Connect van, with an 06-D reg, was driven by Burns into the underground car park of the Belmont apartments after he picked it up from the Drumcondra area. Curtis had handed a set of keys to Smew, who parked an 08-D Ford Mondeo on Stoney Road in East Wall, which was the getaway car. Both vehicles were bought on the DoneDeal website and falsely registered.

The whole plan was now in place, ready to go. Although Burns was concerned about Capper's state of mind. Over the phone, he told Curtis: 'Yeah, I don't think he's up for this, pal, I genuinely don't.' The plan was too far gone to change the main players now. But there was one unforeseen element that the hit team had never planned for: the weather. By that evening, 27 February 2018, the impending arrival of Storm Emma was top of the news headlines. It caused panic as people rushed out to buy groceries, leaving empty bread shelves and milk fridges in the face of what forecasters were warning was a 'once in a lifetime' snowstorm.

Ultimately, the decision of going ahead with the hit was taken out of the group's hands. A snow blizzard descended the like of which Ireland had not seen in years. The country came to a standstill for the following five days and most were left confined to their homes. Smew wasn't one of them. He took matters into his own hands and on 3 March armed himself with a sledgehammer and looted a Centra store in Tallaght, south-west Dublin. That rash decision saw him arrested, charged and remanded in custody. The hit team had lost a key member. But perhaps it was for the best from his perspective because when the snow melted and murder was top of the agenda once more, Smew wasn't available to help. The team would have to find another player to field in the quest to finally take out Patsy Hutch.

17. Planners and Professionals

(28 February 2018 and 10 March 2018:
conspiracies to murder Patsy Hutch)

*'The world's too small for them not to find ya, they have
people everywhere, all over the world.'*
– Robert Browne, member of the hit team

A group of three men sat in the back of the van, ready to strike. One was a former British army soldier disguised with a wig, the other two were brothers and ruthless criminals dressed in dark hooded tops. Full of adrenaline and nerves, they were about to commit a murder. All they were waiting for was the call to move. Their target was about to die, that was for sure.

Six days earlier, on 4 March 2019, the hit team, minus Smew, had gathered once more at Costa Coffee at the Omni Shopping Centre following the short hiatus forced on them by Storm Emma. Mark Capper arrived with Glen Thompson at 5.25 p.m., then sub-cell leader Patrick Curtis landed and they launched into discussion. Also present, but sitting separately, was Michael Burns and Curtis's brother Stephen Curtis.

Later that evening, Capper and Thompson met up with Burns in Clondalkin, and he gave them the Yamaha motorcycle to be used as the hit team's bike for the murder. The following day they rallied around the streets of Finglas on it.

On the night of 6 March, Burns picked up Capper at 10.16 p.m. and the nervy Finglas man informed his boss that he had identified a significant problem. Capper explained: 'When ya red line it [drive at maximum speed], it cuts out.' Burns was displeased: 'Fucking hell, that's no use, is it?' The men made their way out to Collinswood Estate in Dublin 9 and Burns parked his Mercedes close to the 07-KK Ford Connect, which still had the punctured tyre. Despite a second attempt at fixing it, they still couldn't manage it.

The next evening, 7 March, Burns met Capper again. They spoke about the second 06-D Ford Connect van, which had been parked underground at the Belmont apartments, ready to be used to keep the hit team out of sight while they waited for the call to come to tell them to go after Patsy. It was obvious that the extra time afforded to Capper by the snowstorm had not alleviated his nerves about the job: 'See, when I close that door, I'm not going to be able to see out of that van, am I? If I get a text message off yous or whatever to say, right, ready, and I step out, there could be someone there, do ya get me?' Burns reassured him: 'I understand what you're saying, pal, but the reason I drove it in and put it facing the wall, it's facing a bike shed, the reason I put it there was that yas could just sit in the back and watch out then.'

Later in the evening, the third attempt to change the flat tyre on the 07KK white Ford Connect van at Collinswood got under way, and this time Burns and another associate were successful. Once it was fixed, Burns parked it up at the front of the estate. He left in his Mercedes at around 8.30 p.m. But the gardaí keeping an eye on them stuck around and therefore were still there watching on when an 05-D Volkswagen Passat arrived into the area over an hour later. It was being driven by Robert Browne, and the passengers in the car were Capper, Glen Thompson, and his older brother, Gary Thompson. This was the new hit team.

Glen Thompson (b. 26 December 1994) was reared in Finglas and was another criminal whose drug habit had led to him falling into debt. His addition meant he was the youngest member of the cell. His brother Gary (b. 11 October 1984) was a father of four and no stranger to the cops. He had previously been charged with the murder of Graham McNally, a 34-year-old gunned down at Coldwinters, Finglas, on 20 January 2009. However, in 2017 the state dropped the charges against Thompson and his co-accused. That happened just three months before the planned hit on Patsy, and Thompson wasted no time in getting back to work.

Browne (b. 15 February 1983) was originally from the Hardwicke flats in Dublin's north inner city but lived in Phibsborough, although he also spent time in west Dublin with his girlfriend. He was a former British army soldier and had done a number of tours in Afghanistan before leaving the army and falling into drug and alcohol abuse. Although he had not featured in the feud before this point, Browne had close ties to members of the Kinahan gang, and was previously convicted for a robbery alongside gangster Ross Browning in the early 2000s. For the gardaí, this was the first sighting of Browne and Gary Thompson associated with the cell.

Browne and Gary Thompson got out of the Passat and into the bugged 07-KK Ford Connect van at 9.51 p.m. As they drove on, they were followed by Glen Thompson and Mark Capper in the Passat. Browne, like Burns, had reservations about Capper's capability, as he told his pal: 'He better get up, Gary, if he doesn't get up, Gary, and this doesn't happen, he's out.' Gary Thomspon agreed: 'If he doesn't get up, then me and you,' and then added that Capper is 'just comfortable on a bike'. He continued: 'That's what I says to Glen. I said, "Glen, look at the opportunity, if he backs out again, why couldn't Robert do it?"' Browne couldn't drive a motorcycle but added: 'I don't like the way he was sniffing and all, Gary . . . I just don't like the way he wants to do Patsy.'

The conversation turned to the wider feud and Browne referred to the cartel's power as they hunted for Patsy's brother, Gerry 'the Monk' Hutch: 'The world's too small for them not to find ya, they have people everywhere, all over the world.' Gary Thompson weighed in with his insight: 'Here, they have people stationed everywhere in case the Monk turns up in places. I know they've a young fella in Barcelona in case he turns up in Barcelona, I know a fella in Belgium in case he turns up there.' Browne also referenced the vast property empire Christy 'Dapper Don' Kinahan had built up over the years, including in Brazil: 'Gary, all that money, they all have bogey passports and they all get out, plan, get away money, the auld fella owns half of Rio.' The conversation moved on to money for the task ahead of them, with Browne promising: 'I'll get you fifteen grand outta this, Gar.' They parked the van at Plunkett Green, near the Thompson's address in Finglas.

When members of the sub-cell met again on 8 March at Costa Coffee at 4.45 p.m., there was one noticeable absence: Capper did not show. It appeared he had pulled out. The six remaining men discussed what was left to do on the logistical end and, most importantly, who would now be the gunman in Capper's place. Gardaí were not able to listen to these discussions and had yet to figure out what date the team had picked for the execution, but from the nature of the men's behaviour they believed it would be in the coming days.

After the meeting, gardaí watched as Burns and Stephen Curtis travelled into the north inner-city centre and went to various shops buying burner phones, SIM cards and credit. As they shifted from one spot to another, Burns made a number of calls to Patrick Curtis to keep him informed and to clarify any outstanding matters. Stephen Curtis wasn't happy with how things were proceeding, however. He began ranting about his older sibling: 'He gets it wrong all the time, he's always getting it wrong. He's doing it all wrong, bringing people to that coffee shop, that coffee shop is packed with coppers, the Garda station is around the corner. Red hot, running back and forward at the table, swapping over phones, you even do that in a field, for fuck sake, you'd be red hot.' Referring to the van with the flat tyre, he said: 'What kind of gangsters if the tyre hanging off their jeep? Mr always doing my head in, I'm getting outta this gang before I even step into it.' Stephen Curtis (b. 11 November 1987) had worked in a family business before following his sibling into crime. A regular in the gym, Curtis was an enforcer and had no legitimate employment at the time.

In further conversation, the gardaí learned that the gang had hit yet another stumbling block because the relationship between Burns and the woman who lived at the same apartment block as Patsy's daughter had ended. Burns told Curtis: 'I was only with the gee-bag to try and get into that place, you know what I mean, in the heart of there.'

The next day, the Thompson brothers and Browne went to the 07-KK Ford Connect van where it had been parked two days beforehand and got into it at 3.19 p.m. As investigators listened, they figured that this was the final preparation ahead of the hit the following morning, 10 March 2017. Glen Thompson was forensically aware and did not want to leave a trace behind in the van, telling driver Browne: 'You wanna watch what you're touching there.' Browne replied: 'I'm not driving with gloves, I'll wipe it down.' Glen Thompson stated that he had two fresh packets of gloves, ready for their use.

Due to the obstacles that had surfaced with the motorcycle and the element of targeting Patsy's daughter's car, a fresh plan had been hatched. Glen Thompson brought up the weapons and referred to a pistol: 'I'll give you the Makarov and let me use the mack thing coz I'll be getting out as well.' Browne jumped in as he spoke about arming himself with a revolver: 'I'll just use the little small one, you take the 38, I just want something just in case.' The gardaí believed this conversation indicated that the two Thompson brothers would get out and carry out the murder while Browne was to be the driver of the car, but that he wanted protection for himself.

Browne was also anxious about the possibility of being seen getting into the van: 'What I want is to get into this van and no one sees us and no one says I'm after seeing fellas jump into a little white van, then there's a red alert for a white van, ya know what I mean? It's real quiet in there, especially with them guards.' Browne warned his accomplices to prioritize themselves rather than going all out to assassinate Patsy, who he believed might have watchers in place himself. Browne said: 'Just don't get too indulgent getting him, watch them cunts, young fellas there selling tablets, they'll scatter anyway, I'd say. Ya never know, there could be a young fella with a thing watching him, that's what you need to watch. Ya know what I mean? Paying someone to watch his back going in.' As the journey continued, there was more light-hearted chat as the men laughed about previous nights out, pranks, pulling chairs out from underneath each other. Then Browne asked: 'Boys having a party, getting the bag and a few bottles?' Glen Thompson replied: 'Like that Saturday, if this goes down.' Robert giggled: 'Bottle of Grey Goose.'

They parked the van on Stoney Road and drove away in the Ford Mondeo car, which had been parked by Smew on the night of 27 February, before the snowstorm and his sledgehammer incident. Detectives had now become aware of another vehicle of interest, a stolen Audi A6 with bogus 141-T reg plates that was parked outside Gary Thompson's home.

Detective Superintendent Dave Gallagher had been keeping up to date with all the developments on the case as he oversaw the investigation. That evening, he was satisfied that the conspiracy to murder Patsy Hutch was reaching its critical point and he put in place an operation for the next morning that included members of the GNDOCB, the Special Crime Task Force, Crime and Security and the Emergency Response Unit. The cops were as ready as the criminals.

Following a briefing in the early hours of 10 March 2018, gardaí were deployed, ready and watching. At 6.45 a.m. Browne was seen driving in his 05-D Volkswagen Passat over to Gary Thompson's home at Plunkett Green, Finglas. The Thompson brothers and Browne then left in the 141-T Audi A6, which investigators had already identified, and travelled into the north inner city, arriving at the Belmont apartments' underground car park at 7.14 a.m. Browne reversed into the No. 27 parking space. The 06-D Ford Connect van was still in spot No. 30, where it had been left by Burns on 27 February. Browne had disguised himself with a wig and was wearing dark clothes. Front-seat passenger Gary Thompson was wearing a hooded jacket. Glen Thompson, sat in the back seat, was also wearing a dark hooded rain jacket.

At 7.16 a.m. the three men got out of the car and into the back of the van. They were sitting just 250 metres from Patsy's home at Champions Avenue, waiting for the call when the move was made to draw him out. The gardaí had seen and heard enough.

Detective Superintendent Gallagher made the call to intervene. Immediately, officers from the Emergency Response Unit drove down into the car park and up against the Ford Connect van. They jumped out, official Sig Sauer P226 pistols held up, and roared, 'Armed gardaí, show me your hands.'

The Thompsons and Browne were taken from the back of the van and put face down on the ground, then handcuffed. Inside the van, a garda picked up an Audi key that opened the vehicle they had arrived in. Looking into that car, on the rear seat lay three firearms: a 9mm-calibre PM63 RAK submachine gun loaded with a magazine containing eighteen rounds of ammunition and fitted with a shoulder strap; a 9mm-calibre Beretta 92 semi-automatic pistol loaded with a magazine containing twelve rounds of ammo; and a 38 Rossi special-calibre revolver loaded with five rounds. A fourth firearm, a 9mm-calibre Makarov semi-automatic pistol loaded with a magazine containing seven rounds of ammo, was found in the driver's door.

Three black, brand-new balaclavas were also found in the Audi, as was a plastic bag containing two litre-sized bottles of petrol, two red petrol cans and another plastic bag with four 500ml-sized bottles of petrol. Other items in the van included three pairs of gloves, a black wig, three Nokia phones and keys for the various vehicles. Gary Thompson had the fob of the gates for the underground car park in his waistband.

At 7.20 a.m. the men were arrested for conspiracy to murder Patsy Hutch. Gary Thompson and Robert Browne were taken to Store Street Garda Station, while Glen Thompson was taken to Clontarf Garda Station. The Audi and the van in the underground car park were seized, as was the 07-KK Ford Connect that was still in place for the getaway at Stoney Road.

Meanwhile, the plan to lure Patsy Hutch out of his house was proceeding because the rest of the team had no idea what had just befallen their colleagues. The home of Patsy's pal, Anthony 'Scarface' Fitzgerald, was targeted and a rock thrown through the front window. Fitzgerald was a former professional boxer who played no role in the feud. He had fought under the Kinahan-affiliated gym MGM, but later left the boxing management firm. He had carried the coffin of Patsy's son Gary Hutch, who was the first victim of the feud. When he heard the sound of breaking glass, little did he know he had come close to carrying the coffin of his friend, Patsy.

Later that morning, gardaí became aware that Burns was driving his Mercedes in Dublin's north inner city. He was stopped at Gardiners Row, Dublin 1, at around 10 a.m. and arrested. Four phones were seized and the searching officers also found a hotel-room slip in the name of a Kinahan foot soldier. Burns had €245 on him. He handed €15 to one of the arresting officers to get him cigarettes. His car was impounded and he was brought to Clontarf Garda Station.

Burns had been linked to two properties, and also to the one in Tallaght where the 08-D Yamaha motorcycle, originally part of the plan, was stored. The Yamaha keys and more mobile phones were seized. At the second address, in Lucan, gardaí had to force the door open because no one was there. They discovered a silencer for a gun wrapped in a T-shirt, along with five rounds of 9mm ammunition in a blue disposable glove. Also inside the home were car keys and a fob for the car park where Patsy's daughter lived.

At Bellman's Walk in Selville Place, Dublin 1, gardaí knocked on the door of the Curtis family home with a warrant to search the premises. They carried out their search with Patrick and Stephen there watching on. Officers immediately saw ten phones, which were switched on, in the living room. Four mobiles were on the top of the back of the sofa, while five others – including an encrypted Aquarius X mobile – were on the seat cushions of the couch. A tenth phone, a Samsung, was plugged into a socket in the wall. Most of the devices were wrapped in different-coloured elastic bands to identify one from another. Four other mobiles were discovered in a box under the kitchen table.

Handwritten notes found in the home had various amounts of figures under In and Out categories, with the balance beginning at €7,000. Included was €500 spent on phones, with the date 8 March 2018 beside it. There was another figure of €450, which was assessed to have been spent on the first batch purchased in February. 'Nut', the nickname used for Burns, had been given €750 and a further €100 for diesel, and €1,000 on 9 March. In total, expenses and payments of €6,500 were recorded, excluding the cost of vehicles and firearms. Investigators estimated that the gang had access to at least €10,000 for the costs associated with the plot.

When a garda team got to Capper's address at Abbotstown Avenue, Finglas, Dublin 11, he attempted to discard a phone, but it was recovered. Gardaí found nothing of evidential value at the properties linked to the Thompsons or to Browne. No one was arrested during the searches and, after four days in custody, Burns was released with a file going to the DPP.

On 15 March, Gary Thompson, Glen Thompson, and Robert Browne were brought before Dublin District Court and charged with firearms offences. They were remanded in custody.

The phones proved to hold crucial information that gave concrete evidence as to the positions the suspects held in the gang, but officers also hoped they would provide clarity on the identity of the person to whom Patrick Curtis was answering. The BQ Aquarius belonging to him could not be accessed due to its high level of encryption and use on a private network. Luckily for gardaí, Curtis had struggled to retain information passed on in disappearing messages and solved it by taking screenshots. On Curtis's Samsung phone the gardaí uncovered pictures taken from the encrypted device showing messages from a man using the pseudonym 'Lordnose'.

On 23 February, Lordnose had texted Curtis: 'This has to be done military and if there [sic] not able to do that there is no point them doing the work as there [sic] putting themselves and others at risk!!!!! Do they agree????'

On 26 February, two days before the original planned date of the murder, Lordnose wrote: 'So job be done Wednesday morning.' The next day, Lordnose texted: 'Ask can he point out [Patsy's daughter] GAF out . . . Sound, pal, we really need to know that gaf.'

There were messages on 7 March referencing 'The Boxer', who was Anthony Fitzgerald. The man gardaí suspect is Lordnose has long been associated with senior members of the Kinahan gang but works in a legitimate job to cover his tracks. At the time of writing, in May 2024, he remains a free man, always managing to avoid prosecution due to the lack of evidence against him.

A key modus operandi was the use of burner phones. The gardaí examined downloads and records from the phones seized and identified eight Nokias that were activated between 11.48 p.m. and 00.45 a.m. on the night of 20 February into the morning of 21 February 2018, which gardaí knew, from his bugged conversations, had been bought by Burns. The analysis showed Burns used two, gave three to Patrick Curtis, two to Smew and one to Capper.

The second set of nine burners was purchased by Burns and Stephen Curtis on 8 March and activated that evening. From this set, three were recovered from the Thompson brothers and Robert Browne, and one was found at the Curtis household along with four others unopened. The audio recordings from the vehicles used also gave gardaí further evidence as they could establish who was on the receiving end of certain calls from the conversations they listened in on.

Patrick Curtis, Michael Burns and Mark Capper had kept to using the phones bought in the first batch and remained in contact with one another on them, but also with 'L'. As gardaí carried out inquiries, it emerged that the number of 'L' had also been in contact with a phone belonging to Patrick and Stephen Curtis. Gardaí then established that the same number had been given to gardaí at Store Street Garda Station in late 2017 as part of the bail conditions of a man named Ciaran O'Driscoll. In fact, O'Driscoll had taken a call on this number from a garda dealing with his case on 7 March 2018. Gardaí were then able to link this number to the records from a number of commercial businesses, including a pizza delivery restaurant and a taxi company, both of which had him saved under his name on their customer databases along with his address at Avondale House, Cumberland Street, Dublin 1. O'Driscoll had spoken with Patrick Curtis five times over the phone and in two text messages on 9 March. Another number associated with O'Driscoll had been in contact with Curtis on 22 February, revealing that he too was involved in the initial plan.

O'Driscoll (b. 21 February 1995) also had access to a home just doors away from Patsy Hutch on Champions Avenue, where his grandmother lived. O'Driscoll's parents were drug addicts, who have both since passed away, and he was a user himself, with ninety criminal convictions to his name. He was effectively raised by his grandmother in her house on Champions Avenue. As he had every reason to be in the area, he had not raised the suspicions of the gardaí stationed on the road. But according to the gang's list of payments, O'Driscoll had been paid €2,000.

Over a year after the plot, on 27 March 2019, the Curtis brothers were arrested at their home. Each was interviewed seven times but answered 'No comment' to every question. O'Driscoll was also lifted on the same morning, but he was willing to talk with detectives over the course of five interviews.

O'Driscoll told gardaí that he lived in Avondale House with his younger sister and aunt, who took over the home when his mother died in May 2018, but added that his family home was on Champions Avenue, where his grandmother had lived before her passing.

O'Driscoll knew the Hutch clan and Patsy but had not seen any of them for some time as he had been in custody. Giving an insight into the relations, O'Driscoll explained:

'Patsy Snr came into me nanny's home when the coffin was being laid out. He came in, paid his respects and shook me hand like the good man he is. I know Patsy came. I've no problem with Patsy or his wife or his kids. Whenever I see him I'd say hello to him and he'd always say hello back to me. I'd know the whole Hutch family well. I used to sit in the garden and get drunk. I don't know who's living in the house now but I know him.'

Gardaí showed him pictures of the guns seized in the operation and he said: 'Yeah, but this is the first time I've ever seen these guns before. It's disgraceful, isn't it? I've nothing to do with it. It's low. That's what I call the lowest of the low.'

Regarding his whereabouts on 10 March 2018, O'Driscoll told the detectives: 'Trust me, I don't get out of bed until two in the afternoon. I was actually selling crack that day at Avondale. I'd say about 450 to 500 quid worth. About 24 bags of it. I was selling it from about three in the day until about eleven in the night. My customers would ring me and I'd go and meet them.' As the scale of evidence against him was drip-fed, O'Driscoll stopped talking and resorted to 'No comment' answers. He denied any knowledge of the conspiracy and was released from custody.

On 28 March 2019, Capper was arrested in Finglas and brought into Store Street Garda Station for questioning but maintained his right to silence over five interviews. On the same date, Smew was lifted from prison but also answered 'No comment' to everything put to him at Clondalkin Garda Station.

The original three-man hit team were the first to be sentenced in July 2019 after pleading guilty. The Special Criminal Court found that Gary and Glen Thompson along with Robert Browne were caught 'red-handed'. The Thompsons were each hit with a twelve-and-a-half-year sentence while Browne received eleven and a half years' jail time. The men, Mr Justice Tony Hunt said, had shown 'no restraint or reluctance'.

Patrick and Stephen Curtis, Burns, Smew, Capper and O'Driscoll were rearrested and charged in December 2019. They all pleaded guilty the following year. Capper and Smew were sentenced to seven and a half years behind bars and O'Driscoll was jailed for five years for his role as a looker. Those higher up the chain were given varying degrees of jail terms, with Burns sentenced to nine years and Stephen Curtis caged for five years.

At the Special Criminal Court, Patrick Curtis was given a 10-year term in prison for his role as a 'top figure within' the sub-cell. He was the first person ever in Ireland to be jailed for directing the activities of a criminal organization. Before his sentencing, the court heard that jailing the claustrophobic defendant was like putting 'a man with arachnophobia in a cell with spiders'. Dr Conor McGarry said Curtis had been diagnosed with excessive compulsive disorder and blessed himself sixty times daily to compensate for his negative thoughts. He and his brother were allowed to share a cell in Portlaoise Prison to help him deal with his medical issues. It was the first time two inmates had shared a cell at the state's maximum-security prison. Mr Justice Hunt remarked: 'In this first instance, it is tempting to observe that not plotting to murder other people would have been the best way of avoiding this unfortunate situation.'

At Capper's sentencing hearing, Detective Superintendent Dave Gallagher gave evidence based on his twenty-five years' experience investigating organized crime. For the first time in an Irish court, he specifically named the Kinahan

Organized Crime Group (OCG), which the court accepted as 'uncontroverted evidence'. Based on the senior garda's evidence, the court established that the Kinahan OCG is involved in serious criminal offending, including the organization and carrying-out of execution-type murders. These activities primarily comprise organized drugs and firearm trafficking on an international scale. It further accepted evidence that the cartel is organized on the basis of a hierarchical structure, which includes sub-cell structures. The cartel was laid bare and exposed for what it was.

The endless cash the cartel had at its disposal had become all but meaningless in the feud. This was a personal vendetta with no boundaries. The aim was to kill as many Hutch associates as possible – not caring about how close or far they sat from that association. When the feud had kicked off with the murder of Gary Hutch in Spain, it quickly became apparent how serious the Kinahan OCG was about delivering death to their rivals. Those in the know and in the media had predicted up to sixty murders following the Regency attack. That would likely have been the case if the Garda Síochána hadn't stepped up and fought the cartel with every weapon in their arsenal. Their continued interventions and clever policework stripped the Kinahan cartel of the power their drug money once gave them. Again and again they were foiled in their efforts. They thought they were in a fight with the Hutch OCG, but it turned out a much more formidable opponent had stepped into the ring. The assassins had been disarmed.

Epilogue: Disrupt and Dismantle

'The capabilities of the Kinahan organization have been significantly reduced in recent times but it is by no means eradicated. The Kinahan group as it existed in 2016 or 2017 no longer exists.'
– Detective Chief Superintendent Seamus Boland

After Kinahan assassin Michael Carroll received a 22-year sentence for the failed attempts to kill John Hutch and Eddie Staunton, John Hutch's wife, Vera, spoke to *Irish Sun* news reporter Michael Doyle on the steps of the Criminal Courts of Justice in Dublin's Parkgate Street and said: 'We were told the feud is over. We're trying to move on with our lives now.' The last murder connected to the Kinahan and Hutch feud – the killing of Hutch associate Jason 'Buda' Molyneux – occurred in north inner-city Dublin in January 2018. Since then, the Hutch family and others connected to the Hutch Organized Crime Group have not been living with the same level of threat that they witnessed between the end of 2015 and 2018.

In 2023, the permanent Garda checkpoint was removed from the home of Patsy Hutch while photographs of James 'Mago' Gately – stalked by cartel assassins over a 5-month period in 2017 – showed him walking casually around the streets of his home city. The cartel's number-one target at the start of the feud, Gerry 'the Monk' Hutch, was also pictured walking freely close to his home in Clontarf, north Dublin, after he was cleared of the murder of David Byrne at the Regency Hotel. He seemed to be enjoying life as he soaked up the sun in Lanzarote over the 2023 Christmas period. The constant fear of attack is gone, that much is clear.

The same cannot be said for Daniel Kinahan in his adopted home of Dubai. At the time of writing in early 2024, a comprehensive file compiled by the Garda National Drugs and Organised Crime Bureau (GNDOCB) on Kinahan's alleged role in directing the activities of the narco-terrorist gang during the feud had been submitted to the DPP. In a separate file to the same office, gardaí have also recommended that Daniel Kinahan be charged in relation to the murder of the Monk's brother, Eddie Hutch, on 8 February 2016. His right-hand man, Sean McGovern, is the focus of a European Arrest Warrant and will be charged with the murder of Noel 'Duck Egg' Kirwan if he is extradited to Ireland. These aren't the only pressures the Kinahan organization has been feeling in recent years.

On 11 April 2022, at a historic meeting in Dublin's City Hall, $5 million rewards were each placed on the heads of the two Kinahan siblings and their father as part of a global investigation involving GNDOCB, the UK's National Crime Agency (NCA), Europol, the Drug Enforcement Administration (DEA) and the US Treasury Department. At the same time, financial sanctions from the Office of Foreign Assets Control (OFAC) were placed on three companies linked to the cartel.

When announcing details of the million-dollar rewards, the US Treasury Department concluded that the 'Kinahan Organized Crime Group smuggles deadly narcotics, including cocaine, to Europe and is a threat to the entire licit economy through its role in international money laundering. Criminal groups like the KOCG prey on the most vulnerable in society and bring drug-related crime and violence, including murder, to the countries in which they operate. Since February 2016, the KOCG has been involved in a gang war with another group in Ireland and Spain, resulting in numerous murders, including of two innocent bystanders.'

Other senior cartel figures and the companies they were heading up would also come under the international spotlight, including Johnny 'Johnny Cash' Morrissey. Just five months after the announcement of the sanctions, Morrissey was arrested by Spanish police investigating a €200 million cartel money-laundering network. In early 2024, he remains in custody.

Following the unprecedented announcement at City Hall, Daniel Kinahan's trusted lieutenant, Liam Byrne, found himself in custody in the UK on alleged weapons offences alongside Thomas 'Bomber' Kavanagh's son Jack Kavanagh. There have been other blows, too. For example, Daniel Kinahan's old boxing agency, MTK, was closed down, and a former drug addict, Seamus Walsh, was convicted of applying for a passport later used by Daniel Kinahan to travel to Dubai during the feud. Kinahan has also been left isolated after the arrests of key associates and members of Europe's super-cartel, Raffaele Imperiale and Ridouan Taghi.

Due to the global reach of the Kinahan cartel, Garda liaison officers have been posted as far afield as South America, Washington and the UAE. The liaison officer posted to South America was honoured with the Colombian Distinguished Services Medal for his efforts in helping his international colleagues to combat the narco-terrorist groups shipping tonnes of cocaine across the Atlantic. In one of the investigations, over €157 million worth of cocaine was recovered from the MV *Matthew* when it was seized off the County Wexford coast in September 2023.

Alongside the international law enforcement investigations, which have seen police officers from the UAE travel to Ireland for meetings with Garda Commissioner Drew Harris and other senior Garda members, negotiations have also taken place between the Department of Justice in Ireland and its counterparts in the UAE, with a view to establishing extradition arrangements between the two countries.

The developments in tackling organized crime that have been witnessed over the last two years have been incredible, but the initiative to dismantle the structures of the criminal organization started in the midst of their killing spree, as Detective Chief Superintendent Boland explains: 'When you consider the amount of Gardaí, including armed Gardaí, who were on the streets after the Regency happened, the Kinahan crime group were still killing people. The relentless nature of the killings showed they weren't afraid of law enforcement because they were so violent and so confident in their own abilities because this is what they had been doing for many years. When we looked at the structure of the criminal organization, the same names who had been prevalent in the past when it came to violent crime were once again in the middle of the feud. We were looking at people like Alan Wilson and it was important for us to be resilient. The gang was well established by 2016 and they were a high-value priority target for the Garda National Drugs and Organised Crime Bureau because they were the most violent and most proficient gang in the country – they posed a huge threat.

They were a significant threat to society and so we needed to deploy significant full-time resources, no matter how difficult or expensive that was, to ensure we could identify the structures of the gang.'

The gardaí were facing a new type of criminal capability in the Kinahan OCG, one that could use technology as proficiently as weaponry to achieve its aims. This sort of policing was, to a large extent, uncharted territory and the Garda Síochána had to learn and adapt quickly. Gardaí had to devise new strategies to effectively tackle this highly dangerous, highly flexible organization, as Seamus Boland explained: 'We implemented the GNDOCB strategy of disrupt and dismantle and this meant being resilient and focused on continuing to investigate them until they no longer impacted in this jurisdiction. The criminals' perception of law enforcement is that we are results driven and more reactive than proactive, but once we identified key individuals who were working for them, whether it be in logistics, money laundering or contract killers, we proactively targeted them during intelligence-led operations. Once we identified those who were prepared to kill people, they became high-value targets for long-term intelligence-led covert operations until they were apprehended. Our strategy had to be long term because they have been the primary gang impacting this jurisdiction – we don't want them to operate for another twenty years.

'We had great support and collaboration from local gardaí, the Garda National Crime and Security Intelligence Service, the Emergency Response Unit and senior officers, in particular the then Commissioner Noirin O'Sullivan, in terms of support, confidence and resourcing, along with funding from the government. Our investigations proved that the allocation of sufficient dedicated resources to identified national priority policing targets, and ongoing local investigations into the murders and serious crimes already committed, will have a positive impact on community safety. We assessed, at the time, that this focused and resourced approach would impact on organized crime-related murders in Ireland and currently, in early 2024, we are experiencing the least amount of organized crime-related murders or shooting incidents in over two decades. In 2016 we had twenty threat-to-life operations and twenty-six in 2017, and in 2023 there were none. But we must learn from this experience and ensure no organized crime group ever reaches the violent heights of the toxic Kinahan Organized Crime Group again.'

At the time of writing, in early 2024, it is six years since a Kinahan cartel hit team was active in Ireland. In an interview with the authors, Detective Superintendent Dave Gallagher also outlined the Garda strategy to bring the contract killers to justice: 'A key component of the strategy to tackle this organization and bring an end to the violence was to not only target the disposable hitmen but also to develop strong and often complex evidential cases to identify the wider hit team members – those providing the logistical and planning support, those in leadership positions, those deciding who was to be killed and those who were directing the activities of the criminal investigation.

'This strategy resulted in key individuals in the organization who positioned themselves in the background, far removed from the actual commission of the murders, being prosecuted and convicted with long prison sentences imposed. Successful prosecutions of the hit teams removed violent actors from the streets and the successful prosecution of key personnel who believed themselves to be untouchable resulted in loss of capability and confidence in the ability for the organization to commit murders. Achieving these outcomes involved a significant collaborative effort with absolute dedication, perseverance and resilience from the Garda members of all ranks across the multiple investigation teams, the intelligence sections, the tactical sections involved in surveillance and those involved in the high-risk interventions.'

The views of Boland and Gallagher are shared by former Assistant Commissioner Pat Leahy: 'Even though a priority for the Garda organization was the intervention of the cartel hit teams, every resource was made available to the investigators involved in bringing the killers to justice.'

When suspects were arrested, specialist interviewers from the Garda National Bureau of Criminal Investigation were often brought in to support the investigation teams. They were brought in on seven feud-related murders and three attempted murders. Other units across the Garda organization also played key roles in the investigations, as former Assistant Commissioner Leahy described: 'When the Kinahan Organized Crime Group embarked on their killing spree there was a realignment of resources. It was the frequency of violence which caught everybody – everybody was surprised by the frequency of events that took place. The State was never going to let those at the heart of the Kinahan and Hutch feud walk off into the sunset. They had to pursue it to the very end and I think that my former colleagues will be successful in the end.

'The State is duty-bound to investigate every individual connected to this feud, no matter where they are residing. A lot of great work has already been done, but the investigations will continue no matter how long it takes. The level of work that went into the investigations around the Michael Barr and Gareth Hutch murders, along with the investigations into Michael Carroll, was extraordinary. The level of dedication and professionalism shown by everyone involved in all of those investigations was second to none. Every resource of the Garda organization, along with units ranging from community gardaí to specialist units, were used in the response to the threat posed by this criminal organization.'

The former assistant commissioner's views are also shared by Chief Superintendent Patrick McMenamin from the North Central Division, who said: 'The work that was conducted on these investigations, from the first responders to the detectives who were assigned to the investigations, demonstrated the highest levels of professionalism. I mention first responders, who are so vital in establishing the existence of and the preservation of evidence, presence of witnesses and getting things right from the outset. The success in these investigations is testimony to their professionalism, experience, tenacity, perseverance and steadfast determination to bring to justice the perpetrators of these murders. The investigators never give up.'

Reflecting on the standard of investigations during the early days of the feud, Detective Superintendent Colm Murphy, also from the North Central Division, said: 'The investigations into these murders and other serious offences relating to this feud demonstrate how members of An Garda Síochána go about their business in a professional, thorough and diligent manner. We utilized all available means to investigate these horrendous crimes and this included the unwavering support of the community and the world-class experience of Forensic Science Ireland and the Garda

National Technical Bureau. The commitment, dedication and resilience of Garda personnel over a long period of time illustrates the determination of everyone involved in these investigations.'

Nonetheless, eight years on from the Regency Hotel attack, investigations into feud-related incidents are continuing, as the unsolved murders in the dispute remain the focus of ongoing Garda investigations. The repercussions continue to be felt – especially as there were simply so many people involved, from the bottom to the top of the cartel.

During the height of the feud in 2016 and 2017, the cartel, unlike their enemies, had the financial clout to pay the contract killers offering their services. Money talks, of course, and even those from the north inner-city area of Dublin and those who had grown up with the Hutch family declared their loyalty to Daniel Kinahan. As one investigator told the authors: 'I remember speaking to one family who went way back with Gerry Hutch and they said they couldn't get involved in the feud because the Kinahans had too much power and money. There were even young lads who were selling drugs in the north inner city wanted the Hutches dealt with because the Gardaí's Operation Hybrid was affecting their business. It didn't matter if they came from the same community as Gerry Hutch.'

As we have seen, though, while the cartel was regarded as a transnational criminal organization led by 'top tier' criminals, the same could not be said for some of the individuals they recruited to wage war on the Hutch clan. This was evident to former Assistant Commissioner Michael O'Sullivan, who was part of a team of undercover officers who once targeted Christy Kinahan Snr in the 1980s: 'The people who were employed by the Kinahan organization were modern-day bounty-hunters who were promised blood money. You wouldn't send some of these people to the shop for a pint of milk, but here they were running around the city with weapons supplied to them by the Kinahan organization. The Kinahans were throwing money at these clowns. A lot of the hit teams were cobbled together – it was like a free-for-all and many of them didn't know what they were doing, but there were others who were professional who were determined to keep going until they got the job done. Even if an innocent person had been murdered, it didn't matter. They would keep going because they knew the only way they would get paid is if the target identified to them by the Kinahan organization had been murdered. It was a chaotic time, but once the resources were made available the results followed. The professionalism and dedication shown by my former colleagues was exemplary in such difficult times.'

The cartel may have recruited the experienced marksman Imre Arakas and former British soldier Robert Browne, but then they also had people like Joseph Kelly and Michael Carroll on the books. Speaking about Carroll, for example, one former detective told the authors the drug addict was never a 'natural-born killer': 'When he was committing robberies from shops to feed his habit he would threaten people but never use extreme forms of violence. I think he got involved with the Kinahan group under duress because he had lost their drugs and owed Freddie Thompson a lot of money. Carroll, and others like him, were in way over their head. I remember seeing him before the attempt to kill John Hutch and he was in a right state. The fact the Kinahan group also turned to people like him showed how desperate they were. It was very often the case that when people like him were told to kill someone, they did so because they were warned their own lives, or the lives of their children, would be in danger. Michael Carroll wasn't a cartel member and they were scraping the bottom of the barrel when they relied on him to kill people. He was simply someone who could be easily exploited by senior cartel figures for their own selfish ends – they won't care about him or the dozens of people who are now serving time out of loyalty to the Kinahan organization.

Security Analyst Sheelagh Brady believes that while lack of education, deprivation or family circumstances may all contribute to foot soldiers joining gangs, these might not be the core reasons for aligning themselves with these groups. In an interview with the authors, she said: 'One thing that they have by living in environments where gangs are present is the opportunity to join a gang on their doorstep. I don't have that. So we can look at it and say it's the conditions that they were exposed to such as deprivation, maybe not the greatest family circumstances and so on, or maybe it was purely that they had that opportunity.'

After fourteen years of observing crimes and criminals when she was a garda, Brady believes that camaraderie gained from gang membership can fill a void in these men's lives, giving them a sense of belonging that they did not get in school, at home or in their larger community: 'Things that indicate that it may be more about belonging and identity, than it is necessarily about what the people do in these groups, are things like, they all look the same, they all dress the same, they all speak the same, giving a sense of shared identity. It's how you order the influence of factors they're exposed to, as in deprivation, lack of education – it's not to say that they're not huge influences on what drove them there – it just may not be the root cause of it. Opportunity or life experiences may have made them more susceptible.'

Brady noted that just because a person is from a deprived area it does not automatically mean they have poor education or a difficult upbringing; their circumstances might be very decent, and yet they might still decide to join a gang or not. As she sees it: 'I think some people are more susceptible, because groups do give us that kind of emotional feeling of well-being that we may not get elsewhere. We have trust within, we may gain courage from those groups, and we might want to be liked. So when you're part of a hit team, or when they're grooming you to be a runner or eyes on their street, you may feel you belong. If they know your name, you belong. If you're the one that they talk to, rather than your mates, you belong. There's a strength in that and a sense of power can come with this. It's like, if you're a footballer, and you're the one that they always pick to take the penalty. We often explain membership in the context of crime as due to a vulnerability as opposed to natural group behaviour that these individuals are just conforming to by seeking a sense of belonging, albeit in this case, by becoming part of a criminal group.'

The cartel's overall operation in Ireland sucked in a huge number of people in this way, but that influence has been curtailed, taking out their capacity to murder along with their capacity to accumulate more wealth. Former Assistant Commissioner John O'Driscoll, who was key in developing the relationships with law enforcement agencies abroad that saw the US sanctions placed on the gang, believes there is more to come: 'Despite the limitations of dismantling a group who have got to the stage that the Kinahans have got to, An Garda Síochána and law enforcement in general have a long way to go yet, and I suspect will achieve more success.'

O'Driscoll cited concerns about the UAE cooperating in the fight against the cartel. He pointed to the fact that Sean McGovern remains in Dubai, over two years on from the issuing of a European Arrest Warrant for him. He explained: 'The UAE have not cooperated in relation to that. Why do we have such faith in them cooperating down the line with the Kinahans? I don't have as much faith in the UAE as others have. I would think some of the trust that has been put in that State is misplaced.'

That said, he acknowledges that the work of the gardaí has made the world a much smaller place for the members of the Kinahan OCG, and their travel options are extremely limited: 'It's one thing being incarcerated in Mountjoy Prison, or similar, but there is an element of incarceration in the UAE when you can't leave. And you have family members, maybe wives or girlfriends, who did not buy into a scenario where they would never be able to leave the country again, never come back to Ireland. We had the Kinahans coming home for a funeral immediately after the Regency, they have not been able to enter this jurisdiction since. They can't enter Europe, never mind Ireland, they can't go to the US, they can't attend boxing. It can become a lonely and miserable world.'

The Kinahans might have the money, the watches, the designer gear, but looked at in that light, it's a gilded cage. Would you want all that if the price you had to pay was loneliness and misery? It seems fitting that it's ended up this way, given that the Kinahan cartel has done nothing but sow loneliness and misery in every jurisdiction they've cast their long, dark shadow across. Through the drugs and the guns they have taken lives, thwarted lives, stunted lives and blighted lives, creating misery and the loneliness of pure grief. There is perhaps some sense of poetic justice in how they must live their lives now, far from home, rich, but poor in all that matters. In the final reckoning, it really doesn't seem worth it.

Acknowledgements

We offer our sincere thanks to all of those investigators from An Garda Síochána, both retired and serving, who shared their insights into the investigations featured in this book. We would also like to thank the team at the Garda Press Office for their support. Thanks to the various security sources we spoke to about this project.

We are also grateful to some of the families of those murdered by the Kinahan cartel for sharing their stories of the trauma they continue to endure today.

Praise is also due to our editor, Rachel Pierce, for her tireless efforts and suggestions which improved our efforts. Thanks to Michael McLoughlin, Patricia Deevy, Joyce Dignam and the Sandycove team for believing in this project and for all their support. Thanks also to libel expert Kieran Kelly for his direction.

Thanks to *Irish Sun* editor, Fiona Wynne, deputy editor, Declan Ferry, the *Sunday Times* editor, Kieran McDaid, and all of our colleagues at the *Irish Sun* for their support.

Thanks to Jon Lee from the *Irish Sun* picture desk for compiling the images for the picture inset. Copyright as follows: 4 – Solarpix; 6 – used courtesy of the *Irish Sun*; 7 and 11 – Press Association; 19, 32, 36, 69 and 71 – Crispin Rodwell; 24, 51, 68 and70 – Collins Picture Agency; 31 – Rollingnews. ie; 50 – Pacemaker. All other pictures supplied by the authors.

And on a personal note:

Stephen: Thanks to my family for their support and for putting up with me during the writing process. Thanks also to

Chrissie's parents for taking care of our kids when I was working on the book. Thanks also to the 'Big Man' and 'The Jedi' for all their help and guidance over the years.

John: I would like to thank a number of colleagues for their ongoing support and assistance throughout this process and my career, particularly the *Irish Independent's* crime correspondent, Robin Schiller, *Reach* deputy news editor, Owen Conlon, and RTÉ's crime correspondent, Paul Reynolds. Thanks also to the *Sunday Times* Ireland associate editor Mick McNiffe, the *Irish Sun's* Barry Moran and photographer Mick O'Neill for their encouragement. Love to my family, who have always supported me, and to my friends.

THE CARTEL:

THE SHOCKING STORY OF THE KINAHAN CRIME CARTEL
STEPHEN BREEN AND OWEN CONLON

THE NUMBER ONE BESTSELLER

The definitive account of the rise of the Kinahan Cartel and the deadly feud that shocked a nation and brought the gang to the edge of destruction.

February 2016. A daring gun attack in the Regency Hotel brings Dubliner Christy Kinahan and his international criminal cartel to a horrified public's attention.

Kinahan's son Daniel, the target of the attack, escapes. A trusted henchman dies at the scene. And the deadly rivalry between the Kinahans and the family and associates of the veteran Dublin gangster Gerry Hutch becomes all-out war. It results in a never-before-seen level of international cooperation – including between Irish, UK and US police forces – to topple the Kinahan gang.

The Cartel offers a unique behind-the-scenes account of how the Kinahan crime organization got so big, and why a local feud sowed the seeds for the gang's destruction.

'It's incisive, it's intriguing, it's fascinating'
Ryan Tubridy, RTÉ

'Fascinating!'

Keith Ward, FM104

THE HITMEN:
THE SHOCKING TRUE STORY OF A FAMILY OF KILLERS FOR HIRE
STEPHEN BREEN AND OWEN CONLON

THE NUMBER ONE BESTSELLER

Meet the Wilsons – the deadliest family in crime

Brothers Eric, Keith and John Wilson, their cousin Alan and nephew Luke shared a trade: assassination. Working for Ireland's criminal gangs they brought bloodshed and chaos to the streets.

The Wilsons were not choosy about their targets. Hutches, Real IRA chiefs or random opponents from pub rows – they were all the same to them. Nor were they picky about motives – as long as the price was right, they asked no questions.

The Hitmen is the shocking story of how a family cornered the market in intimidation and vengeance. It details the terrible cost in human suffering, particularly the death of an innocent teenage girl, Mariaora Rostas, when she randomly crossed their path. And it reveals how, one by one, each of the Wilsons was put out of business.

The Hitmen draws on exclusive access to wire taps, case files and interviews with sources close to the gang who have never spoken before. Number one bestselling authors Stephen Breen and Owen Conlon have written an extraordinary account of a family business like no other.

'A triumph'

> Nicola Tallant, *Crime World* podcast

'An incredible catalogue of mayhem . . . amazing'
> Pat Kenny, Newstalk

'Riveting'

> *Irish Times*

FAT FREDDIE:
A GANGSTER'S LIFE – THE BLOODY CAREER OF FREDDIE THOMPSON
STEPHEN BREEN

THE NUMBER ONE BESTSELLER

'Fat' Freddie Thompson first appeared in court in 1997. He was sixteen and already aspiring to be a major crime boss. Over the next twenty years his criminal career would be marked by mayhem, brutality and murder.

In 2000 a row over a failed drugs deal ignited a murderous feud in Dublin's south inner city. The Crumlin–Drimnagh feud's first victim was a friend of Thompson's and he led his Crumlin crew in a series of tit-for-tat killings. Sixteen young men would lose their lives over the next fifteen years.

Meanwhile, childhood friend, Daniel Kinahan, had become a senior figure in his father Christy Kinahan's international crime cartel. Working with the Kinahan Cartel, Thompson launched himself as a drug dealer in Dublin.

When another deadly feud broke out in 2016 – between the powerful Kinahans and veteran Dublin criminal, Gerry 'The Monk' Hutch – Thompson was ready to get his hands dirty. But Thompson's loyalty would be his undoing. In August 2018 he was convicted of murder and jailed.

Fat Freddie is a gripping account of the rise and fall of Freddie Thompson. Award-winning crime journalist Stephen Breen, co-author of the number one bestseller *The Cartel*, has written the definitive portrait of a notorious Dublin gangster, a shocking story of double-crossing, vengeance and murder.

'A fascinating read'

Seán O'Rourke, RTÉ Radio One

'Explosive'

Irish Sunday Mirror